Beautiful Things
IN POPULAR CULTURE

As always, to John Hartley, who is right
about most things

Beautiful Things
IN POPULAR CULTURE

Edited by
ALAN McKEE

Blackwell
Publishing

Blackwell Publishing
© 2007 by Blackwell Publishing Ltd
except for editorial material and organization © 2007 by Alan McKee

BLACKWELL PUBLISHING
350 Main Street, Malden, MA 02148-5020, USA
9600 Garsington Road, Oxford OX4 2DQ, UK
550 Swanston Street, Carlton, Victoria 3053, Australia

First published 2007 by Blackwell Publishing Ltd

1   2007

Library of Congress Cataloging-in-Publication Data

Beautiful things in popular culture / edited by Alan McKee.
    p. cm.
  ISBN-13: 978-1-4051-3190-2 (hardback : alk. paper)
  ISBN-10: 1-4051-3190-X (hardback : alk. paper)
  ISBN-13: 978-1-4051-3191-9 (pbk. : alk. paper)
  ISBN-10: 1-4051-3191-8 (pbk. : alk. paper)
1. Popular culture.   2. Aesthetics, Modern—20th century.   I. McKee, Alan.

  CB430.B387   2006
  306'.0973–dc22
                          2006001715

A catalogue record for this title is available from the British Library.

Set in 10 on 13 pt Galliard
by SNP Best-set Typesetter Ltd, Hong Kong
Printed and bound in Singapore
by Markono Print Media Pte Ltd

The publisher's policy is to use permanent paper from mills that operate a sustainable
forestry policy, and which has been manufactured from pulp processed using acid-free
and elementary chlorine-free practices. Furthermore, the publisher ensures that the text
paper and cover board used have met acceptable environmental accreditation standards.

For further information on
Blackwell Publishing, visit our website:
www.blackwellpublishing.com

Contents

List of Figures

Notes on Contributors

John Banks has been an avid gamer since playing the arcade game *Defender* at the local corner shop as a teen in the early 1980s. His favorite videogames include the *Grand Theft Auto* series and *Halo* 1 & 2. Recently, he has been spending far too much time playing Blizzard's *World of Warcraft*. He works with the games development company Auran, as well as being a researcher with the Australasian Cooperative Research Centre for Interaction Design. He has researched the relationships among computer games, their audiences, and game development companies, among other things.

Marc Brennan's first and only encounter with Kylie Minogue was a personal appearance by the pop star at the Perth nightclub Pinocchio's in 1987. An arch Indie boy at the time, his intention was to heckle the diminutive starlet – an aim that was thwarted by his two autograph-hunting friends. Age has weathered such prejudiced tendencies, as has a greater appreciation of the art of the pop song encouraged by years of viewing such Australian televisual staples as *Countdown, Rage*, and *Video Hits* (but not *So Fresh*). He now finds pleasure in cutting the rug to remixes of pop songs, drinking beer at live performances, and busting some Janet Jackson moves for his students. He will, one day, manage a boy band.

Will Brooker grew up on Denny O'Neil's Batman in the 1970s, Frank Miller's Batman in the 1980s and Grant Morrison's Batman in the 1990s. While researching his PhD thesis, a cultural history of Batman's first 60 years, he spent two weeks in DC Comics' NYU offices and interviewed Denny O'Neil about Miller and Morrison. On the publication of his book

Batman Unmasked in 2000, he was interviewed by Gloria Hunniford on a sofa with the 1960s Caped Crusader, Adam West. Brooker knows seven working defenses. Three of them disarm with minimal contact. Three of them kill. The other . . . hurts.

Simon Frith is old enough to be described these days as a pioneer of popular music studies – his first academic book, *The Sociology of Rock*, appeared in 1978. In university terms, his disciplinary expertise has always been a little unclear – he has been a lecturer in sociology, a professor in departments of both English Studies and Film and Media, and now holds the Tovey Chair of Music at the University of Edinburgh. His first published reviews (of records by Gene Vincent and the Small Faces) appeared in *Rolling Stone* in 1970 and in the 1980s he became rock critic of both the London *Sunday Times* and the *Observer*. For much of this period he reviewed singles, and his "Thesis on Disco" (an homage to Karl Marx's "Thesis on Feuerbach") appeared in *Time Out* on the occasion of the UK release of *Saturday Night Fever*. He has been the chair of the judges of the Mercury Music Prize since its inauguration in 1992 and is the author of *Performing Rites: On the Value of Popular Music*. He may not know much about disco, but has every confidence in his expertise in what is meant by "the best."

Claire Gould would like to think she has the best-dressed feet in the world. A former university lecturer and newspaper journalist, she crossed the floor to online media when they adopted the more casual combat trousers and trainers dress code. She currently edits the *Daily Telegraph* online (www.dailytelegraph.com.au) in Sydney, has broadened her footwear horizons and wears thongs (flip flops) in summer. She stares at her feet for at least three hours a day.

Sara Gwenllian Jones has researched and written extensively on *Xena: Warrior Princess* in particular, and cult television generally, in her books *Cult Television* and *Worlds Apart: Essays on Cult Television* (edited with Roberta Pearson). She has also published on the topic in journals including *Continuum, Screen*, the *Journal of Television and New Media*, and in book collections including Mark Jancovich and James Lyons' *Quality Popular Television*. Her next book will be a cultural history of pirates.

John Hartley lived in Wales for 19 years and fell for Humphrey Jennings while taking a film production course at Chapter Film Workshop in

Cardiff in 1979. His interest in propaganda stems from having made an "agit-prop" film about working conditions for cinema projectionists. Called *We're Dying to Please You*, it played at art houses and film festivals and led to the replacement of Chapter Cinema's carbon arc lamps with xenon bulbs. Hartley visited Cwmgiedd with a view to making a film about *The Silent Village*, but emigrated to Australia instead. He went on to write about Jennings and propaganda more generally in several books, including *Tele-ology*, *The Politics of Pictures*, *Uses of Television* (all Routledge) and *A Short History of Cultural Studies* (Sage).

After a long and expensive apprenticeship in shiny, fast, and beautiful Italian objects – namely racing bicycles – **Margaret Henderson** eventually progressed to beautiful two-wheeled objects with engines. Four Japanese sports bikes later, and one ride of a friend's Ducati F1, she finally got the economic base in place and bought her first Ducati, a 750 Monster. She now rides a Ducati 800 Supersport – red, of course, with white GT stripes. She has published widely in cultural and literary studies, including a study of motorcycle magazines.

Henry Jenkins once received a fan letter from Neil Gaiman after Jenkins testified before the US Senate Commerce Committee hearings on "Marketing Violence to Youth." DC Comics president Paul Levitz returns his phone calls. In fact, he is working with Gaiman, Levitz, and Harlan Ellison to organize the Julius Schwartz lecture series at MIT in honor of the Silver Age editor who revitalized The Flash and Green Lantern and created The Justice League of America. He regularly teaches courses on comics as the DeFlorz Professor of the Humanities and Director of the Comparative Media Studies Program at MIT. He is the author or editor of more than 10 books on various aspects of popular culture, including *Textual Poachers: Television Fans and Participatory Culture*, *From Barbie to Mortal Kombat: Gender and Computer Games*, and the forthcoming *Convergence Culture*. He is now turning his attention to the challenge of understanding what it means when a genre – superheroes – totally dominates a medium – comics. He should confess, however, that this topic is in part a scam to get his endowed chair to support his comic-book-buying habit.

Alan McKee is a connoisseur of *Buffy the Vampire Slayer* (best episode: "Hush"); Terry Pratchett novels (*Carpe Jugulum*); Andrew Lloyd Webber musicals (*Phantom of the Opera*); action movies (*Aliens*) and gay porn

(*Frisky Summer*, although Johan Paulik isn't really his type). He's 5′10″, 35 years old, gym fit, cute, and currently single. For a photograph, email a.mckee@qut.edu.au.

Thomas McLaughlin is a lifelong pickup basketball player, beginning on the playgrounds of Philadelphia, and including more than 20 years in an ongoing faculty/staff/community "oldguygame." His main claim to hoops fame is that he has played with a guy who used to play with Michael Jordan. He is also a lifelong fan who practically cries when basketball season begins every Fall. As a scholar interested in cultural studies and everyday practices, he has published articles on basketball ethics and on basketball as an improvised group movement practice. His book *Give and Go: Basketball as a Cultural Practice*, is currently being considered for publication.

Mark McLelland researches gay culture and the Internet in Japan and is the author of *Queer Japan from the Pacific War to the Internet Age* and co-editor of the collection *Japanese Cybercultures*. In his cyber travels he has made numerous important discoveries, including the fact that more gay porn is written by straight Japanese women than by gay Japanese men and that the largest audience for these "boy love" stories is Japanese schoolgirls. When not annoying Western feminists with this observation, he likes to drink Earl Grey tea and read literary biographies of famous homosexuals.

Once, while **Glen Thomas** was in conversation with Emma Darcy, she asked him to describe his favorite sexual fantasy. He is still trying to think of an answer. He does, however, know a lot about other people's. He has read more romance novels than he can count, interviewed some of the most successful romance writers in Australia, and has spoken with hundreds of devoted romance readers. He is a member of the Romance Writers of Australia, and has become something of a fixture at the RWA annual convention. He has also published articles and book chapters on romance, the romance market, and romance readership. More recently, Emma Darcy told him that his work on romance would give him any number of insights into the female mind, which he should be able to use to his advantage. Sadly, this is yet to eventuate.

Sue Turnbull has been a co-convenor of the writers and readership network Sisters in Crime Australia since 1992. In this capacity, she has been a judge of the Scarlet Stiletto Short Story competition and the Ned

Kelly Awards for Australian Crime Fiction. She regularly reviews crime fiction for the *Age* and the *Sydney Morning Herald*. Her academic essays on crime fiction have appeared in such journals as *The Australian Journal of Law and Society* and *The International Journal of Cultural Studies*. She teaches Media Studies at La Trobe University when she is not contemplating crime, and is currently writing her own book about popular culture and aesthetics, entitled *Moments of Intensity*.

Introduction

Alan McKee

Shit Books

When I was much younger than I am today I bought a historical romance novel – a "bodice ripper" – for my mother's birthday, knowing that she enjoyed the occasional foray into the romantic past. Using all of the fine discrimination at my disposal, as a non-reader of the genre, I bought one that looked suitably florid. On the cover, the sky was bloodshot dark and a hero who looked like Fabio boasted a flouncey pirate's shirt and a swooning heroine in his arms.

When she opened the present and saw the book, my mother was suitably delighted. But several weeks later I noticed that it was still lying on her bedside table, obviously unread. I asked her why. She looked a bit embarrassed, but finally admitted: "That's not really the kind of book I like. That's shit." This last was said, not angrily, but apologetically. I, looking in from the outside, knowing nothing about the detail of the genre, had casually assumed that any bodice ripper was as good as any other – that these texts were completely anonymous and interchangeable, and that their readers would like any one as much as any other. I didn't know – as my mother evidently did – that there are rules for the genre. There are rules about what makes a good bodice ripper, and what makes a bad one.

It All Sounds the Same to Me

I was young then, but it's not only young people who make this mistake. The consumption of popular culture is going on around us every day.

Hundreds of millions of people are consuming films, television programs, computer games, pornography, trashy magazines, pop music, heavy metal, rap, country and western, crime novels, romances, and hundreds of other kinds of culture. And as they do so, they are making judgments about whether they are good or bad – whether this particular T-shirt or skateboard or website is a good T-shirt or skateboard or website. The everyday consumption of popular culture involves the use of popular aesthetic systems. And yet – amazingly – the intellectuals whose job is to understand and comment on the cultures in which they live continue to know very little about these systems. Indeed, when it comes to understanding how the masses decide what examples of popular culture to consume, many intellectuals assume that it is in fact the *producers* of popular culture who make the decision – that consumers simply accept whatever is offered to them.

The reason for this mistake isn't difficult to understand – for most intellectuals, popular culture is simply not their culture, and they don't know very much about it. They may know a lot about what Theodor Adorno, Stuart Hall, or Harold Bloom say about popular culture – but very little about popular culture itself. The fashionable philosopher Slavoj Žižek, who is taken seriously by many intellectuals as a useful thinker on culture, famously wrote a book in which he claimed that *Star Wars* was directed by Steven Spielberg.[1] Because they don't know the culture, they don't see the differences between different television programs, films, trashy magazines, or pornographic videos. Like grumpy old men kvetching about rock music, they say "It all sounds the same to me" – not realizing that this tells us more about them than it does about the music in question. Television researcher Sonia Livingstone quotes a group of academics complaining that: "One would have to have a passion for sameness, amounting to mania, if after *six* years of viewing *Coronation Street* or *Hawaii Five-O* one still looked forward eagerly to the next episode."[2] She points out that in fact: "Soap operas present a vision of endless 'sameness' only to a non-viewer: to those who know the programme well, a wide range of subtle, complex and historically informed meanings are involved."[3] As anyone who regularly watches large amounts of television can tell you, some episodes of soap operas are better than others – and some are standout classics (the Moldavian Massacre in *Dynasty*; the birth of Sonia's child to Martin in *EastEnders*; the wedding of Kylie and Jason in *Neighbours* . . .).

Some branches of intellectual thought – the much maligned "cultural studies" for example – have acknowledged that popular aesthetic processes exist.[4] And we have recently seen researchers begin to explore and report on some of these systems. It is now possible for the interested reader to find out how the consumers of popular music decide what is good music, and how horror film aficionados engage in processes of aesthetic distinction; how baseball fans decide which is the best team; the ways in which television viewers distinguish between good and bad sitcoms; how karaoke singers decide which performances are best; what rock fans look for in their music; how fans of television science fiction exercise their discrimination; the criteria for deciding what is good graffiti; and what the consumers of soft-core porn value in their videos.[5] But there still remain vast areas of popular culture where only the expert consumers themselves understand how they are making the distinctions between good and bad examples; and outsiders – including people whose job it is to understand the culture around them – do not even know that these systems exist.

How do the readers of serial killer fiction decide which books are particularly good? As an expert on Internet porn sites, how would you know which ones can safely be dismissed as worthless? Why would the cognoscenti refuse Britney the title of best pop princess? Welcome to *Beautiful Things in Popular Culture*. The aim of this book is to bring together a collection of experts in various areas of popular culture, and have them explain – through the medium of "the best" example in their area of expertise – just how these popular aesthetic systems work. The chapters have been chosen to try to offer a wide range of different kinds of popular culture – literature (Thomas, Turnbull, Jenkins, Brooker), the visual arts (Jenkins, Brooker, Banks), music (Frith, Brennan), design (McLelland, Banks), material culture (Henderson, Gould), performance (McLaughlin, Brennan) and drama (Gwenllian Jones, Hartley, Banks). Of course this collection cannot be exhaustive. There is much, much more to learn about popular culture than there is about high culture, simply because the area of popular culture is massively larger than high. The number of texts being produced and circulated in popular films, television, magazines, novels, computer games, music, and every other medium is many orders of magnitude greater – thousands, perhaps even hundreds of thousands of times greater – than that area of human endeavor that rejoices in the title of "high culture." And as the respected music critic and academic Simon Frith (who has contributed an account of "the best disco record" for this collection) has pointed out, even within a single area of popular culture there are many different evaluative systems, employed by the people who make it, the people who distribute it, and the people who consume it, taking account of different genres and historical traditions, and focusing on different aspects of the texts.[6] This collection does not even pretend to be representative – but hopefully the range of topics covered is, at least, indicative of the wide variety of kinds of production that we can bring under the title of "popular culture"; and shows that across these areas, aesthetic systems for judging their worth are in play.

―――――――――― **Whatever They're Given** ――――――――――

But why does any of this matter? Who really cares how consumers of *Batman* comics work out which is the best story – or even if they do so in the first place?

The answer is simple. On the left and the right of intellectual politics – and continuing into wider public debates about "dumbing down," trashy media, globalization, and media ownership – there is a shared assumption underpinning much intellectual theorizing about culture: that the masses cannot distinguish between good and bad culture. They lack the faculty for discrimination. They take whatever they are given by the producers of the culture machine.

On the right we have writers like Allan Bloom – author of *The Closing of the American Mind* – and Harold Bloom – who wrote *The Western Canon*.[7] These Blooms (no relation, as far as I can tell) seem very grumpy. Both received substantial publicity for their defense of the "canon" – "the good old Great Books approach" to teaching culture at university.[8] Both contend – and were received sympathetically in the media for their contention – that it is the job of universities to teach students discernment: how to discriminate between good culture (the "canon") and trash culture (that is, mass culture). If we do not do this, they say, culture will fall into "chaos," "mere anarchy,"[9] or a "sea of democratic relativism."[10] They argue that there are "only a few" people in any nation who have "cultivation"[11] or "the discerning spirit."[12] These people are not in the masses. Harold Bloom argues that "it seems clear that capital is necessary for the cultivation of aesthetic values. . . . This alliance of sublimity and financial and political power has never ceased, and presumably never can or will"; and that "[v]ery few working class readers ever matter in determining the survival of texts";[13] while Allan Bloom condemns the "vulgarities" (vulgarity, *OED*, "the quality of being usual, ordinary or commonplace; an instance of this") of the world outside the university.[14] For the Blooms, it is only educated people who are able to distinguish good culture from bad culture: "Lack of education simply results in students' seeking for enlightenment wherever it is readily available, without being able to distinguish between the sublime and trash."[15]

But it is not only elitist conservative intellectuals who believe this to be the case. A large proportion of left-leaning intellectuals draw on similar assumptions in developing their models of culture. The German philosopher Jürgen Habermas is also a popular public intellectual – indeed, he made it into *Time* magazine's 2004 list of the top 100 "most powerful and influential people in the world," as one of the most important "scientists and thinkers," one of those whose "words and deeds have an outsize effect on the rest of us."[16] Habermas's most commonly cited book is called *The Structural Transformation of the Public Sphere*; in it he argues that the public sphere in Western countries is collapsing back into feudalism because of multinational corporate greed. The problem as he sees it is that the *producers* of popular culture have control over what is consumed. He says that the masses who consume popular culture have an: "inarticulate readiness to assent" to whatever culture they are offered.[17] His belief is that working-class audiences are "intellectually lazy"[18] and lack the ability to discriminate between good and bad culture, "because under the pressure of need and drudgery, they had neither the leisure nor the opportunity to 'be concerned with things that do not have an immediate bearing on their physical needs'."[19] "The part of consumer strata with relatively little education" tend to like "relaxation and entertainment."[20] But it is the job of education to provide "guidance of an enlarged public towards the appreciation of a culture undamaged in its substance."[21]

It is true that the right and left wings of intellectual politics disagree on just *why* the masses need to learn to appreciate high culture. On the right it is argued either that high culture is simply better, in a transcendental way, than popular culture; or that its consumption shapes consumers into being better, more moral citizens. On the left it is argued that art, unlike popular culture, challenges the status quo and leads people to think for themselves, thus having politically progressive effects. But on both political sides of the intellectual spectrum there is agreement on this fundamental issue: that the masses consume indiscriminately. The fact that they choose to consume trash is taken as all the evidence that is needed to prove that they lack the ability to distinguish between good and bad culture.

This assumption isn't limited to writing within universities. As noted above, commentators like Harold Bloom and Jürgen Habermas are public intellectuals. And the idea that the consumers of popular culture are indiscriminate also informs many public debates about culture. In worries about globalization, media imperialism, media ownership, and dumbing down, consumers are always presented as being incapable of making informed choices about culture. In these debates, it is always the media owners, producers, and transnational companies who are held to be responsible for negative changes to culture. It is very rare for commentators to acknowledge that consumers might be playing a part in – or even driving – these changes, by the choices they make about what to consume.

The belief that consumers of mass culture lack the ability for discernment is often articulated in public debates by writers contending that they will take "whatever they're given": "Most Americans feed on whatever they are given at the trough of ABC, CBS, NBC, CNN, Fox and newspapers that are by and large owned by the same companies"; "Kids will suck up whatever they are given"; "Most of America is all too eager to accept whatever they are given"; "The one-way character of broadcast media . . . encourages passivity, receptivity, inaction . . . [and consumers] learn how to be better passive recipients of whatever they're given."[22] If we believe that consumers are indiscriminate, that they don't make informed and intelligent choices between different trashy television programs, pornography, pop songs, or comic books, then we can blame everything about the changing media on the producers – for after all, it is they who give the consumers "whatever they're given."

Savvy and Discerning

The odd thing is that the only people who believe that the consumers of popular culture are indiscriminate are those who are ignorant about the area. Whenever writers do research into everyday consumption practices, they discover – without exception – that they involve discrimination, decision-making, and the application and assessment of many competing criteria. The anthropologist Daniel Miller studied the culture of grocery shoppers in London, finding out – among other things – how consumers made their decisions about which material goods to buy. He was not specifically studying the use of aesthetic criteria; but his analysis of everyday purchasing decisions (groceries) shows that even the most quotidian moments of consumption involve complex decisions about what is a good and what is a bad product. He spent a year working with 76 families, watching what they bought in supermarkets, listening to them talk about why they bought what they did, and spending time in their houses watching how those provisions were used. Grocery buying is a massively important part of consumer society. Few people buy Porsches, but everybody needs food and drink on a daily basis. The common view of shoppers who buy junk food and heavily advertised household brands is that they see the adverts for these products and then reflexively go and buy what they see. We pay little attention to the complex intellectual work involved in choosing one brand of meat pie over another. But Miller found that the housewives and other women who still make up the majority of grocery shoppers make complicated decisions about what to buy based on who they are buying for (husbands, children, other relatives), what official authorities say these people should be eating (healthy foods, of course), what these people will actually eat when it's put in front of them, the relationships they have with these people (trying to make them happy and show them love, sometimes trying to influence and change them), the messages that advertisers have circulated around products, and the question of "quality" – whether a more expensive product might, in the long run, prove cheaper if it is better made and will last longer.[23]

Everyday purchasing decisions involve complex intellectual work. Aesthetic criteria play their part in making these decisions – and not just for highly educated, middle-aged American professors of literary studies. The journalist Alexis Petridis spent an afternoon with a 9-year-old girl who loves pop music – perhaps the ultimate icon of the helpless consumer in thrall to the decision-making of multinational corporations – and found that even here, consumption is never indiscriminate:

> Olivia is nine years old and she loves pop. These days, troubled music journalists spend a lot of their time clutching their brows in despair and demanding to know who buys all these dreadful, anodyne, manufactured pop singles . . . Olivia does . . . I have given her 20 pounds, let her loose in HMV and told her to buy what she wants . . . [A] lot of older music fans . . . like to believe that your average pre-teen fan is devoid of musical taste, susceptible to the most basic advertising techniques and incapable

of making a considered choice about what music they like . . . Kids will buy anything as long as it's been on the telly [they say] . . . But [they] haven't watched Olivia carefully dissecting her morning's purchases . . . She's . . . savvy and discerning . . . Olivia seems to have eclectic taste, and her opinions about music worked out . . . She prefers Pink to Britney Spears, not because of her hair or clothes, but because "her lyrics are better, she sings about different things, about herself and being angry. Britney's songs are all the same as each other" . . . [Later] she lets out what sounds suspiciously like a cynical cackle. I came here expecting to be horrified by the insane caprices of a weenybopper, but, frankly, I rather like the cut of Olivia's jib[24]

When research is done into the decisions involved in the consumption of popular culture, it repeatedly shows that these decisions do involve discrimination. By contrast, the assumption that consumers of popular culture are indiscriminate seems to rest on the following chain of reasoning: these people consume trash; it is not possible that anybody could make an informed decision to choose trash rather than high culture; therefore they are not making informed decisions. But this syllogism doesn't follow. It assumes that it is not possible for aesthetic systems to exist against whose criteria trash might be judged as "good" culture. And this is wrong. For there do exist just such systems: detailed aesthetic systems by which the consumers of popular culture come to decide that *Red Dragon* is a good serial killer novel, while other serial killer novels are less worthwhile; that Michael Jordan is an outstanding basketball player; that Brian Michael Bendis stands out for the quality of his super-hero comic book work.

How do we know this? We have the research. You have the research – here in your hands, with this guide to *Beautiful Things in Popular Culture*. Each chapter in this book lays out in detail the criteria that can be used to distinguish between good and bad popular culture, and shows that connoisseurs are using these in their discussions about their areas of interest. Which is not to say that social scientists have it right, and that we can explain consumer behavior as a series of rational decisions following straightforward logical rules – any more than we can reduce the history of Shakespeare criticism to a series of diagrams, lists of attributes, and statistical processes.[25] The creation, discussion, and circulation of these popular aesthetic systems are imaginative, unruly acts requiring inspiration, intelligence, and occasional bouts of extreme irrationality. Just like any other act of creativity.

And when we see the creative intellectual work involved in making popular aesthetic judgments, it changes the way that we imagine culture working. We can no longer accept that popular consumption is indiscriminate. We can no longer believe that consumers will take "whatever they are given." Which means that we cannot argue that consumers have no place in explaining important structural changes that we observe in our cultures – globalization or dumbing down, for example. For consumers are making informed decisions about what is "good" and "bad" in their preferred areas of popular culture. We must at least acknowledge their voices as contributing to the debate about what should be available in culture, what kinds of texts should be consumed, and what value those texts bring to the people who consume them. Too often we think about computer games, violent television, pornography, and even popular music as having "effects" on people. But there is intellectual work involved, discriminating work involved, in the choices about which pornography, which pop music, which computer games to consume. Consumers do not just do whatever they are told, or buy whatever they are offered.

Are We the Masses?

Each chapter in this collection is written by a connoisseur in the area. Each of them is an intellectual – or so I am claiming, although not all might be happy with the label – in the sense that the writers hold jobs in the "knowledge class" and make their money through the intellectual labor of generating and disseminating ideas.[26] Most – though not all – work as academics, but they're also journalists, book reviewers, music critics, presidents of fan clubs, and judges of prizes.

These writers are not typical of popular culture consumers – they're unusually intelligent, articulate, and often very funny. That's why I asked them to contribute to this collection. But at the same time, they are ordinary consumers in the sense that although their discriminating consumption of their area of culture might differ in degree from those of other consumers, it does not differ in kind. Not all consumers are connoisseurs of every kind of culture; but the authors demonstrate that the evaluative systems they are drawing on in making their choices about what is best also belong to the wider communities of consumers – not just those who work as intellectuals. For intellectuals have now begun to realize that there is no line between them and "the masses"; that the masses "may be just like them";[27] or indeed, that the masses may even *be* us. As one media researcher puts it: "Although my status as an academic defines me as a member of an elite group . . . I am at the same time a fully paid member of the mass audience."[28] The contributors to this collection are all consumers of popular culture at the same time as being outstanding intellectuals.

They also all understand – precisely because they know their areas and the ways in which popular aesthetic systems are employed in the practices of everyday consumption – that claims about what is "the best" in each area are always provisional. Such claims never tell a simple truth – they are always gambits, claims to power, and to the right to have one's own tastes validated. There is no final agreement among the aficionados of sneakers that the Nike Air Max Classic TW is the best sneaker; there will always be experts on *Xena: Warrior Princess* who will argue that Ares is the best villain; while a certain contingent of gay male porn connoisseurs will insist that *straightcollegemen.com* must be acknowledged as the best website for men who have sex with men. The claims offered in this book are not objective truths. Rather, the authors are playing the game. In every case, the claim that is made for "best" is a *reasonable* one. Other connoisseurs in each area would at least recognize the "best," would realize that it is uncontroversial for an expert in the area to make such a claim, and understand the criteria used and the arguments made for it – even if they do not personally agree that this is the absolute best. The authors all know that the question of which people are allowed to legitimate their tastes as "the best" is a politicized one.[29] The call to the authors in this collection was a cheeky one – to take the methodologies of exegesis and appreciation, which are agreed by intellectuals to be acceptable ones when applied to art, and to turn them onto vulgar, trashy objects that are not normally granted such a dignity. The object of the collection is not to provide a canon which interested students in popular culture must learn off by heart (although I personally have found the descriptions of the "beautiful things" to be fascinating and convincing). It is rather to give us a glimpse into popular aesthetic systems, and how they function in the consumption of mass culture. In most other contexts these authors would spend their time deconstructing the social functioning of traditional aesthetic systems; I'm grateful to them for indulging my call to a strategic use of them in this collection – and for playing the game so well.

Of course, given that my interest is ultimately in the systems of popular aesthetics used by consumers in deciding what is good and what is bad culture, I could equally well have put together a collection called *Absolute Crap in Popular Culture*, where aficionados wrote excoriating essays describing the very worst examples of their areas of expertise – "The worst romantic comedy" (*Forces of Nature*, perhaps); or "The worst rapper" (Vanilla Ice?). There are two reasons I chose to go with the Beautiful Things instead. First, I don't think that *Absolute Crap in Popular Culture* is quite as catchy a title; and second, it's my feeling that there's quite enough commentary already in circulation that's keen to focus on the worst examples of popular culture – and not enough looking at the beauty of the best of it.

Guidelines For Their Choices

What will happen to our cultures if the masses cease to look to intellectuals for guidance about what is good culture and what is bad? Do we necessarily face "chaos" and "anarchy," a "sea of relativism," as the critics on the right worry? With those on the left, should we be concerned that the working classes, if we do not lead them to appreciate art, will be lost to the "intellectually lazy" world of popular culture, unable to distinguish for themselves between what is valuable and what is worthless? With those who worry about the globalization of the media, and about dumbing down, should we be concerned that consumers of popular culture will take "whatever they're given"?

I am confident that none of these is true. When audiences don't rely on intellectuals to guide them in their cultural consumption, what actually happens is that they engage for themselves in detailed debates about what's good, what's bad, and how you would make these judgments. The consumers of popular culture already have aesthetic systems in place, which play a part in the intellectual work involved in making decisions about which trashy magazines to buy, which vulgar television programs to view, which dirty websites to visit. We may not approve of everything that they consume – but we can't leap from that fact to a claim that therefore there is no discrimination involved in their choices. Harold Bloom writes, with a flourish as though he is making an irrefutable point about the intellectual bankruptcy of those who challenge the traditional Western canon: "Batman comics, Mormon theme parks, television, movies and rock . . . where will the social changers find the guidelines for *their* choices?"[30] Start on pages 33–48. You'll find the answers right here.

Notes

1 Slavoj Žižek, *The Plague of Fantasies* (London: Verso, 1997).
2 H. T. Himmelweit, B. Swift, and M. E. Jaeger, quoted in Sonia Livingstone, *Making Sense of Television: The Psychology of Audience Interpretation* (London and New York: Routledge, 1998), p. 54.
3 Ibid.
4 Pierre Bourdieu, *Distinction: A Social Critique of the Judgement of Taste* (London: Routledge, 1984); Charlotte Brunsdon, "Problems with quality," *Screen* 31/1 (1990): 67–90; Simon Frith, "The good, the bad and the indifferent: defending popular culture from the populists," *Diacritics* 21/4 (1991): 102–115; Ava Collins, "Intellectuals, power and quality television," *Cultural Studies* 7/1 (1993): 28–45; Sarah Thornton, *Club Cultures: Music, Media and Subcultural Capital* (Cambridge: Polity, 1995); John Frow, *Cultural Studies and Cultural Value* (Oxford: Oxford University Press, 1995); Timothy Leggatt, "Identifying the undefinable – an essay on approaches to assessing quality in television in the UK," in Sakae Ishikawa, ed., *Quality Assessment of Television* (Luton: John Libbey Press, 1996), pp. 73–87; Robin Nelson, *TV Drama in Transition: Forms, Values and Cultural Change* (London: Macmillan Press, 1997); Daniel Miller, "Why some things matter," in Miller, ed., *Material Cultures: Why Some Things Matter* (London: UCL Press, 1998), pp. 3–21; Jim Collins, "High-pop: an introduction," in Collins, ed., *High-Pop: Making Culture into popular entertainment* (Malden and Oxford: Blackwell Publishing, 2002), pp. 1–31.
5 Simon Frith, *Performing Rites: Evaluating Popular Music* (Oxford and New York: Oxford University Press, 1996); Mark Jancovich, " 'A real shocker': authenticity, genre and the struggle for distinction," *Continuum: Journal of Media and Cultural Studies* 14/1 (April 2000): 23–36; Leo Trachtenberg, *The Wonder Team: The True Story of the Incomparable 1927 New York Yankees* (Bowling Green, Ohio: Bowling Green State University Popular Press, 1995); Bradley S. Greenberg and Rick Busselle, "Audience dimensions of quality in situation comedies and action programmes," in Sakae Ishikawa, ed., *Quality Assessment of Television* (Luton: John Libbey/ Luton University Press, 1996), pp. 169–96; Robert Drew, " 'Anyone can do it': forging a participatory culture in karaoke bars," in Henry Jenkins, Tara McPherson, and Jane Shattuc, eds., *Hop on Pop: The Politics and Pleasure of Popular Culture* (Durham and London: Duke University Press,

2002), pp. 254–69; Kembrew McLeod, "*1/2: a critique of rock criticism in North America," *Popular Music* 20/1 (2001): 47–60; Alan McKee, "Which is the best *Doctor Who* story? A case study in value judgements outside the academy," *Intensities: The Journal of Cult Media* 1 (2001): <www.cult-media.com/issue1/Amckee.htm>; Susan Stewart, "Ceci Tuera Cela: graffiti as crime and art," in John Fekete, ed., *Life After Postmodernism* (New York: St Martins Press, 1988), pp. 161–80; David Andrews, "Convention and ideology in the contemporary softcore feature: the sexual architecture of *House of Love*," *The Journal of Popular Culture* 38/1 (2004): 5–33.

6   Frith, *Performing Rites*, pp. 52–74.

7   Allan Bloom, *The Closing of the American Mind* (New York: Simon and Schuster, 1987); Harold Bloom, *The Western Canon* (New York: Harcourt Brace & Company, 1994).

8   Allan Bloom, *The Closing of the American Mind*, p. 344.

9   Harold Bloom, *The Western Canon*, p. 1.

10   Allan Bloom, *The Closing of the American Mind*, p. 351.

11   Ibid., pp. 260, 254.

12   Harold Bloom, *The Western Canon*, p. 9.

13   Ibid., pp. 33, 38.

14   Allan Bloom, *The Closing of the American Mind*, p. 337.

15   Ibid., p. 64.

16   "Table of contents," *Time* magazine (April 26, 2004), p. 5.

17   Jürgen Habermas, *The Structural Transformation of the Public Sphere: An Inquiry into a Category of Bourgeois Society*, trans. Thomas Burger and Frederick Lawrence (Cambridge, MA: The MIT Press, 1989 [1962]), p. 201.

18   F. Von Holtzendorff, cited with approval in ibid., p. 240.

19   Ibid., p. 102, quoting Wieland.

20   Ibid., pp. 165, 166.

21   Ibid., p. 165.

22   Sheepwatch '04, "Ministry of disinformation-related program activities," *Wither in the Light* (March 4, 2004); <www.mushika.blogspot.com/2004/3/sheepwatch-04-ministry-of.html> (accessed July 7, 2004); John R. McEwen, "*Rugrats in Paris*: the movie," *FilmQuips* (2000), <www.filmquipsonline.com/rugratsinparis.html> (accessed July 7, 2004); John Cannon, "Where should we go from here?" *Another Perspective* (2004), <www.anotherperspective.org/advoc118.html> (accessed July 7, 2004); Michael Jensen, "Opportunity, responsibility and the edutainment war." Keynote speech given at the Association of American University Presses Second Electronic Publishers Workshop, Washington DC, June 1994, <www.nap.edu/staff/mjensen/aaupwk94.htm> (accessed 7 July 2004).

23 Daniel Miller, *A Theory of Shopping* (Ithaca, NY: Cornell University Press, 1998).

24 Alexis Petridis, "Pop of the tots," *Guardian* (August 30, 2002), p. 2.

25 See Del Hawkins, Cathy Neal, Pascale Quester, and Roger Best, *Consumer Behaviour: Implications For Marketing Strategy* (Sydney et al: The McGraw-Hill Companies Inc, 1994).

26 Frow, *Cultural Studies and Cultural Value.*

27 John Hartley, *Popular Reality: Journalism, Modernity and Popular Culture* (London, New York and Sydney: Arnold, 1996), p. 239.

28 Brian McNair, *Journalism and Democracy: An Evaluation of the Political Public Sphere* (London and New York: Routledge, 2000), p. 3.

29 Bourdieu, *Distinction.*

30 Harold Bloom, *The Western Canon*, pp. 519, 526.

1

Best Contemporary Mainstream Superhero Comics Writer: Brian Michael Bendis

Henry Jenkins

In *Ultimate Spider-Man* 28 (henceforth *U.S.*), Mary Jane (M.J.) comes racing into the Midtown High School library and asks her boyfriend, Peter Parker, whether he brought his costume. Rhino is smashing up downtown Manhattan and no one has been able to stop him. Asking M.J. to cover for his fourth period French class, Peter races to his locker and grabs his Spider-Man costume (hidden in his knapsack), only to run into his Aunt May who is at school for a parent–teacher meeting. As Peter squirms in his chair, the teacher accuses him of being "distracted" and "unfocused" in class. Begging off, he races for the door, only to spot the school principal, and then spins off down another hallway. He cuts through the school cafeteria where he catches the lunch lady grumbling that the Rhino coverage is interrupting her soaps, then out the door, where he runs into his friend Gwen, who is sobbing that nobody cares about her. Extracting himself from this emotional crisis, Peter races out of the school, stopping long enough to shout to M.J. to go see after Gwen. A few seconds later, Peter gets clocked by a football and chased by the school bullies, before scaling over the walls, scampering across rooftops, and riding on the tops of cars, arriving just in time to see Iron Man taking kudos for stopping the Rhino's rampage.

Whew! We've all had days like this.

I always wondered how even an ultra-nerd like Peter could manage to skip classes so often (all in the call of duty, of course) without ending up flunking out or spending the rest of his life in detention. From the start, Stan Lee and Steve Ditko conceived Spider-Man as sharing the flaws and foibles of his teen readers.[1] Forget Metropolis and Gotham City: Marvel set its stories in actual locations in Manhattan. They relied on the sudden introduction of real world problems, such as not having enough money to buy a new costume or not knowing how to explain why you just stood up your hot date, to increase audience identification. What counted as comic book realism in the 1960s doesn't necessarily work for contemporary kids. Through the *Ultimate Spider-Man* series, Brian Michael Bendis retools Ol' Spidey for a generation that has grown up on *Buffy the Vampire Slayer*, creating a comic that is as hip and "postmodern" as it gets.

Bendis has fleshed out the core characters, changing the way they dress and talk to reflect contemporary mallrat culture, but not altering their core. In this case, the supportive M.J., the concerned Aunt May, and the "drama queen" Gwen are used as comic foils to amplify Peter's struggle to escape the gravitational pull of his high school. Bendis also reconceptualized some members of the Spider-Man rogue's gallery to up their "coolness" factor – turning the usually dorky Rhino into a powerful mecha-man who tosses city buses through Starbucks' windows. The well-crafted issue maintains a frantic pace that keeps you turning pages. It contrasts with previous issues, coming right after an angsty story arc that took us inside the head of the Green Goblin and almost cost M.J. her life. It builds on evolving character relations, such as M.J.'s new involvement in Peter's superhero life; and it prepares for future plot developments, such as the growing rift in Gwen's family. Artist Mark Bagley distills the essence of the characters into telling gestures, such as M.J. waving frantically from an upper window for Peter to get moving, Peter staring off into space during the parent–teacher conference, or a frustrated Spider-Man watching as Iron Man throws his hands up in victory.

The Bendis Moment

Film critics used to write about "the Lubitsch touch."[2] Ernest Lubitsch melded European sophistication with classic Hollywood storytelling, adding one more layer of suggestion to the basic building blocks of the romantic comedy. Today, comic fans might talk about the "Bendis moment." Bendis always adds his own distinctive twist to the familiar characters and situations of the superhero genre, creating "memorable moments" which will be discussed, debated, and savored by the fan boys. Half the time Bendis infuriates us by doing the unthinkable; the other half, he rewards us by taking us places we never imagined we'd get to go; but no matter what, he produces comics we want to talk about. A Bendis moment can be as innocent as Peter Parker, sprawled on the floor cradling his crumpled Spider-Man costume and sobbing over his breakup with M.J. (*U.S.* 33) or as crude as the controversial sequence in *Alias* (1) (henceforth *A.*), where it is implied that the protagonist Jessica Jones is having anal sex with Luke Cage.

One of the most memorable Bendis moments came when Parker gets rescued by three of the hottest mutant "babes" from the *Ultimate X-men* cast. As Spidey "fans," they are just tickled to death to meet him. The telepath Jean Grey gushes that he's the first guy she's met in months that hasn't tried to imagine her naked (*U.S.* 43). Across 14 awkward panels, Bendis and Bagley cut between Peter and Jean, as he tries, without success, not to think of her naked and as she waits impatiently for him to get over it. Any guy who has wanted desperately to be "better than the others" and has had their hormones get in the way must surely feel for Peter's predicament confronting a girl who can read his every conflicted thought. Such moments grow organically out of the interplay between characters we know and love and exploit the juxtaposition between the fantastical situations we associate with superhero comics and a much more mundane reality we live in most of the time.

Bendis, Who?

Bendis writes what industry insiders call "buzz books," managing to be a critical darling who racks up awards and a commercial success who tops the charts. Bendis won both the Wizard award (from fans) and the Eisner award (from fellow pros) for best writer in 2003 and 2004. Most months, he writes 4 or 5 of the 25 top-selling comics. *Wizard* has called Bendis the "Michael Jordan of Marvel," citing this most valuable player as one of the key factors behind the company's commercial and critical revival over the past few years.[3] (Somewhere around here, I keep wanting to toss off a "Bendis like Beckham" pun.) As Marvel President Bill Jemas explains, "Brian delivers hundreds of thousands of fans every month. He makes all of those fans happy and brings them back."[4] Current *Wonder Woman* scribe Greg Rucka praises Bendis as *the* consummate professional: "He has a complete command of the art. Every aspect of the writer's job, he can do it well, and understands it intuitively. He's got every trick in the toolbox and God knows, he knows how to use them."[5]

And to top it all, he is amazingly prolific, cranking out 5–8 different titles every month over the past several years. *Ultimate Spider-Man* alone adds up to 18 issues a year. When Marvel needed a pinch hitter for *Ultimate X-Men*, Bendis crossed over and added another biweekly title to his workload, even as he was helping to launch *Ultimate Fantastic Four* and knock off the *Ultimate Six* mini-series.

His commercial success and professionalism have earned Bendis the creative freedom to take risks and the power to reshape the Marvel universe. As he notes: "I get paid whether I kick ass or phone it in. Why not kick ass?"[6] And kick ass he does, month after month.

Why Writer?

Comics, after all, are a medium that combines words and pictures and often involves a collaboration between a writer and an artist. During much of its history, artists were the fan favorites, each representing a distinctive visual style that changed how we looked at and thought about superheroes.[7] If anything, contemporary comics include a broader array of styles and a more nuanced color palette than ever before, and there are certainly fans who buy comics for the art. But many comic fans and critics would agree that the present moment represents a kind of golden age for comic writers. DC Comics President Paul Levine argues that comics represent a kind of sweet spot for popular writers – a place that pays well and still allows a high degree of creative freedom – and as such, it is the place both where many writers get started and where they return when they want to stretch and retool themselves.[8] So, you can see novelists like Brad Meltzner (*Green Arrow*) or Michael Chabon, television writers like Joss Whedon and J. Michael Straczinski, or filmmakers like Kevin Smith writing comics – and at the same time, top comics writers, from Howard Chaykin to Bendis himself, are being pulled toward other media.[9] Bendis acts as story-editor for the MTV animated *Spider-Man* series, is working with Frank Oz on a film adaptation of *Powers*, and is consulting with the game companies making interactive entertainment out of Marvel properties. And he's written a very funny book, *Fortune and Glory*, about his experiences trying to deal with competing (and ultimately fruitless) bids to make *Torso* into a movie.

In comics, the writer is the guiding creative intelligence.[10] In some cases, especially in indie comics, the writer and artist are one and the same. Bendis started out that way on his early projects, such as *Jinx*, *Goldfish*, *Torso*, and *Fire*. He developed a distinctive visual style based on staging and photographing each panel, then pushing them into high contrast, and rotoscoping the images. Mimicking Film Noir, he uses highly kinetic and canted compositions which rely on sharp contrasts between light and shadow. He deploys some of these same framing techniques in his later works – as in the ways he captures the monotony of police work in both *Torso* and *Powers* by showing a two-page spread of dozens of identically framed reaction shots of various suspects denying any knowledge of the case.

In other cases, the writer develops a detailed screenplay that is given life by the artist. As a top talent at the most successful contemporary comics company, Bendis gets his pick among artists and each of his comics has a distinctive visual style which serves his content well. Although I found his Kewpie-eyed characters cloying at first, I have come to appreciate the Manga-influenced style which Mark Bagley brings to *Ultimate Spider-Man*; Bagley amplifies his teen character's emotional responses through the use of exaggerated facial expressions and gestures. Michael Avon Oeming's artwork for *Powers* is, if anything, even more stylized, but far less cutesy-pie, emphasizing the iconic quality of his superhero and detective protagonists, while Alex Maleev's scratchy drawing style and more somber palette captures *Daredevil*'s moodiness. Bendis uses David Mack's arty pastels for the covers of *Alias*, signaling its more female-friendly tone and content. Bendis also uses Mack's collage-like images in "Wake Up!" (*Daredevil* 16–19; henceforth *D.D.*) as clues into the psyche of a child who has been traumatized by watching Daredevil battle his father, Leap Frog. In *Ultimate Marvel Team-Up* each issue is drawn by a different artist, often allowing little-known or fringe artists their first shot at doing mainstream comics.

Why Mainstream?

Why mainstream? Comic fans are sharply divided into two camps: on the one side, there are fans of comics as popular culture (with a focus on the creative reworking of genre elements and plays with continuity) and their voice is perhaps best represented by *Wizard*; on the other side, there are fans of comics as art (with a focus on aesthetic experimentation and unconventional content) and their voice is perhaps best represented by *Comics Journal*. At my local shop, the two types of books are divided off from each other by a partition designed to keep the kids from mangling the adult books, but also working to signal a certain cultural hierarchy at play. To praise Bendis as one of today's best writers is already to take sides, since the *Comics Journal* crowd will look down their noses at you if you admit to reading superhero comics.

The most interesting contemporary comics fall somewhere between these two extremes – including work published by smaller companies like ABC, Oni, Image, Dark Horse, or Wildstorm, which put their own spin on the superhero genre or works published by the boutique labels, such as Vertigo at DC or Max at Marvel, which are maintained by the mainstream publishers. Increasingly, the lines between mainstream and indie comics are breaking down. Much as indie filmmakers are getting a shot at directing Hollywood blockbusters, indie comic creators (such as Gilbert Hernandez, John Strum, or Peter Bagge) are venturing into the mainstream without risking their street cred. Bendis started out doing edgy black-and-white crime comics whose visual style owed plenty to John Alton and verbal style owed almost as much to David Mamet. Bendis still keeps a toe in the indie realm with his creator-owned *Powers* series, even as he shapes such flagship Marvel properties as *Spider-Man*, *Fantastic Four*, *X-Men*, and *Daredevil*.

Alias helped to launch Marvel's more mature-themed Max line, allowing Bendis to put an indie spin on the Marvel universe. In the first issue, his detective protagonist accidentally videos Captain America sneaking out of a married woman's apartment in the middle of the night and putting on his costume on a shadowy rooftop. Some argue that the self-proclaimed "potty mouth" was brought over from the fringes precisely to break the lingering hold of the Comics Code. Curiously, his Ultimate books have had the opposite impact, opening comics to hordes of younger readers. Every year the core comic market gets older and older and demands more and more mature content, hence the need to break free from 1950s vintage content restrictions. At the same time, the future of comics depends on attracting newbies, who come to the medium without a lot of background on its characters. Whatever the problem with the current comics market is, Bendis is at least part of the solution.

Why Superhero?

Why superhero? Let's face it: When most people think about American comics, they are thinking buff men in tights. There are certainly other genres thriving today; crime comics, fantasy comics, romances, and kid's comics are all undergoing a revival – mostly on the fringes. Vertigo has made its reputation as the place where DC does everything but super-heroes. That's where someone like Neil Gaiman rules supreme (and he would clearly be in the bidding for best contemporary comics writer if I excluded the superhero modifier). Bendis is one of those writers who make it safe to lust after superhero comics again.

The challenges of writing superhero comics are unique in popular culture. For one thing, the main DC titles have been in continuous publication since the 1930s and the main Marvel titles since the 1960s. And there are readers who have stuck with those characters, across all of those decades and who know chapter and verse of what they call "continuity." Continuity can give emotional realism, ensuring that later stories build upon rather than contradict what comes before, but continuity can also be a bottle-neck restricting the flow of new ideas into the genre.[11] Hardcore fans may take pleasure in a plot point that pays off years after it was first introduced, but new readers balk when they feel like they have joined the story mid-process.

Bendis has said that his greatest excitement as a writer comes when he paints himself into a corner and then has to figure out how to get back out again. He constantly takes risks that a lesser writer would avoid and then makes them pay off for the reader, inviting us to think about the superheroes, their rogues galleries, their supporting characters, and their worlds in fresh new ways. Sometimes that pisses off the old-timers. Bendis sparked controversy with some of his earliest work for Marvel from fans who felt that he was putzing around with Elektra, a character introduced by Frank Miller during his acclaimed run of *Daredevil*.[12]

The main point of the Ultimate series was to allow writers like Bendis to scuttle a lot of baggage while allowing Marvel to continue to publish other books that follow the well-established continuity. The Ultimate books operate in a world apart from the other Marvel titles. Mark Millar, the other author who shaped Marvel's Ultimate series, explains:

> The Ultimate line was designed to remind us about the strong concepts which have carried these characters for four decades. It's like slimming down a fat chick. . . . I found Marvel's complex history and three-and-a-half-thousand super characters daunting. Starting from scratch gave me and Brian the same excitement there must have been in 1962. There was no feeling of restraint when putting this together.[13]

The recent history of the superhero genre has been marked by several movements between deconstructionist writers (such as Frank Miller, Alan Moore, Rick Veitch, or Grant Morrison) who critiqued the genre's fascist fantasies, and reconstructionist writers (such as Mark Waid, Kurt Busiek, Mark Millar, Jeph Loeb, or Greg Rucka) who have sought to put the "Wow!" back in the genre.[14] Bendis's deft writing allows him to move back and forth between the two camps, chipping away at clichés, critiquing underlying assumptions, while at the same time offering the kind of slobber-knocking fight scenes and high-flying adventures that make comic fans grin. Each Bendis book offers a different angle on the superhero genre: depicting a young man learning the ropes and facing adult dismissals (*Ultimate Spiderman*); a more mature superhero whose world seems to be coming apart before his eyes (*Daredevil*); a former B-level superhero who sometimes has trouble getting the A-listers on the telephone (*Alias*); and a bunch of beat cops who have to unravel the scandals and conspiracies celebrity superheroes hope to hide from their tabloid-reading public (*Powers*). Bendis clearly loves the genre, but he's more than willing to take the piss out of it.

Why Contemporary?

Why contemporary? The current comic market is divided between fans who buy the individual issues as they come into the comic shops and those who wait to buy a paper-bound "graphic novel" compilation at the local booksellers. These two competing readerships mean that writers have to balance long-term plot developments with memorable moments that pay off in each issue. Bendis is the master of the cliff-hanging final panel. Consider, for example, *Powers* 9, which ends as Deena Pilgrim grabs the arm of a mob boss, just as he is teleporting away. The final page shows his arm come off in her hands and we know that all kind of mayhem – legal, verbal, and physical – will follow.

For most of their history, superhero stories had to be contained within a single issue, since there was no guarantee that any given reader would be able to get their hands on a particular title off the spin rack at the corner drugstore. As comics moved toward specialty stores, which offered a more reliable system of distribution, continuity and serialization became more and more central. Today, most plotlines extend across five, six, or seven issues. Writers like Bendis exploit this slower pace to flesh out the characters and to get the maximum emotional impact from each moment in the hero's journey. Stan Lee's version of Spider-Man's origins was told in a single issue, where many scenes were related in single panels. Bendis retold that story across the first five issues of *Ultimate Spider-Man*, and thus was able to spend more time building up, say, the relationship between Peter and his Uncle Ben, the other students' reactions to the initial manifestations of his power, or the wrestling company where he first tries to earn some bread through his newfound strength.

There's no point comparing Bendis with Stan Lee, the writer who created so many of the Marvel characters that Bendis is now retooling. Lee and Bendis wrote in such radically different contexts, for such different audiences, and under such different constraints that there is no basis for making a meaningful comparison. All we can say is that Bendis is doing exactly what the genre needs right now and that in the current context, it's hard to think of anyone who is doing it better.

Bendis is the man in the middle – between the indies and the mainstream, hardcore fans and newbie readers, deconstructionist and reconstructionist impulses, memorable moments and elaborate story arcs. So, what is it that makes reading a Bendis book one of the grand pleasures in contemporary comics?

Dialogue

Wizard praises Bendis for "dialogue that pops and snaps more than a fresh bowl of Rice Krispies."[15] Some of Bendis's best dialogue is laugh-out-loud funny: Spider-Man reading fat jokes off index cards and then tossing them into the Kingpin's face – like a more aggressive version of David Letterman (*U.S.* 12); Deena Pilgram, the working stiff cop in *Powers*, wandering through the lobby of a superteam's skyscraper head-quarters, obviously modeled after the Fantastic Four's Baxter Building, and mumbling, "the Windex bill alone" (*Powers* 15; henceforth *P.*) or chiding a suspect because he actually paid to buy the DVD of *Runaway Bride* (*P.* 13). In an exchange that winks at Stan Lee's tendency to put Yiddish words in the mouths of his WASP protagonists, M.J. demands to know where Peter "picked up" a word like "Mishugas" and then urges him to "put it back" where he found it (*U.S.* 47).

Superhero comics are notorious for their clunky or over-inflated dialogue, dating back to a time when the pictures were crude and the writers sometimes had to fill in plot information the artist never got around to drawing. So, you have the situation where characters describe things that would be obvious to anyone standing at the location or where villains spell out their entire plans. Sometimes the entire book is nothing but exposition as the writer tries to cram an ambitious story into far too few pages. Only belatedly did comic writers see dialogue as a means of defining the characters or setting the emotional tone. When Peter Parker first realizes that he has spider strength, Stan Lee has him exclaim, "What's happening to me? I feel – different! As though my entire body is charged with some fantastic energy," and then has him go into a long wonkish discussion of how his various powers parallel those of the common spider.[16] (Come to think of it, maybe that is how the geekish protagonist would react!) Bendis deals with a similar discovery in *Alias* in a far more down-to-earth manner. An angry adolescent is trudging along through a city park, her mind a million miles away, and then, suddenly, realizes that her feet are no longer touching the ground and that she has no idea how to land again. Her: "Shit! Oh Shit!" economically expresses her shift between giddy excitement and gut-wrenching terror.

Bendis has noted, "If anything, my goals for dialogue come from the fact that I so abhor exposition. Information has to be given to the reader, but I always ask myself if this dialogue I have written is something that someone would say out loud."[17] Bendis makes limited use of thought balloons or even titling, using dialogue primarily to depict communication between characters, and relying on vivid images to carry the weight of exposition.

At the same time, Bendis adopts more naturalistic patterns of communication, including a focus on the various ways people struggle, in real life, to adequately express their ideas. A recent anthology, *Total Sellout*, shares a series of his monologues, some autobiographical, others based on things he overheard on the street, which shows his early fascination with human speech patterns. Bendis loves to weave complex layers of word balloons across the page, allowing a well-drawn character study to hold our interest in the absence of more visceral action sequences. This technique came into its own in *Jinx*, which includes rambling debates between various low-life characters on such issues as the letterboxing of movies that recall the debate about Madonna songs that opens *Reservoir Dogs* or the famous "Royale with Cheese" exchange in *Pulp Fiction*.

As Bendis moved from realist works toward superhero fantasies, he draws on these same rambling exchanges to add authenticity, as when a coroner in *Powers* 2 grumbles about the challenge of doing autopsies on super beings, the police at the opening of *Daredevil* 32 grumble about being called out of bed in the middle of the night, or when a groupie in *Powers* 13 describes her various sexual encounters with the cape and cowl set. Here's an exchange between Gwen and Peter from *Ultimate Spider-Man* 40 which takes the awkwardness of adolescent interaction to a comic level of absurdity, but could have come off any teen chat room:

Gwen: Are you going to that party tonight?
Peter: What party?
Gwen: There's a party at this guy's house.
Peter: I don't even know about it. Who told you?
Gwen: No one. I overheard. No one tells me about parties.
Peter: No one tells me either.
Gwen: Know why?
Peter: Because we have no friends.
Gwen: We're losers.
Peter: Sure, but you know, by choice.
Gwen: Not really.
Peter: Not really?
Gwen: No. I don't want to be a loser. I want people to like me.
Peter: But you hate everyone.
Gwen: Yeah, but I don't want them to hate me.
Peter: Allrighty . . .
Gwen: Do you want to go to the party?
Peter: Not even in the slightest.

Gwen: It's just at some guy's house from the other school.
Peter: Which other school?
Gwen: I don't know – that school that isn't ours – that you hear the idiot
         guys always being in a rivalry with . . .

Bendis fits all of this dialogue in only two frames – and continues the sequence for the rest of the page.

Critics accuse Bendis of being verbose and he certainly uses more words per page than anyone else. Yet, Bendis knows when to pull back and let his images speak for him, making effective use of wordless montages which convey the characters' thought processes. Consider the moment in *Ultimate Spider-Man* 14 where the meat-headed Kong almost discovers Spider-Man's secret identity but is unable to hold all of the pieces of information together in his mind; or the scene in *Alias* 21 where we see a teenaged Jessica's thoughts as she masturbates to a pinup of Johnny Storm (ending with a close-up of her curling toes). Perhaps most spectacularly, an entire issue of *Powers* (31) includes only the grunts of subhuman apes as Bendis traces the origins of the superhero back to prehistoric times. Throughout *Alias*, Bendis contrasts the information-dump that Jessica receives from her clients with wordless shots showing the detective absorbing and reacting to the information.

Bendis fans come to admire his verbally intensive passages, especially moments when the action stops and characters confess some aspect of their worldview. The "ReBeCCA, PLeaSe CoMe HoMe," storyline in *Alias*, for example, uses a series of interviews and confessions to depict the self-dread and claustrophobia experienced by a small town teen who becomes convinced that she must be a mutant and the various ways that she is misunderstood by her parents, teachers, classmates, and the local minister.

In *Alias*, Bendis's dialogue often walks a thin line between profane and profound, exploiting the freedom a "Mature Readers" title gives him to break traditional taboos. Near the end of the series, Bendis ironically comments on the gap between the world he is depicting and the way these same characters talk in other Marvel titles. He inserts Jessica's origin stories in the margins – literally as well as figuratively – of the first *Spider-Man* comic, including an exchange where Jessica and Peter compare notes on Flash, the school bully, who torments them both:

Peter: I just saw what happened. That Flash is a real class-A jerk.
Jessica: He's a fucking depressed dickhead retard.
Peter: I, uh, ok. I wouldn't use those words exactly but . . .

Realism

If Bendis's inarticulate but emotionally expressive characters recall the impact of method acting on the American cinema, Bendis prepares for writing such scenes in much the same way Robert DeNiro gets into his roles – by going out in the streets, connecting with real people, and observing their work culture. When he wrote *Torso*, a police procedural, he spent time riding in patrol cars. When he wrote *Jinx*, he interviewed scam artists, bounty hunters, and petty gamblers. He told an interviewer, "There's something true in everything I write, including Spider-Man."[18] Obviously, Bendis can't sling webs and scamper across the rooftops, but he works to surround his superheroes with more realistic cops, detectives, reporters, criminals, and victims. And he did spend time hanging out in malls and on chat rooms to try to understand better the speech patterns and lifestyles of contemporary teens in order to make the high school culture in *Ultimate Spider-Man* as convincing as possible.

Alias, in particular, is noted for its blunt insertion of more mundane human realities into a superhero context. Jessica, rescued by Thor, gets motion sickness and vomits on the mighty Norse god's boots (*A.* 23). Spider-Woman explains that she doesn't wear her old costume any more because it makes her butt look too big (*A.* 20). Two superheroes complain about how suspicious they are of all kinds of relationships when everyone they know has at least one secret identity (*A.* 15). Jessica has trouble explaining to her mom what she does or why it matters (*A.* 7). Jessica gets snubbed when waiting in line at a hot night spot because she wasn't even an Avenger (*A.* 18). If superheroes existed, these are precisely the kinds of exchanges they would be having behind closed doors. And the institutions have adjusted to the point that it is standard medical procedure in checking someone into the emergency room to ask whether or not they are mutants. One of my favorite panels (*A.* 7) shows Jessica thinking about a case while sitting on the john. Sure, Bendis has an earthy – some might say, vulgar – streak (and sometimes it gets the best of him), but then, given the sanitized world of traditional comics, it is refreshing to read a story where a superhero takes a crap.

Characterization

Bendis's naturalistic dialogue and realistic details contribute to some of the most compelling characterization in contemporary comics. *Ultimate*

X-Man artist David Finch notes that "What Bendis does best is he can put himself inside anybody he wants without judgment. The characters he writes are real people, with real human feelings. They're just so vivid."[19] *Wizard* concurs: "Bendis doesn't seem to speak through his characters so much as they use him to channel their fears, worries, and most intimate thoughts."[20]

For the guys at *Wizard* the ultimate demonstration of Bendis's skill is his retooling and rehabilitation of Aunt May: "Anyone who can elevate Peter Parker's doting, septuagenarian Aunt May from a wheat-cake-baking-worrywart to a younger, self-assured magisterial matriarch of the household deserves high accolades."[21] Throughout *Ultimate Spider-Man*, Bendis helps us to feel the pain and loneliness she feels after the brutal murder of her husband and the growing isolation she faces as Peter keeps running out of the house in the middle of the night or doesn't come home because, unbeknownst to her, he's battling Venom. For all of the fascination with secret identities in comics, people rarely examine what a wedge a secret on that scale can drive into a relationship, how many lies get told, how many promises get broken. In "Guilt" (*U.S.* 45), the better part of the issue centers around May's visit to her shrink. She withstood the death of her sister and the death of her husband without seeking counseling, but then finds herself struggling to deal with the death of Captain Stacey, Gwen's father, with whom she has experienced only a mild flirtation. She talks about the ways that the emergence of Spider-Man has contributed to her feelings that the world around her has stopped making sense.

Similarly, an earlier issue, "Confessions" (*U.S.* 13), takes us through the process of Peter's coming out as Spider-Man to M.J., which moves from shock and disbelief, into giddy excitement, and then burning passion, before it is cut short by a worried Aunt May who is convinced that the two teens are doing something they shouldn't up in his bedroom. From here, Bendis can build on the relationship through throwaway scenes, having laid down a believable foundation for the on-again, off-again romance between two teen characters who are getting involved in situations they neither fully understand nor fully control.

Bendis's Peter Parker really doesn't know if he's ready for grown-up realities, still gives himself over to sophomoric pranks like pulling down Doc Ock's pants in the middle of a battle (*U.S.* 20), still thumbs his nose at adult authorities – including the fine folks at SHIELD who are monitoring his development – and still refuses to overlook the hypocrisy of newspaper editors who jump into bed with petty politicians and then run smear campaigns against the friendly neighborhood Spider-Man. Bendis powerfully depicts Peter's confusion and outrage when the Kingpin literally gets away with a murder that was recorded on video and none of the grown-ups seems the slightest bit shocked (*U.S.* 48). Like many teens, there are days when Peter feels like "everyone on the planet Earth is picking on me" – only in his case, the bullies include men with robotic arms or green skin (*U.S.* 47).

Trajectory

Perhaps the most remarkable thing about *Alias* is that it had an ending. Umberto Eco famously described the impossible, inhuman reality created around characters like Superman who are not only indestructible but also move no closer to death.[22] Bendis takes Jessica not toward death but toward a new beginning which addressed the central emotional issues that have driven the character throughout the series. From the opening book, he has depicted a woman who has turned her back on her superpowers and tried to distance herself from her former friends. She consistently deflects all questions about why she hung up her cape, but the subject comes up in almost every issue. From the first, we see that she is depressed and engages in a wide array of self-destructive behavior. On her first date with Scott Lang (The Ant-Man), he refuses to order her a drink, insisting that they see what it's like to deal with each other sober (*A.* 15). We watch her drawn toward and back away from a series of men. As often as not, her investigations into crimes end up being investigations into her own psyche. To be sure, all of this is consistent with the genre conventions of the hardboiled detective story (especially as they have been fleshed out by people like Sara Paretsky).

So, on first reading, it is easy to take it all for granted, until you get to the final story arc, which takes us through the exhilaration of her teenaged discovery of her own powers and then the prolonged mental and physical debasement she faces as she spends several years under the mental control of Kilgrave. She finally breaks down and tells Luke Cage what happened, for the first time in the books leaving herself totally vulnerable to someone else. Her description of the complex psychological aftereffects of her subjugation is at once fantastical and totally convincing:

He put it in my head. He made me *do* it. He made me *say* it. It doesn't – you have to understand – it doesn't *change* the fact that I *did* it or *said* it. No one understands. They say they do, but they don't. In your head – it doesn't *feel* any different that when you think it *yourself*, you see? It feels – Not only does it feel the *same*, it actually feels *better* because the thought, the command is pure. It's strong. It's there. Loud and clear. It's almost sooth-ing. In my mind I can't tell the difference between what he *made* me do or say and what I do or say on my own. The only reason I know I wasn't in love with him is that I say to myself: How could I be? I hate him. (*A.* 25)

Without making it clear at first, Bendis has taken us through the mental processes of someone who has survived the most horrific sexual assault, whose dignity and ability to consent have been stripped aside, and who has been left to live with the consequences. No wonder she has seemed so guarded and so self-destructive. No wonder she has been depicted so many times with her eyes turned downward or as if she felt faintly sick to her stomach.

In the final pages, she seems ready to put the pieces together: a case forces her to confront and overpower Kilgrave and finally move beyond that chapter of her life. While Luke up till now has been depicted as the wrong man for her, he is someone who actually understands her con-flicted feelings, appreciates her strength in withstanding all of this, and shows her the support she needs. In the final panels, we learn that she is pregnant with Luke's child and that he will stand beside her. This is not the kind of place you expect a Superhero comic to take you. How telling that Bendis ends where most other superhero titles begin – with an origin story rooted in trauma.

Last Thoughts

Bendis himself sets the terms by which we evaluate his work. He told interviewers at *Write Now!*:

I heard a quote from Sting, that rock-and-roll is a bastard art form. That there is no one thing that makes rock-and-roll, rock-and-roll, that it only really succeeds when somebody makes the conscious personal decision to pull something new into it from outside like jazz, country, or opera. Some-thing vital happens then. I think comics are the same way. There is no one thing that makes a great comic. Each time someone's gone outside of comics and pulled something into it for their own reasons, something really exciting happens. A lot of artists have done that, but not a lot of writers[23]

Bendis has helped to revitalize the modern superhero comics by pulling into the genre a range of techniques which in other art forms ensure naturalism: his reliance on fragmented and sometimes incomplete dialogue; his interest in documenting the perspectives of professional groups or youth subcultures; his attention to the mundane details of everyday life; his ability to allow characters to grow and develop over time. He talks about his comics alongside the work of writers like David Mamet or Richard Price, refusing to accept a second-class status for his own medium. Rather, his work does something theirs cannot – build on a 30- or 40-year history of our relationships with these characters, push these ideas into alternative realities and use them to comment on our own lived experiences, and, oh yeah, capture the hearts and imaginations of hundreds of thousands of teenagers.

We really are living in a golden age of comic writers and there are many people pulling at the superhero genre from lots of different directions. But nobody writes comics quite like Bendis does.

Notes

1 Stan Lee, *Origins of Marvel Comics* (New York: Simon and Schuster, 1974); Gerard Jones and Will Jacobs, *The Comic Book Heroes: The First History of Modern Comic Books – From the Silver Age to the Present* (New York: Prima, 1996).

2 Herman G. Weinberg, *The Lubitsch Touch: A Critical Study* (New York: Dover, 1977).

3 Casey Seijas, "The Marvel renaissance," *Wizard* 124 (January 2002): 40–6.

4 Mike Cotton, "The Bendis Bunch," *Wizard* 141 (June 2003): 90.

5 Seijas, "The Marvel renaissance," p. 44.

6 Cotton, "The Bendis bunch," p. 94.

7 Bradford W. Wright, *Comic Book Nation: The Transformation of Youth Culture in America* (Baltimore: Johns Hopkins University Press, 2003); Matthew J. Putsz, *Comic Book Culture: Fanboys and True Believers* (Jackson: University of Mississippi Press, 2000).

8   Personal interview, 2003.

9   Lee Atchison, "In Search of Fortune and Glory," *Sequential Tarts* (2000) <http://www.sequentialtart.com/archive/apr00/bendis.shtml> (accessed September 11, 2005).

10   Alan Moore, *Writing for Comics* (London: Avitar, 2003); Dennis O'Neil, *The DC Guide to Writing For Comics* (New York: Watson-Guptill, 2001).

11   Putsz, *Comic Book Culture.*

12   Jocelyn Reid, "Elektra-Fying News," *Sequential Tarts* (2001) <http://www.sequentialtart.com/archive/july01/bendis2.shtml> (accessed September 11, 2005); Alex Hamby, "Never Say Never Again," *Hero Realm* (2002) <http://www.herorealm.com/Interviews/b_bendis1.htm> (accessed September 11, 2005).

13   McDonough and the *Wizard* Staff, "The ultimate move," *Wizard* 135 (December 2002): 73.

14   Geoff Klock, *How to Read Superhero Comics and Why* (London: Continuum, 2002); Scott Bukatman, *Matters of Gravity: Special Effects and Supermen in the 20th Century* (Durham: Duke University Press, 2003).

15   Richard Ho, "Ultimate man: Brian Michael Bendis," *Wizard* 147 (January 2004): 78.

16   Lee, *Origins of Marvel Comics*, p. 142.

17   Danny Fingeroth, "Alias: Spider-Man," *Write Now!* 1 (August 2002): 10.

18   Ibid., p. 6.

19   Ho, "Ultimate man," p. 78.

20   Ibid.

21   Ibid.

22   Umberto Eco, *The Role of the Reader* (Bloomington: Indiana University Press, 1979[1962]).

23   Fingeroth, "Alias: Spider-Man," p. 8.

2

The Best Batman Story: *The Dark Knight Returns*

Will Brooker

You have . . . a relationship with a man, an older man, for around three years. You get used to people asking how he's doing when they meet you; you're treated as a couple, your names joined in friends' minds. It ends amicably, affectionately. No big split, just a drifting, a sense that this period of your life is now over. You take his pictures off your wall, file the souvenirs away. People ask you about him as if you should know; you tell them that was years ago. Gossip about him filters through to you from time to time: he's revamped his image; he's been seen with a new partner or an old flame. You wish him well.

And then someone asks you to name the best time. To pick out one adventure, one great day, one moment.

Batman, to me, is more than a character from comics, films, and television: Batman is a phase of my life, from 1996 to 1999, when I holed up in Cardiff – in an apartment as tiny as a monk's cell, the shower in a cupboard next to the kitchen sink and the bathroom a dank cubicle – and plastered images of my chosen icon across the walls, loading the shelves with graphic novels. Even now, five years and five books later, I still carry the label the tabloids gave me when they discovered my PhD research, one day in spring 99: Doctor Batman.

Batman, to me, is a photo-album of moments; a montage compiled of snatched clips from 60 years; a flick-book of images, each with its own charm, each tugging with it a rush of memories. The "Negative Batman," reverse-processed and fleeing the light, from an annual in the 1970s; the

Adam West Batman, always heroic rather than ridiculous when I watched him as a child; the Denny O'Neil "Shaman" Batman, which gave me fever dreams during a week of flu; the stark, ludicrously brutal Batman of the first, late-'30s episodes, dealing out death and rough justice; the thin-lipped, scar-hardened Batman of Grant Morrison's *Justice League* comics, which I followed religiously every month; the stylized Expressionist Batman of the animated TV series, swooping across the city with more grace than any human actor could hope for.

To pick just one is to betray all the others, but if it must be done then I have my criterion for choosing: it is simple and subjective, and it would make for a chapter of 100 words, so what follows are the harder, more objective reasons – not my soft, personal reading, which barely deserves to be called "reason" – why Frank Miller's *The Dark Knight Returns*, published in four parts during 1986 and reprinted as a graphic novel, should be in the running for the most important single Batman story since his first appearance in the issue of *Detective Comics* dated May 1939.

Of course, there can be no absolute "best text." There are as many best Batman stories as there are Batman fans, and mine will be just one love letter among millions. However my discussion here is not entirely solipsistic, and it does operate within a context – within a community. This is true in four significant ways.

First, my choice of *Dark Knight* as favorite Batman story is shared with many other fans. Of course, my evidence to support this is selective – isn't all evidence selective? – and offers no kind of absolute proof in itself, but a brief survey of online testimonies will indicate that my opting for *Dark Knight* is by no means a decision totally out of left field. These results were thrown up by the simple but effective method of a Google search for "best Batman story." A query on the cinema site *Chud.com*, "Best Batman Graphic Novel?" elicited the following rapid response from Wilco: "Frank Miller's *The Dark Knight Returns*. You must own this if you want to know what Batman is," followed by a confirmation from LowShot, "*The Dark Knight Returns* is obviously the best." Michelle, listing "The Best of the Best: Batman" on *Amazon.com*, celebrates *Dark Knight* as "Hands down, the GREATEST Batman story ever!!" A fan-reviewer at *SF-Z.com* muses: "There have been many Batman stories. Most come and go, but this particular story, *The Dark Knight Returns* . . . is truly a must-read." A second fan on the same page reminds readers that in 2000 *Wizard* magazine voted *Dark Knight Returns* second only to Moore's

Watchmen, offering an enthusiastic correction: "I personally believe that *The Dark Knight* is the greatest comic book story ever told."

Second, however, my stress that there can be no absolute "best" text is supported within the community of Batman fans by the fact that there are many who disagree that *Dark Knight* is the best Batman story. Other online readers propose a myriad of other titles for the honor – *Knightfall*, *Arkham Asylum*, *A Death in the Family*, *Alien vs Batman*, *Contagion*, *Cataclysm*, *Hush*, or *Killing Joke*. Indeed, others go further, insisting explicitly that *The Dark Knight* is, in one fan's words, "not a very well-written comic book" or that Frank Miller's representation of the Dark Knight character was "too far from what I understand as the core concept of Batman." So, while my choice of *Dark Knight* may unite me with a significant group, even a majority, of Bat-fans, there are many who wouldn't identify with my choice, but who would approve of my resistance to absolute notions of a "best Batman." Whether *Dark Knight* works for the individual depends, amongst other things, on that individual's personal conception of what Batman is, how he looks, how he operates as a character, what the tone of his narratives should be, and which supporting elements of the mythos are necessary to a classic story. My preference for *Dark Knight* is, for instance, bound up with the fact that it was my dad who brought home the first two episodes in 1986 – the first comics I'd looked at in years, and a revelation. For me, the ageing Batman in *Dark Knight* comes across as a powerfully loving father figure. Other fans must have equally personal reasons for their affection toward a specific version of the character.

The third and fourth ways in which this chapter relates to the critical agenda and quality criteria of a broader fan community lie in my approach to evaluating *Dark Knight*'s "importance," and in my celebration of its pleasures. The assessment of importance, an approach which explores issues of institution, genre, form, and authorship, was echoed by contributors to the discussion forum *Barbelith.com* in their own assessment of *Dark Knight*, and, crucially, was treated as an objective measure of value entirely distinct from whether they actually liked the book. A brief survey of quotations is bound to seem anecdotal, but will give a flavor of the response.

> I think if you took a straw poll of great Batman stories *DKR* would have to be odds-on to top it, just because very little else would appear to have that iconic, stand-alone quality. There's *Arkham Asylum*, *Batman Year*

One, and *The Killing Joke*, possibly, and apart from those I can't think of
anything. And there's clearly a fairly strong argument for *DKR* as the
ultimate Bat-story, if only in terms of its general pop cultural impact. While
it's no doubt a long way behind the movies, the Sixties TV show, and even
quite possibly the recent cartoons, *DKR* still has to be streets ahead of the
competition as a Batman series that's lodged itself in the broader public
imagination, and also in terms of its influence on the Bat-mythos thereafter
– even as someone who loathed *DKR* with a burning passion, I think you'd
be hard-pushed to deny that really. (Flight of Dragons)

Barbelith contributors agree that *Dark Knight Returns* made its
impact by redefining expectations of the comic book in both form and
content. "It was an actual solid piece of writing that came out in a time
before comic writers were expected to be solid writers by even the most
minimal standards generally applied to writers of books," Simplist
explains:

> It appeared in a then-unique glossy perfect-bound format at a time when
> most comics were still on newsprint. Pretend you've never read a comic
> before, and read a couple of archive volumes. Really let it sink in that prior
> to the late '80s, that's pretty much how comics were written. Then pick
> up *DKR*, experience the contrast, and you'll have a much better sense of
> what this book did to comics the year it was released.

Others view it as a "seminal" work (Bobossboy) that "reshaped Batman
so thoroughly that it's hard to un-see it" (Diztastic Voyage). Bobossboy
goes on: "it is hard to imagine the sheer shock and awe impact . . . unless you were there at the time." Duncan Falconer, while expressing a
preference for the sequel *Dark Knight Strikes Back* and the prequel *Year
One*, accepts that *Dark Knight Returns*: "set the tone for Batman for
the last 19 years," while Benny the Ball argues that the story's "resonance . . . carried through the DC Universe." As Phyrefox concludes:
"I think almost all Batman stories since then have been hugely influenced by the tone and feel of *DKR*." These contributors also agree that
we can recognize this importance regardless of personal feelings about
the story: "I don't think it matters whether or not you think Miller is
a good writer, I don't think you can deny the power and influence of
DKR" (Phyrefox).

From these comments, a clear distinction emerges: that personal
enjoyment of a book, or connection with its vision of Batman, can and

sometimes must be separated from a more objective appraisal of its "importance." This latter quality is gauged in terms of the text's impact on the mythos (the character, the city), on the genre (the DC Universe), on the form (the actual production and marketing), and on the audience, within both the comic book community and the broader cultural sphere (popular imagination, media importance). There is a stress that these qualities have to be examined within a specific historical context – that the fan has a duty to place him or herself back in 1986, and try to reimagine what comics were like before *Dark Knight* in order to appreciate its impact.

This surprisingly unified community voice arose in response to my original draft of this chapter, making it clear to me that my own criteria were shared with at least my immediate online fellow-fans; yet the discourse about "importance" as an objective measure of worth is not confined to this one Internet forum. As suggestion of its broader use, consider the preamble on a long-running, dedicated Batman page, Patrick Furlong's *The Dark Knight*. Though Furlong's entire website, from its title onwards, is shaped by Miller's interpretation of the character, his review of the text sticks to the facts: a retelling of the narrative, and the following argument for the book's merits:

> No story in the Batman world is probably more important than Frank Miller's *The Dark Knight Returns*. This story was released in 1986, and was responsible for the rejuvenation of Batman as a dark character, and for the comics industry as a whole. Read the following overview of *The Dark Knight Returns*, and see why this story is so powerful . . .

Finally, and the fourth way in which this chapter relates to the intellectual work of the broader fan community, toward the end of this chapter I am allowing my personal love of *Dark Knight Returns* free, unashamed rein, liberated from caveats and caution. In this hymn to the text, I am also sharing in an approach I have witnessed on *Barbelith's* community: the celebration of a comic book for its "moments," its resonant images and lines of dialogue that lodge deep in the memory to give lasting pleasure. While this form of appreciation is not entirely separate from the discourse of "importance" – the "moments" are what give *Dark Knight* its immediate impact and longer-term resonance with the individual – this is an engagement with the text that ditches the talk about paper format, broader cultural influence, or assessment within a historical context, and allows a joyful communion with the world created in those words and pictures.

Hunt the Dark Knight: assessing importance

The Dark Knight Returns, written and penciled by Frank Miller, inked by Klaus Janson, colored by Lynn Varley, and lettered by John Costanza, is set 10 years after Batman's retirement from crime-fighting. An older, slightly creakier Wayne, unable to repress the dark archetype inside himself, returns to the streets of Gotham to take apart a vicious, cyberpunk subculture called the Mutants, then face a final, fatal date with his arch-nemesis the Joker. In the last chapter, Batman does the unthinkable and bests Superman, moments before his own apparent death. All the familiar elements are there, made unfamiliar: Robin is an intelligent but rebellious girl called Carrie, the Joker is a cold Bowie-type, and the police commissioner is a hard-ass woman, Yindel, with none of Gordon's patience for vigilantes. Superman is a godlike being: Batman is more vulnerable than ever before, but built like a tank.

While *Dark Knight* was received as groundbreaking at the time of its original four-part publication and book-length reissue, its impact caused further-reaching, delayed tremors that did more than shake down the concept of Batman and his immediate mythos. Even at the time of writing, almost 20 years later, Miller's creation of an alternate future for Batman is reverberating through the DC Universe, shaping the timelines, the origins, the rules, and possibilities for every other character in the company's fictional world of demigods and titans.

When it first appeared, *Dark Knight* stood outside the structures of comic book convention, its departure from the accepted structures of Batman's continuity justified as a one-off experiment by an iconoclastic, star creator. In a retroactive shuffle typical of the superhero industry, though, *Dark Knight* was subsequently rebranded – much as *Star Wars* was titled *Episode IV* a year after its initial release – and imprinted with the logo "Elseworlds." "In Elseworlds," as the official back-cover blurb runs: "Heroes are taken from their usual settings and put into strange times and places – some that have existed, or might have existed, and others that can't, couldn't or shouldn't exist. The result is stories that make characters who are familiar as yesterday seem as fresh as tomorrow."

According to linear chronology, the first Elseworlds Batman tale was Augustyn and Mignola's *Gotham By Gaslight* (1989), featuring a Victorian Dark Knight in a thick, clumsily bricolaged outfit dealing with the Ripper, followed by further exploratory departures such as Moench, Jones, and Jones's *Batman and Dracula: Red Rain* (1991), Chaykin, Moore, and Chiarello's *Batman/Houdini: The Devil's Workshop* (1993) and Chaykin's *Dark Allegiances* (1996), which could have been subtitled *Batman/Hitler*. With hindsight, however, it was *Dark Knight* that opened up the potential for what used to be called "Imaginary Stories," paving the way for speculations outside rigid continuity.

Dark Knight's lasting influence was, appropriately for a Batman comic, twofold, two-faced and entirely paradoxical. On the one hand, as I'll detail below, it set the tone to grim, grainy, rainy, and gritty, and convinced a host of subsequent writers and artists that the key to an "adult" comic was hard-hitting vigilantism with an edge of political commentary and an S&M twist to the superhero costumes. In this context, it was the prime text of the "post-Crisis" period: the *Crisis on Infinite Earths* maxiseries had forced DC's universe into a slimmed-down, supposedly more manageable form, razing off worlds that didn't fit and mercy-killing swathes of characters. It was a holocaust not just of geography but of history, as origins were rebooted and the past wiped out. From this point onward, whole pockets of history were buried: and invariably, it was the more embarrassing, campy episodes that were repressed, never included when the origin was retold. Batman's early days now officially involved pilgrimages to train with Asian martial artists and mystics, and trials by combat in Gotham's red-light district: there was no Ace the Bat-Hound, no science fiction alien adventures, no Rainbow Batman costumes in this history, and anyone clinging to that kind of nostalgia was suffering false memory syndrome. It wasn't a dream, it wasn't an imaginary story. It never happened anymore.

Dark Knight, then, with its rock-hard man-mountain of a Batman, his costume armored and his vehicle a military monster – the girl-Robin deadening those troublesome homoerotic associations that had persisted since the 1950s, and the Joker taking the mantle of sexual deviance away from the hero – suited the mood of tough, no bullshit gravity that had been imposed on a colorful but messy universe, a circus of pseudo-science and careless inconsistency. The compression of multiple universes into a single, serious earth was echoed by the insistence on the new term "graphic novel," replacing the light and infantile "comic book": one hefty hardback volume carrying far more weight than a dozen flimsy monthly titles, and earning superhero adventures a temporary place in mainstream bookstores as "post-literate" visual culture. *Dark Knight* embodied the genre's tightening-up into a masculine, muscular form, perfect for the key market of heterosexual teenage boys and young men who wanted superheroes they could finally be proud to admire, comics they could read in public. It was a heavy-duty mother of a vehicle itself, crushing the old jokes about caped crusaders and Boy Wonders, powering through expectations and prejudices, and planting a reinforced new Batman in the ruins, staring anyone down who dared mention Adam West.

On the other, *Dark Knight* was inherently playful, striking out from the accepted codes and breaking away from established conventions – a female Robin, a new Commissioner, a tank-like Batmobile, the death of the Joker, and the end of the Batman – and as such, it planted generic seeds that flowered in the alt-historical Elseworld experiments and continued growing under the surface, blooming suddenly again in the mid-1990s. Mark Waid and Alex Ross's four-part Elseworlds series *Kingdom Come* (1996) gave Batman another possible future, its vision of a snowy-haired, cynical technocrat distinct from *Dark Knight*, but indebted to it for the very concept of alternative timelines where iconic, never-changing characters are allowed to age, growing weaker but wiser.

In 1998 Waid and a team of artists revisited this future in an experiment more ambitious than any previous Elseworlds: *The Kingdom* broke the rules further by meshing with mainstream continuity and bringing the alternate timeline into contact with the official "present-day," culminating in the revelation of Hypertime, a temporal theory that explained how all the Elseworld universes could co-exist along parallel, possible strands. For the first time, the playful experiments were permitted within the official mythos, albeit through a science fiction get-out clause that only allowed restricted travel between temporal flows, on special occasions. Even more importantly, the double-page spread that introduced Hypertime, with glimpsed scenes from possible alternatives, included tantalizing flashes from comics that had been officially ruled out of continuity since the Crisis: old, illogical versions of characters, silly pets, giants, and doppelgangers, whimsical misfits like the fifth-dimensional sprite Bat-Mite. Among the half-forgotten faces was Superman's dog, Krypto, guaranteeing that Ace the Bat-Hound must, by rights, be back in permitted continuity too.

The Dark Knight's bold carving of a possible future for the character outside the normal boundaries of monthly comic books had – ironically, given its reception as a tough and uncompromising revision of a camp hero – ultimately led to an upheaval of the rules laid down in 1986 and a reopening of the gloriously untidy treasure-chest that Crisis had intended to bury.

The success of *Dark Knight* – its unprecedented sales beyond the traditional comic-buying market, and its grabbing of headlines in daily newspapers and hip magazines – had dramatic repercussions for the comic book industry. Once more, contemporary trends in superhero comics can be identified as further ripples from that 1986 shockwave, and again, the longer-term effects are in some ways surprising, revealing the complexity of *Dark Knight* beyond its initial impression of a macho jackboot on the mythos.

At the time, *Dark Knight* was often reviewed alongside Moore and Gibbons's *Watchmen* and Art Spiegelman's *Maus* as exemplars of the "graphic novel" phenomenon, and while the form failed to wedge itself firmly into mainstream popular culture – the traditional novel turned out not to be dead after all, and the comic book remained, by and large, in comic shops – this newfound kudos gave the industry an incredible ego-boost. The ephemeral medium of four-color funny-papers was treated to luxurious production values: glossy paper, painted art, hardback covers. Monthly titles that would have been remembered only in fans' collections were dug out and reprinted in handsome volumes and "archive" editions. The entire career of *Kingdom Come* co-creator Alex Ross, whose talent is for photo-realistic, Norman Rockwell-style portraits of DC heroes, would have been very different without these changes in the basic production process, and the perception that comics could also sell as coffee-table editions.

While this pumped-up confidence led to pretentious, overwrought, and overpriced follies like Morrison and McKean's *Arkham Asylum* (1989) – illegible lettering, quotes from Lewis Carroll, textured endpapers, but very little story beneath the impressionistic art – it also enabled the reprinting of innovative but relatively obscure work like Bryan Talbot's *Adventures of Luther Arkwright* (1990), led to book-length celebrations of newspaper classics like Herriman's *Krazy Kat*, helped find a market for indie, girl-friendly titles like the Hernandez Brothers' *Love and Rockets*, and encouraged the publication of experimental "commix" such as *Raw*. Even in recent years, the fact that Chris

Ware's *Jimmy Corrigan: The Smartest Boy On Earth* (2001) was even reviewed in the *Guardian*, let alone that it won that newspaper's First Book Award, is a subtle but significant after-effect of the mid-'80s graphic novel hype.

Dark Knight Returns helped to shape the physical form and appearance of comic books, but more directly it cast a shadow over the superhero genre, dominating the way costumed characters were represented: even when the trend for grim and gritty vigilantism abated, the new mood was itself a reaction to the post-*Dark Knight* tendency for hardboiled revisionism. In the new Batman's wake, a series of DC's key icons and second-string characters were given rewritten origins, many of them borrowing from both *Watchmen* – literary prose, epigrams, psychosexual complexity – and *Dark Knight*'s approach with its radical, often brutal spin on familiar visual tropes. Inevitably, few of the imitators matched the standard of either Miller or Moore – the most notorious example of mismanaged "maturity" and "dark revisionism" remains Mike Grell's Green Arrow reboot, *The Longbow Hunters* (1987), which used the implied rape and graphically depicted violation of his female partner, the Black Canary, to justify the hero's gear-shift from crime-fighting with trick arrows to sadistic, uncompromising vengeance.

However, the late-'80s obsession with reinvented superheroes – which frequently meant digging up obscure, ridiculous, or redundant characters – also led to some fascinating challenges and work of lasting value. Neil Gaiman followed his prestige three-part musing on the forgotten heroine *Black Orchid* (1988) with an experiment in horror fantasy, transforming *Sandman* (1989 onward) from a guy in a gas mask to a gothic personification of Dreaming and creating a minor cultural phenomenon, one of the biggest crossover successes of the 1990s. Grant Morrison transformed the freakish adventures of the *Doom Patrol* (1989 onward) into a heady, fragmentary trip, with episodes based on Smiths lyrics and Dadaist aesthetics. Peter Milligan revived the minor character *Shade: The Changing Man* (1990 onward) and took him on a Lynchian road trip through the contemporary American nightmare.

These slightly skewed monthly titles – distinct in mood and tone from the mainstream DC Universe – earned a dedicated indie following and, in time, a separate corporate imprint, Vertigo, replacing their previous vague description of "dark fantasy." This dark, charming little pocket of the DC mythos flourished during the 1990s and continues to house acclaimed, intelligent regular monthlies such as Milligan's *Human*

Target, Azzarello and Risso's *100 Bullets*, and Brian K. Vaughan's *Y: The Last Man*.

While the Vertigo brand can be traced clearly back to *Dark Knight*'s adult-oriented revisionism, its development includes a further interesting twist. Just as *Dark Knight*'s bold experiment with a possible future can now be seen as a precursor of Elseworlds and, in turn, Hypertime's continuity apertures, so Miller's rewriting of Batman, despite its apparently lantern-jawed heterosexuality, effectively enabled Vertigo as a space for creators like Morrison, Milligan, and Gaiman to play with other superhero characters: and that play frequently embraced gay, lesbian, bisexual, and transsexual identities.

This separate area within DC, with its "for mature readers" label on the cover of each title, became a space for surprisingly queer adventures and heroes, of whom *Doom Patrol*'s transvestite stretch of real estate, Danny-the-Street, was perhaps the most surreally flamboyant example. With hindsight, Miller's apparently grimly straight Bat-mythos can be seen to involve a fair amount of cross-dressing and boundary-blurring itself: the Joker is a lipsticked Bowie look-alike, with feminine manners but a bodybuilder's physique, and even the Dark Knight, in one scene, disguises himself as a woman while wrestling a Nazi uber-wench called Bruno.

For better or worse, *Dark Knight* and the mainstream credibility it attracted also jumpstarted development on the *Batman* feature film, directed by Tim Burton and released in 1989. The movie was, like the graphic novel, touted as a "dark" corrective to the dayglo flamboyance of the Adam West TV series that remained the dominant popular image of Batman in the mid-1980s, and incorporated several of Miller's revisionist tropes – the military edge to the costume, vehicle and utility belt, the modern gothic of the architecture, the terse growl of the protagonist – along with at least one shot inspired directly by the graphic novel, where Batman suspends a perp off the roof of a building. Trailers for *Batman Begins* (2005) suggest an even more immediate debt to *Dark Knight Returns*, with the Batmobile-tank and glimpses of the origin sequence apparently based on specific frames of Miller's art.

It's worth noting that, in this respect too, *Dark Knight*'s legacy involved an unexpected twist into the camp playfulness it had – or so it seemed – been explicitly intended to stamp out. Just as the homoerotic potential of Batman and Robin's relationship, brought to light by Dr Fredric Wertham's *Seduction of the Innocent* (1954) and strenuously repressed in the comic books that followed the mid-'50s clampdown, had nudged back to the surface in the 1960s TV *Batman*'s knowing double-meanings, so Tim Burton's relatively dark, angst-ridden, and lonely vigilante gave way to Joel Schumacher's two feature-length pantomimes, *Batman Forever* (1995) and *Batman and Robin* (1997), complete with meaningful glances between a dynamic duo in sculpted codpieces.

On a fundamental level, it may be the case that Batman, particularly when teamed with Robin, contains inherently camp and homoerotic aspects that simply cannot be permanently denied and will always edge back into the mythos; more specifically, as I suggested above, Miller's *Dark Knight* may be more playful, less containing, more embracing of Batman's mythos in all its facets – not just the grim brutality, but the flamboyance, the grotesques, the masquerade, the queerness – than was perceived at the time of its publication.

In authorial terms, Miller's approach to both writing and art in *Dark Knight* can be traced back to his work on the Marvel comic *Daredevil* (1980 onwards), where he began to introduce first-person, Chandler-esque captions in place of the more conventional third-person voice-over narration, and rely on sequences of wordless visuals like a film storyboard. *Dark Knight*'s hard-nosed breakdown of fight scenes into wincing technical detail – a short-circuited nerve, a severed muscle, a shattered pelvis – is rehearsed in Daredevil's duels. Miller's science-fiction samurai epic, *Ronin* (1983), brought a Japanese sensibility to his work, with even bolder use of silent panels, often building up in a sequence of rhythmic smaller frames to a huge splash page. The layout patterns of *Dark Knight* are all here, with an increasingly stylized use of heavy black inks: the fascination with samurai and ninja would emerge in *Elektra: Assassin* (1986) and the starkly contrasting lights and darks subsequently lent themselves to the expressionist modern *noir* of *Sin City* (1992).

The impact of Miller's mid-'80s techniques on superhero storytelling was both obvious and subtle, ranging from blatant lifts to unconscious influence. Miller's frame-by-frame depiction of the Wayne parents' murder underlies countless subsequent glimpses of the origin sequence, including those in *Gotham By Gaslight* and *Arkham Asylum*. His use of cinematic, storyboard-style pacing, and his device of dramatically foregrounding sound effects as integral to the image, were both played up further in the jazzy graphics of Howard Chaykin's late-'80s revisionism such as *The Shadow* (1987) and *Blackhawk* (1987), while the high-contrast *noir* of Gotham's streetlife clearly shapes Risso's work in the more recent *100*

Bullets. The shift from third-person narrative captions to fragmented stream-of-consciousness, revealing Batman's internal thought process, became the standard convention: see, for instance, Loeb and Lee's best-selling, year-long saga *Hush* (2003).

Miller's borrowing of manga's dynamism, with its kinetic blurs around speeding objects, gave Anglo-American superhero art a jab in the arm; its after-effects can be detected in the graphics of Steve Yeowell's *Zenith* (1988–93) and Bryan Hitch's *The Authority* (1999). More specifically, *Dark Knight*'s use of TV screens as miniature panels, and the spectacular breaking of this steady rhythm with heroic splash pages, are borrowed in what seems deliberate homage by one of 2004's most critically acclaimed titles, Morrison and Quitely's *We3*.

The Dark Knight Triumphant: Communion With Moments

So, *Dark Knight* helped shape the space/time boundaries of the DC Universe; it helped change the shape, form, and readership of comic books. It cast a long shadow over the portrayal not just of Batman but of superheroes in general during subsequent decades; it helped clear the way for the still-vibrant imprint of Vertigo, and made a space for creators like Neil Gaiman and Grant Morrison to experiment with their own costumed characters. It prompted a four-feature film franchise and, in *Batman Begins*, inspired a fifth. Finally, it also changed the way comic book stories are told. These are the reasons I'd give if asked why *The Dark Knight Returns* was the most important, the most influential Batman story since 1939: I'd draw on ideas of institution, genre, author, form.

But if asked why *Dark Knight* is *my* best, I'd use a different criterion; one I also share with other fans. On *Barbelith*, discussions of new comics quickly become a celebration of moments: picking out "cool bits," cherishing snatches of dialogue or stunning splash pages. Rather than the considered discussions I quoted above, these posts are often simple lists, a communal reliving and replaying of the reading experience. Sometimes it's enough just to repeat the best sound effects and captions, like a kid imitating his favorite TV show: "BOOM TUBE ENGAGE!" one fan posts. "BOOM!"

When connecting with a single issue, rather than having to draw back and face the challenge of picking "the best ever," there is a confessional quality to these fans' writing: an unashamed embracing of the emotional response comics can produce. Men in their twenties and thirties praise a comic because it gave them a lump in their throat or tears in their eyes. These threads become a storytelling session – a retelling session, transforming the text and perhaps beginning to mold it into a folktale that belongs to the community – a group activity where the great memories are rebounded off like-minded fans. One comments: "I knew I'd be late for the thread, and this is the best part of the comic apart from the comic itself." There is an unselfconscious communion with both the comic book – which in turn gives a sense of connection with the author, often referred to in these threads by his first name – and the group of fellow readers.

This liberated, joyous rush of response is permitted, I think, by the immediacy of the engagement with a brand new text. Sharing initial feedback on a monthly title you and all your online friends have just bought allows for a different kind of reaction than does the question as to whether a graphic novel from 1986 qualifies as the best Batman comic ever. The latter challenge prompts a far more reserved, objective, and considered response, one that falls back on notions of importance, influence, and institution. It had that effect on the *Barbelith* contributors I quoted above, and it clearly had that effect on me too.

The responsibility of choosing a "best ever" is enough completely to change the mood and the register: it makes fans like me shift from an enthusiastic, childlike embracing of the text to a chin-stroking, guarded evaluation of its context. As Bobossboy admitted, before retreating into the safer ground of assessing *Dark Knight* as "a seminal work": "It is hard to imagine the sheer shock and awe impact . . . unless you were there at the time."

He has a good point. To tap back into that rush of personal engagement with *Dark Knight*, you may have to strip away the after-effects, forget its generic importance in the subsequent two decades, and imagine yourself back there at the time, at the first time; and my time, as I said, was when my dad brought home two issues of a comic unlike any other I'd seen before. Reading it for the first time was like a grenade in your face: explosively shattering your ideas of what comics could be like, and shooting its shrapnel into you, where it wedged deep.

The Dark Knight Returns is my best Batman story because it has the best *moments* of Batman: the best memories of any single Batman story. The images that lodge in your mind, familiar now as family photographs.

The lines of dialogue or narration that stick to your memory, triggered like touchstones. I can recite them now without looking, just as I can see the pictures. Cold poetry. *A wolf howls. I know how he feels.* Bitter lyricism. *I watch them kick him around for a while. I've had worse times.* The laconic growl. *Lucky old man . . . This would be a fine death . . . welcome to hell.* Lines that echo in your own life at unexpected moments, 20 years after first reading.

And the visuals, still breathtakingly vivid: the panels that come alive into a moving sequence in your head, a short film clip. The revelation when you realize the blackness in front of your eyes was fingers, and that they're sliding away to reveal a stomach-clenching drop from the top of a skyscraper. The joyous leap of a 50-year-old man built like a brick out-house with a chirpy, red-haired kid at his side, both soaring across the city in defiance of gravity, age, sense. The physical affection finally allowed them, this new Batman and Robin; permitted now, perversely – as man and little girl, rather than man and teenage boy – to embrace and cling to each other, needing each other. *Good soldier. Good soldier.* The growing trust and playfulness between them. Batman in the back of the copter, trying to command the voice-recognition. *Boosters. Boosters. What . . .* Robin coolly giving the reprogrammed software her own, hipper shorthand: *Peel.* And the rockets fire, taking them back to the cave. *I'm not fired?* she checks. Batman narrows his eyes, with a smile so rare you'd kill to earn it. *You're not fired.*

This story alone is a miniature history in itself, containing other stories within it: taking us from Bruce's childhood to middle age, giving his career a fitting end and setting a template for all origin stories to follow. It predicts, with uncanny prescience, the death of Robin in 1989 and reflects with canny self-awareness the transformation from the 1970s Batman, still in cyan blue with a yellow target on his chest, to the darker, harder figure who would dominate the 1990s. *The Dark Knight Returns* is the best Batman story because it is about so many of the Batman stories that went before – the grim loner of 1939, the introduction of the canary-costumed sidekick in 1940, the political propaganda of the 1940s, the street-level detection of the 1970s, even, in the huge, iconic splash pages and massive sound effects, the Pop Art aesthetic of the 1960s – and, fittingly in a fictional universe where time is repeatedly reshuffled, history unwritten and reworked, lifetimes looped, and origins contained in endings, it also contains, in some form or another, many of the Batman stories that came after.

The Batman comes in many guises. This man – built like a city-block, but with the cracks showing; cold, violent, but also brutally loving – is the one I'd cling to.

Works Cited

In previous work, I have explicitly located myself on the boundary between fandom and academia, an approach that in theory at least combines personal passion with the objective analysis of scholarship. The two fields are not as clearly separate as sometimes imagined, and they muddy a great deal in the middle, but nevertheless they are considered to have distinct qualities and weaknesses.

In this chapter, by contrast, I let myself cross that line and write primarily from the position of a Batman fan, albeit a Batman fan who did a PhD about him. In practice, what this means is that I haven't followed the academic practice of quotations and footnotes. Almost all of the above was written entirely from memory: as a fan, I found I knew it all, and could tell it as readily as I'd recount family history.

However, apart from the primary texts referred to, I owe a debt of thanks to the following secondary works, some of which I looked at during the writing and some of which have, I know, lodged in my memory and shaped my perceptions of Batman. Certain of my observations above are borrowed from these authors, but I hope they will take it as a tribute that their work is forever in my head:

Mark Cotta Vaz, *Tales of the Dark Knight* (London: Futura, 1989).
Gerard Jones and Will Jacobs, *The Comic Book Heroes* (California: Prima, 1997).
Geoff Klock, *How To Read Superhero Comics and Why* (London: Continuum, 2002).
Andy Medhurst, "Batman, Deviance and Camp," in Roberta E. Pearson and William Uricchio, eds., *The Many Lives of the Batman* (London: Routledge, 1991), pp. 149–63.

I offer my thanks to the Comic Book forum at <www.Barbelith.com>, particularly Gumbitch, Nine Ladies Dancing, Madfigs, Stoatie, BillR, Grant, DaveBCooper, and all the contributors cited above.

This chapter is respectfully dedicated to Will Eisner, who passed on while I was writing it.

3

The Best Serial Killer Novel: *Red Dragon*

Sue Turnbull

Red Dragon *simply comes at you and comes at you, finally leaving you shaken and sober and afraid . . . the best popular novel published since* The Godfather.

So blurbs writer Stephen King on the battered cover of my fourth-hand Corgi paperback reprint of Thomas Harris's *Red Dragon*. Frankly, King's recommendation leaves me somewhat indifferent since I associate him with the thriller/horror genre rather than with crime fiction. What this blurb therefore reveals is who the publisher thinks their potential readership might be. You can imagine the marketing rationale: "This crime novel is so horrific, we'd better market it to the King readers who are clearly up for such stuff rather than the crime readers who probably aren't." In any case, as an avid crime reader, I rarely pay much attention to book blurbs, although my all-time favorite is that of columnist P. J. O'Rourke for Carl Hiaasen's black comedy crime novel, which declares *Double Whammy* to be simply "Better than Literature."[1] On the other hand, I do take very seriously the recommendations of fellow crime readers and knowledgeable reviewers who can place a crime novel within its specific sub-generic context, or make an association with another author's work, giving me enough information to ascertain whether or not it is worth tracking down. After a while, you get to know whose recommendations to trust even among your otherwise valued friends: who shares the same aesthetic criteria and sensibilities, who knows a "good" crime novel when they read one. Ultimately, however, it is my own aesthetic judgment as a crime reader which determines my choice, and if a crime novel does not pass what in my circle of readers we have come to call the "first paragraph test," rapidly engaging me with its premise and prose style, then unless I am compelled to read for some other motive than my own pleasure, it goes into the "pass it on" pile.

Although originally published in 1981, *Red Dragon* arrived on my "to be read" pile sometime in the late '80s with an already established reputation and a set of recommendations which frankly put me off. "*Red Dragon*," I was told by a trusted other, "is the scariest crime novel I have ever read." "Don't read it when you are alone, it is deeply disturbing." The comments on my favorite crime fiction email list, *Dorothy-L*, didn't exactly encourage me either; as one female poster put it: "My list of most harrowing begins and ends with *Red Dragon*."[2] Now, I don't mind being unsettled when reading crime fiction; indeed, a frisson of fear may well be part of the pleasure, but "deep disturbance" or a "harrowing" experience is not necessarily what I look for in the literature with which I choose to lull me to sleep. And so *Red Dragon* kept being moved down the pile, waiting for the moment when I would be brave enough to give it a go.

In the meantime, I read Patricia Cornwell's first (and arguably best) serial killer thriller, *Postmortem*, published in 1990, which went on to win such prestigious crime fiction awards as the Edgar, the Creasey, the Anthony, the Macavity, and the French Prix du roman d'aventure all in the one year. These awards, voted for either by fans, fellow crime writers, or both, are but the tip of a vast anthill of crime fiction conventions, associations, and networks that operate internationally, sustained by a welter of on-line lists and websites devoted to the genre in all its diversity. Cornwell's recognition within this network subsequently enabled her to secure a record-breaking three-book contract for $US24 million and encouraged her to write (so far) another twelve novels featuring beleaguered (and increasingly right-wing) medical examiner Dr Kay Scarpetta, thus proving that at the very least crime fiction awards are useful for securing lucrative deals.[3]

Sadly, as Cornwell's royalty checks have waxed, so has her critical reception waned amongst aficionados of the genre, suggesting that as a crime writer becomes more popular, they may not necessarily become much better. Part of the problem may have to do with the imperatives of publishers who demand a book a year from their star performers, who are then caught in a commercial treadmill, churning out the next installment rather than waiting for the next best idea (although there are some notable exceptions, such as Minette Walters). As a crime reader, I am not necessarily impressed by large sales and annual outings – indeed the opposite is more often the case as I search for surprise and innovation. Contrary to suppositions about the formulaic nature of crime fiction, I'm always looking for interesting breaks with tradition and a new voice or perspective – as I know, are many of my fellow readers. Sadly, therefore, by the time I came to read *Red Dragon*, I was already well over the serial killer sub-genre and had been foreshadowing its (hopeful) demise in my own crime fiction reviews for some time.

This was largely an effect of the '90s, when it was almost impossible to avoid the serial killer in crime fiction as so many of my favorite authors decided to give the sub-genre a go. And so I read Val McDermid's fine but unsettling *The Mermaids Singing*, which won the 1995 Gold Dagger Award of the British Crime Writer's Association – thus bringing her to the attention of the highly lucrative American market – and eventually inspired an internationally successful television series, *The Wire in the Blood*. Its title taken from "The Love Song of J Alfred Prufrock" by T. S. Eliot and its chapter epigrams taken from Thomas De Quincey's biting satirical essay "On Murder Considered as One of the Fine Arts," *The Mermaids Singing* took us inside the head of a highly literate and refined transvestite thrill-killer preying on men as he anticipated, rationalized, and relished his gruesome torture scenarios (the term "thrill-killer" comes from Robert and Stephen Holmes's typology of serial killers[4]). It was a tough read, taking me to the edge of pleasure in crime fiction. Let me try and explain what I mean by this "edge" before we head back to *Red Dragon*.

The Edge of Pleasure

I started reading crime fiction at the age of 9. Sentenced to bed by a bout of scarlet fever, I ran out of books. Resourceful in her desperation, and determined to get back to her *Telegraph* crossword, my mother hit upon the Sherlock Holmes solution. Dressed in her best weekday hat, she trudged to and from our local lending library lugging the entire Conan Doyle oeuvre as I devoured it volume by volume. The story which got me hooked was "The Speckled Band," the quintessential Watson and Holmes outing which Sir Arthur Conan Doyle himself nominated as his favorite story.[5] With its gothic setting, the mysterious and agonizing death of a young woman, and a haunting whistle in the middle of the night, "The Speckled Band" combined all the thrills of a ghost story with all the pleasure of a satisfying clue-puzzle mystery. I can still recall the frisson of fear with which I raced to the conclusion, caught between the pleasure of an unsettling text which I did and didn't want to finish and the epistemological desire to know what all these mysterious signs might mean in the end. I was scared, but not too scared, trusting in Sherlock Holmes and Conan Doyle to deliver me to a satisfying and safe denouement.

In the process of this compulsive reading, I forgot I was sick, discovering instead the power of a compelling narrative to take us somewhere else, into a realm of the imagination which gives us relief from the pressing insistence of the self. This was my fix – and I've been in search of it ever since. My desire to get "lost in a book" even led me to study English at London University, where I discovered (as did Janice Radway in her similar account of childhood illness and compensatory reading) that such immersive reading, particularly the kinds of books in which we chose to immerse ourselves, was not what was expected of an English Literature graduate with a refined taste for the classics and a dispassionate critical gaze.[6] And so I gave up crime fiction, conspicuously reading Tolstoy on the bus as a kind of aesthetic style statement.

It was not until the 1980s when a new wave of feminist crime writers, headed by Marcia Muller, Sara Paretsky, and Sue Grafton, began to reinvent the genre that I turned to crime once again, and rediscovered the ways in which a good crime novel grabs you by the scruff of your neck, shakes you up, and deposits you, more or less gently, at the end. Like many others, I also began to wonder from a feminist perspective what inspired me to read such stories, which often deal quite confrontationally with violent death. In this regard, I canvassed my fellow members of the Australian branch of Sisters in Crime in 1997 to find out how they rationalized their reading, receiving a diversity of responses which included everything from "because it has a STORY" to "because I work in the caring professions, I like to come home and read about murdering someone," a comment which inadvertently realizes psychoanalytic literary critic Slavoj Žižek's suggestion that "We *are* murderers in the unconscious of our desires."[7] What was perhaps most interesting about the majority of responses I received was what the Sisters liked least in crime fiction was violence, even though, it could be argued, crime fiction so often depends on that most heinous of violent acts, murder.

But not all crime fiction is the same. As has often been pointed out, not least by Raymond Chandler, there has been a long and enduring

strain of crime writing (often quite mischievously and erroneously associated with female British crime writers of the Golden Age between the
two world wars such as Agatha Christie or Dorothy L. Sayers) in which
the violence occurs off-stage, thus providing the narrative impetus for a
story of detection without ever offending the more delicate reader's sensibilities. Chandler, of course, wanted to make a case for his own particular brand of "realistic" romantic-hero private-eye story featuring Philip
Marlowe, whose connection with the mean streets was much more
tenuous than that of his forebears such as Sam Spade created by Dashiell
Hammett, not to mention a swag of *noir* writers in the '30s and '40s,
including James L. Cain, *The Postman Always Rings Twice*, and later, Jim
Thompson, the creator of possibly the most disturbing serial killer novel
of all time, largely because it is entirely narrated from the killer's point
of view, *The Killer Inside Me.*[8]

Crime fiction has always had a hard edge as well as a soft center, and
crime fiction readers (and writers) usually know precisely where their own
boundaries lie. I imagine this boundary as what I have come to call the
aesthetic frame of a crime novel, a frame composed of the setting, characters, stylistics, plot, and prose style which locate it very precisely within
its own specific sub-genre. This frame may be either a cozy clue puzzle
mystery where death occurs off-stage, or a social realist police procedural
in which the emotional problems of the investigation officers may be of
as much significance as the crime, or a comedy-caper novel in the manner
of Janet Evanovitch, who adds elements of romance and soap opera to
her mix.[9] This aesthetic frame not only assures me that what I am reading
is a fiction, but that I will be safely delivered to knowledge at the end,
thus allowing me to contemplate at a comfortable distance that which I
might find too horrifying or too disturbing to entertain in another
format. And here I might offer another insight provided by the Sisters in
Crime survey which suggested that the least favorite sub-genre of crime
amongst this group of crime readers was "true crime" in which, I would
argue, the violence depicted is not held within the aesthetic framework
of crime fiction, but is located within the narrative framework of the
true-crime account which insists that what it is describing is "real." For
the majority of the Sisters, this is not an adequate aesthetic framework
within which to contemplate death.

Sometimes, however, even the aesthetic framework of crime fiction
cannot contain the experience of reading about violent crime. The boundary of our comfort zone is breached and we can't go on. I recently had

this experience reading the dour but not usually disturbing police pro-
cedurals of Swedish writer Henning Mankell. Several pages into *Before
the Frost*, the perpetrator deliberately sets fire to some swans after dousing
them with petrol and watches them die.[10] I put the book down and
wondered why on the one hand I could entertain reading a book about
a serial killer which, as Stephen King suggested, just came at me and at
me, leaving me shaken, sober, and afraid, but on the other I was completely unable to continue reading a book in which fictional swans met
an entirely fictional death. Although the answer may lie somewhere
between my analyst and Mankell's strategies as a writer, suffice it to say
that I was once again made vividly aware of how crime fiction can take
us by surprise, can stop us in our tracks and throw us off course, even
as it compels us to read on, if we dare.

The eighteenth-century philosopher Edmund Burke knew all about
this negotiation of aesthetic frames and boundaries. In his essay on the
sublime and the beautiful, Burke argued:

> Whatever is fitted in any sort to excite the ideas of pain and danger; that
> is to say, whatever is in any sort terrible, or is conversant about terrible
> objects or operates in a manner analogous to terror, is a source of the
> sublime . . . [However] when danger or pain press too nearly, they are
> incapable of giving any delight, and are simply terrible; but at certain dis-
> tances and with certain modifications, they may be and they are delightful,
> as we every day experience.[11]

And so not wanting to be confronted by the terrible, but in search of the
sublime, I finally read *Red Dragon*, 23 years after it was originally published in 1981.

────────────── **"More than a little truth"** ──────────────

Red Dragon begins quietly enough: "Will Graham sat Crawford down
at a picnic table between the house and the ocean and gave him a glass
of iced tea."[12] This modest, well-balanced sentence gets a number of jobs
done economically: it tells us who, it tells us where, and it implies a world
of domesticity and calm which we anticipate is likely to be ruptured.
There's a lot at stake here. By the time we get to page 8 we know that
former FBI profiler, Will Graham, stands to lose not only his idyllic family

life on Sugarloaf Key in Florida but also his sanity. Graham is a forensic specialist whose ability to empathize with those around him enables him to intuit not only how his nearest and dearest may be thinking, but also the thought processes of psychotic killers. This is a gift he would rather not have as it has already almost cost him his life, as we discover on page 6, when he "connected" almost fatally with Dr Hannibal Lecter in the process of securing his incarceration.

A mad psychiatrist with a penchant for eating people, Lecter is the character who has (unfortunately in my opinion) dominated Harris's fiction ever since *Red Dragon*. This is the character that Anthony Hopkins brought to the attention of a non-crime fiction reading public in Jonathan Demme's 1991 film, *The Silence of the Lambs* – which won five Oscars, including a best actor for Hopkins. Before Hopkins, however, Lecter was played by another much less mannered actor, Brian Cox, in Michael Mann's underrated 1986 adaptation of *Red Dragon* – renamed *Manhunter*. This latter title invokes the title of criminologist John Douglas's book, *Mindhunter*, about the work of the FBI's real-life serial crime unit. Here Douglas suggests that Harris picked up his idea for *Red Dragon* while sitting in FBI courses at Quantico.[13]

While fan sites and on-line biographies make much of Harris's scrupulous research and attention to detail, characteristics which are often associated with his training as a general assignment reporter for the Associated Press from 1968 to 1975, good research does not necessarily make a good crime novel, especially when the author pauses in the action to give you the benefit of their scholarship.[14] Harris, however, avoids such pedantic display here. All we need to know about serial killers for the purposes of *Red Dragon* is revealed slowly and organically as the plot develops.

In his study of murder in romantic literature and contemporary culture, Joel Black suggests that it is only in "high" art, in the work of Aeschylus, Shakespeare, Dostoyevsky, or Gide, that we are allowed to focus on the figure of the murderer or the witness to murder. In "low" art, and Black includes the detective story here although no examples are given, our attention is redirected to either the victim or the detective, and hence "Towards the rational, epistemological and hermeneutic problem of detection, on the one hand, and towards the artistic 'game' of ingenious plot construction, on the other." This leads Black to the conclusion that "Detective fiction is the most inauthentic and artificial of all the varieties of crime literature."[15]

Black, I would argue, is quite simply wrong. Serial killer creators Jim Thompson and Val McDermid would probably agree with me. Crime fiction regularly dares to explore the mind of the killer, although it may choose, as does Harris in *Red Dragon*, not to stay there for too long in case our experience shifts from one of the sublime to that of the simply terrible, and we risk, like Graham, identifying with the killer and losing our way back.

As for inauthenticity, I'm impressed by the number of references to *Red Dragon* and Harris's writing in the work of academic psychological profilers Holmes and Holmes, who have this to say about the difference between the academic and popular portrayal of serial killers:

> Since the tremendous interest in serial murder began, the knowledge base has grown dramatically, and much has changed. . . . Oddly, we have found some works of fiction that are perhaps more close to the mindset of the serial killer than what the academic experts say. The writings of Thomas Harris come to mind. Certainly the academic community snickers at these types of books, but in our dealings with the serial killers themselves, more than one has said that there is *more than a little truth* [my italics] in the characters depicted in those books.[16]

In support of this latter point, author Ronald Holmes admits that frequently in the cases he has profiled for police departments across the United States, he has found himself echoing the words of Will Graham as he tries to reconstruct the mindset of the serial killer known as The Tooth Fairy in *Red Dragon*: "You had to touch her, didn't you!"[17] It might be noted that Graham never actually says these words in the book, although this is indeed a conclusion he reaches.

In order to furnish us with "more than a little truth," Harris chooses in *Red Dragon* not to present his serial killer to us from the first person narrative point of view, using instead the device of a third person omniscient narrator and a kind of "multi-perspectivism" which includes not only Will Graham as the primary investigator, but also such minor characters as Hoyt Lewis the meter reader and Freddy Lounds the hack reporter enacting the media obsession with serial killers in the '80s. Graham does, however, begin his interior dialogue with the serial killer in chapter 2 as he explores the scene of crime, such sections being italicized in the text:

Why did you move them again? Why didn't you leave them that way? Graham asked. *There's something you don't want me to know about you. Why, there's something you are ashamed of? Or is it something you can't afford for me to know?*

Did you open their eyes?

While Graham flounders in ignorance of either identity or motive, the reader is introduced to the killer, Francis Dolarhyde, in chapter 9. Harris thus completely alters the dynamic of the narrative. No longer are we entirely with Will as he struggles toward enlightenment, we are ahead of him.

Harris thus achieves a considerable feat. At the same time as we are invited to share Graham's moral abhorrence of Dolarhyde's terrible crimes against the two families which he has destroyed, we are given information which, even if it does not make us sympathetic to Dolarhyde, at the very least enables us to understand the mad logic of his motivations. As readers we are made privy to Dolarhyde's experience, his fantasies and in the three chapters which occur in the central section of the book, his tragic and abusive early life. As one of the posters to the email list, DorothyL, points out, this insight is absent in the film versions of the book:

> The real problem . . . is that the moments that define Dolarhyde in Harris's book can't really be filmed. Specifically the chapter where Francis's history is recounted, including the unforgettable scene where Francis introduces himself to his grandmother [I think this should be mother and that the poster has conflated two scenes]. That's the moment that is burned into my memory and that makes Dolarhyde a truly haunting character.[18]

The book thus engages us in a double narrative, the story of detection which is Graham's, and the story of the crimes in the past which have produced the killer Dolarhyde.

Graham and Dolarhyde thus vie for our sympathies as their stories move toward an inevitable convergence. What makes Dolarhyde an even more affecting character is that Harris sets up the possibility of his redemption through a relationship with a blind technician, Reba McClean, who works in the same photographic processing plant. When she innocently seduces him, he experiences the possibility of a loving connection to another human being for the first time. It's a poignant and suspenseful moment, full of anxiety for Reba as well as anxiety both for the reader and Dolarhyde. How will he react? Will he be able to silence the demon which drives him to kill, the Red Dragon?

The symbol of the Red Dragon which is central to Dolarhyde's delusions is taken from a series of four paintings by poet and visionary William Blake, which depict Satan as described in the biblical Book of Revelation envisioned as the Great Red Dragon.[19] On the flyleaves of my cheap Corgi edition, a color reproduction of *The Great Red Dragon and the Woman Clothed in Sun* is reprinted both at the beginning and the end of the book. It's a powerful and disturbing image of the devil from the back, his thick phallic tale curling downwards between his legs as he stands over the golden woman who looks up at him in awe. It is this image of Blake's which Dolarhyde has tacked to the wall of his bedroom, tattooed on his body, and which he physically consumes on a trip to the Brooklyn Museum in an effort to annihilate the demon within.

In his psychotic and delusional state, Dolarhyde would therefore appear to fit the pattern of serial killer identified by Holmes and Holmes as "the visionary" who suffers from a "severe break with reality."[20] However, a closer reading of their typology suggests that such a killer selects his victims randomly, is geographically stable, and is disorganized. In this regard, Dolarhyde does not fit the profile. But then, as Holmes and Holmes are at pains to point out, who does? Despite the considerable attention devoted to serial killers in the media and in criminology, it would seem that very little is known about their formation and motivation which can hold true for all cases:

> We believe that those who commit fatal violence are compelled by forces that are currently beyond our understanding. . . . The best answer (at least at this time) may rest with the unique combination of the three basic sources of personality development: biology, psychology (including psychiatry), and sociology. The blending of these three components of personality produces who we are. Any parent knows how different one child is from the others in the family.[21]

Frequently cited in this regard is the case of real-life serial killer Ted Bundy, whose childhood seems to have been unexceptional and happy, he himself describing his mother as being like June Cleaver in *Leave it to Beaver* and his step-siblings as quite normal.[22]

Harris, however, is not writing criminology but crime fiction. Whilst real-life violence may be random and arbitrary, senseless and confusing, crime fiction offers us the panacea of rationality and understanding. And so we come to understand Dolarhyde's deranged logic and begin to see the pattern which Harris has so artfully established, at the center of which is the problem of the family. As a consequence of his treatment by his mother and grandmother, Dolarhyde seeks his revenge on others, particularly the mothering figures which are a source of both his desire and his despair.

There is, therefore, a particular poetic justice in Harris's denouement when Dolarhyde and Graham finally meet. Abandoned by his own mother because of his facial disfigurement, Dolarhyde attacks Graham at home, disfiguring his face with a knife. Graham's wife Molly, however, comes to the rescue, disarming Dolarhyde with a fishing rod before shooting him in his own disfigured face. But there's no happy ending in sight. By the end of the book, Molly knows that staying with Graham may endanger both her and her son. Hannibal Lecter is still at large and it is he who has directed Dolarhyde to their home. Graham, with his newly disfigured face, is therefore abandoned by his family as surely as was Dolarhyde. What Graham feared the most has come true, he has to all intents and purposes become one with Dolarhyde.

A Terrible Beauty

What makes *Red Dragon* the most beautiful serial killer novel I have ever read is therefore located for me in the aesthetic experience of its deep and immensely satisfying structure, a structure which involves a doubling of narrative and character as well as powerful images delivered in vivid economical prose. I much prefer it to its more celebrated sequel, *The Silence of the Lambs* (1989). In this I am supported by many of the crime fiction fans who post on DorothyL, including Vince, who uses the authority of American crime writer James Ellroy to make his case:

> I heard James Ellroy speak a few years ago, and he said that it's very rare for someone to invent and perfect a genre in the same book, but that Thomas Harris accomplished it with the serial killer novel and *Red Dragon*. I'm sure there are earlier examples of the form, but I'm hard pressed to think of a better one.[23]

In my opinion, what makes *Red Dragon* so good, *Silence of the Lambs* less good, and *Hannibal* really bad has to do with the character of

Hannibal Lecter. Shelley spells it out for me on the DorothyL list when she writes:

> I'm not afraid of Hannibal Lecter, because I don't really believe in him. Francis Dolarhyde has just enough twisted and pitiful humanity that I *do* believe in him, and even feel a sort of horrified compassion for him. As a result, I still can't read *Red Dragon* except in crowded places in broad daylight, and there are whole chapters I have to skip.[24]

Clearly, as far as Harris and his publishers are concerned, Lecter is the character with "legs," although I would argue he has already outrun his course since he is a one-dimensional figure of horror, edging ever closer to Stephen King territory. Overblown and over-written, *Hannibal* (1999) is simply terrible rather than sublime, not only in terms of its content but also in terms of its aesthetic frame. Harris, unfortunately, seems committed to Lecter and a fourth book in the series, *Behind the Mask*, is forthcoming.

In the film versions of *Silence of the Lambs* (1991) and *Hannibal* (2001) and the remake of *Red Dragon* (2003), as portrayed by Anthony Hopkins, Lecter is the serial killer as monster, a monster Mark Selzer would argue (somewhat xenophobically) that was the most powerful and enduring symbol of an American fascination with "wound-culture" in the twentieth century:

> Compulsive killing has its place . . . in a public culture in which addictive violence has become not merely a collective spectacle but also one of the crucial sites where private desire and public culture cross. The convening of the public around scenes of violence has come to make up a *wound culture:* the public fascination with torn and opened private bodies and torn and opened psyches, a public gathering around the wound and trauma.[25]

Discussing the case of a notorious real-life serial killer whose story was said by one newspaper "to illustrate the end of the nineteenth century," Selzer goes on to ask: "But what exactly does it mean to understand persons as illustrations of conditions, melting persons into place?"[26] What this usually means, I would argue, is that popular culture in all its representations, either factual or fictional, is routinely and perhaps inevitably treated as a symptom of societal issues, concerns, or obsessions. Thus Selzer discusses Harris's *Red Dragon* not in terms of its aesthetics and affect, but as "a realization in pop-fiction of the pop-psychologists' nightmare vision."[27]

While this symptomatic impulse may be what drives the cultural theorist, it's not necessarily what drives the ardent reader of crime for whom a symbol of cultural anxiety is only ever as interesting as the aesthetic frame (the crime novel) in which it occurs. Regular poster Kevin Bacon Smith reveals his critical assessment of the sub-genre on the email list DetecToday:

> I dunno about serial killer books. I've read a handful of okay ones, but most of them are pretty bad. Sometimes I think they are like the new cosies. You don't have to have people kill "for reasons" as Chandler put it about Hammett. No need for real motives, or well-developed antagonists . . . just use a bunch of psychobabble gleaned from bad movies and have a bunch of young lovelies sporadically dispatched in increasingly gruesome detail throughout the book. Hey he's a nutjob serial killer – that's supposed to be enough explanation for anyone.[28]

To which David White replies:

> I tend to agree on this one. I've only read a few serial killer novels that I like. . . . I liked *Red Dragon* and *Silence of the Lambs* and *Darkness Take my Hand*. *Hannibal* was terrible as a novel, and as much as I don't like the lack of motive found in these novels, giving Hannibal a motive and setting him loose was wrong. Second, what's the deal with making all the serial killers super intelligent? Every one of them has read Dante, seen the greatest paintings ever and can escape from a maximum security prison . . .[29]

For crime fiction fans a serial killer novel is clearly judged by a broad range of aesthetic criteria which include its use of generic conventions, its characters, narrative choices, and credibility. In this way, I perceive the crime fiction fan to be compelled less by the spectacle of the "wound culture" which Selzer describes, and more by the desire for a satisfying and compelling work of art which moves them. These are the terms of the debate in which crime fiction readers engage on-line and off as they discuss how well a crime novel meets the criteria for a "good read" which they are always in the process of defining.

For my own part, while the novelty of the serial killer sub-genre in crime fiction may have worn off, and interest in the serial killer as a significant social symbol has certainly waned in power to be replaced by the a new bogey-person, the terrorist, I can look back at Thomas Harris's *Red Dragon* and assess it as the complex, poetic, and ultimately sublime work of crime fiction which, in all its terrible beauty, I find it to be.

Notes

1   Sue Turnbull, "Better than literature: discourses of value and reading crime," *Australian Journal of Communication* 25/3 (1998): 9–24.
2   Shelley cited in Vince Keenan's posting, DorothyL Archives 2003, <www.dorothyl.com> (accessed August 27, 2003).
3   Sue Turnbull, "Bodies of knowledge: pleasure and anxiety in the detective fiction of Patricia D. Cornwell," *Australian Journal of Law and Society* 9 (1993): 19–41.
4   Ronald M Holmes and Stephen T Holmes, *Serial Murder*, 2nd edn. (Thousand Oaks, London, New Delhi: Sage Publications, 1998).
5   Arthur Conan Doyle, *The Annotated Sherlock Holmes*, ed. William S. Baring-Gould (New York: Clarkson N. Potter, 1967).
6   Janice Radway, *A Feeling for Books: The Book-of the-Month Club, Literary Taste and Middle-Class Desire* (Chapel Hill and London: University of North Carolina Press, 1997).
7   Mark Selzer, *Serial Killers: Life and Death in America's Wound Culture* (London and New York: Routledge, 1998), p. 221.
8   James L. Cain, *The Postman Always Rings Twice* (Harmondsworth: Penguin, 1952[1934]); Jim Thompson, *The Killer Inside Me* (Vintage Books, 1991[1952]).
9   Sue Turnbull, "'Nice dress, take it off': crime, romance and the pleasure of the text," *International Journal of Cultural Studies* 5/1 (2002): 67–82.
10 Henning Mankell, *Before the Frost* (London: The Harvill Press, 2002).
11 Edmund Burke, *A Philosophical Inquiry into the Origin of our Ideas of the Sublime and the Beautiful* (Glasgow: Glasgow University Press, 1818), p. 36.
12 Thomas Harris, *Red Dragon* (New York: Signet, 2001[1975]), p. 1.
13 Selzer, *Serial Killers*, p. 16.
14 William Striebling, "Thomas Harris," Mississippi Writers Page, May 2001, <www.olemiss.edu/depts/english/ms-writers/dir/harris_thomas/> (accessed September 11, 2005).
15 Joel Black, *The Aesthetics of Murder: A Study in Romantic literature and contemporary culture* (Baltimore and London: The John Hopkins University Press, 1991), p. 45.
16 Holmes and Holmes, *Serial Murder*, p. ix.

17 Ibid., p. xi.

18 Vince Keenan, posting to DorothyL Archives, 2003, <www.dorothyl.com> (accessed August 23, 2003).

19 'The Great Red-Dragon paintings of William Blake', *Artscyclopedia*, <www. artscyclopedia.com/red-dragon-william-blake.html> (accessed September 11, 2005).

20 Holmes and Holmes, *Serial Murder*, p. 62.

21 Ibid., p. 59.

22 Ibid., p. 56.

23 Keenan, posting to DorothyL Archives.

24 Shelley McKibbon, posting to DorothyL Archives, <www.dorothyl.com> (accessed October 4, 2001).

25 Selzer, *Serial Killers*, p. 109.

26 Ibid., p. 204.

27 Ibid., p. 114.

28 Kevin Burton Smith, posting to *DetecToday* email list, April 18, 2001.

29 David White, posting to *DetecToday* email list, April 19, 2001.

4

The Best Australian Romance Novelist: Emma Darcy

Glen Thomas

Emma Darcy is the best Australian writer of romance novels. There: I've said it. But on what basis can I make this claim? Romance fiction as a genre is notoriously suspect; it is derided by many commentators, be they academics, literati, or just plain snobs. "Mills & Boon" is often a pejorative term or synonym for "rubbish," and not only in the context of the printed word. The phrase is a handy catch-all that appears in various fields, such as, for instance, a museum review: "This is not so much a new kind of museum as a tired old story published by Mills & Boon";[1] or in sports commentary: "You don't expect Mills & Boon from Middlesbrough."[2] A common refrain in discussions of romance writing is that "anyone could write one," or, even more pompously, "I'd write one myself if I had a spare weekend" – to which the logical response is, of course, "Why don't you then, if it is so easy and lucrative?" Such remarks are invariably followed by knowledgeable discussions of "The Formula" for writing romance novels and the many millions of dollars that writers of romance make, merely by adhering to "The Formula." Rumors even abound that there is a computer program (somewhere) that merely requires the author to enter the characters' names, descriptions, and the novel's settings, and hey-presto: out pops a fully written romance novel, ready for the publisher (and, by extension, for the haplessly duped, indiscriminate readers who mindlessly consume whatever is put in front of them).

It should go without saying (but often, it does not), that this is non-sense. There is no computer program, nor is there a formula, at least in the sense of a formula that is used to produce the same element, like NaCl is always salt. A formula implies that something must be the same all the time, every time. If the formula is changed, then a different element is produced: NaCl is salt, but NaHCl is chlorine bleach, which you most certainly do not want with your chips. Romance novels are certainly governed by generic conventions, but they are not formulaic.

Those who speak so knowingly about romance novels tend, in the main, never to have read one. I suspect that, in simple Freudian terms, this dismissive attitude conceals a deeper truth: those who disparage romance novels would secretly like to write one (and perhaps have even tried), but cannot. One of the curious aspects of romance writing is the sheer number of people who do try to write a romance: the London office of Harlequin (the parent company of Mills & Boon) receives between 4,000 and 5,000 unsolicited manuscripts each year, of which maybe 12 are accepted.[3] A corollary of this desire to write romance fiction is the astonishing growth in the number of "How to" books on romance writing, such as Beard's *The Complete Idiot's Guide to Getting Your Romance Published*.[4] Aspiring romance authors can also attend conferences, seminars, and writers' support groups dedicated to romance fiction and how to write for this genre. Despite its questionable status, romance fiction remains the most popular form of writing in the world at the moment. To be, or to name, the best writer in this genre, then, presents a set of challenges, among them the dismissive attitude toward romance fiction and the sheer volume of works published and authors.

And out of these books and sales, Emma Darcy is the best Australian writer of romance. I say this on the following grounds. First, her output and sales exceed those of other Australian authors. This in itself does not guarantee her status: but beyond this, she never rewrites herself; she maintains a strong sense of justice and fairness in her novels; and her novels display an interesting awareness of their own place as a part of popular culture.

Emma Darcy's output and sales are impressive by anyone's standards. Since she began writing for Harlequin in 1980, she has completed more than 90 novels (and she is still writing, on average, four new novels each year). Worldwide sales of her romance novels now exceed 60 million copies in 26 languages. By comparison, Valerie Parv, another successful Australian romance author, has in roughly the same amount of time written more than 60 novels, with worldwide sales of more than 20 million copies. The sheer volume of Emma Darcy's output and sales makes her a very successful romance novelist, but these figures are indicative of her success, not a reason for it. The reason why Darcy sells so well, and why she is the best, is because of the quality of the novels she writes.

One of the key reasons for her success is that her plots are always original. While she certainly remains within the generic conventions of romance (as opposed to adhering to the non-existent formula), Darcy has shown herself willing to experiment with her plots and settings – unlike some romance authors who will repeat the same plots across their novels. For instance, Helen Bianchin, an Australian author of more than 40 Harlequin romances, will reuse the same plot structure, to the extent that she can be said to specialize in plots where the heroines are forced into a marriage against their will in order to achieve a wider good, usually for their families. Therefore, Bianchin's *The Wedding Ultimatum* (2002) and *In the Spaniard's Bed* (2003) share the same basic structure: the heroines are heiresses to a business empire that is struggling with financial difficulties, so in order to save the family business these women either marry, or become involved sexually with, men who bail out the family company, despite the fact that the heroines initially cannot abide their new husbands/sexual partners. In both these cases, the sexual passion between the hero and the heroine is enough for the heroine to overcome her initial revulsion (suggesting a strong market for readers who empathize with heroines who either marry or have sex with men they dislike. This is an intriguing situation, but outside the scope of this chapter).

For Darcy, though, the plots and settings of her novels are highly varied. While many of her books are set in and around Sydney and its surrounding beaches, there are plenty that are not. Settings range from the Australian outback, North Queensland, and the Great Barrier Reef to France, China, the United Kingdom, Las Vegas, and (fictional) Middle-Eastern countries. This variety of settings makes Darcy a truly global romance novelist, yet at the same time she is able to maintain a strong sense of "Australian-ness" in her novels – what cultural historian Juliet Flesch calls "the beetroot in the burger."[5] Australian romance authors tend to maintain a stronger sense of place in their novels than do their overseas counterparts. In part this is due to the perceived exoticism of the Australian settings, and the sheer breadth of available settings: the Barrier Reef, the Outback, metropolitan Sydney, Melbourne, or Brisbane, small beachside towns, and so on. As one of Darcy's fans notes with regard to a book set in Melbourne: "It is authentic Melbourne City – right down to Stalactites restaurant on Lonsdale Street."[6] But on another level, even in books with non-Australian settings "Australian-ness" is evident at the level of characterization, in that international readers see Australian characters as "more 'real'. By this they mean that the characters use language differently, and react to situations differently, from the characters in romances by American and British authors."[7] Key character attributes to emerge from Australian settings are a sense of humor, independence, and a sense of fair play[8] (the last of which I will discuss later). Susanna Carr highlights similar points in her observation that the Darcy hero is: "a bit of a rogue, but has a great capacity for tenderness."[9]

Darcy's various settings and sense of Australian-ness are combined with plots that are always contemporary. Indeed, this element sets Darcy's plots apart from other romance authors. She ensures that her books are in tune with contemporary ideas and preoccupations by keeping an alert eye on the culture at large. For example, the initial impetus for *The Blind-Date Bride* (2003) was the results of Harlequin's annual St Valentine's Day Report. Darcy explained this to me in conversation:

> Two years ago they [Harlequin] produced a St Valentine's Day Report which was about sexual fantasy, what's your favorite sexual fantasy. High on the list was on a beach, and I though right, if that has this huge appeal across the board, then on the beach it's going to be.[10]

This short comment explains a large part of Darcy's appeal. Research (albeit somewhat unscientific) suggests that people like the idea (if, perhaps, not the practice) of sex on the beach, so this becomes a central feature of Darcy's next book. This for me is one of the defining elements that will make a work genuinely popular. The book takes an element of culture (sex) and places this element in with contemporary concerns and issues. Darcy's other skill is to make the sex scenes in her novels (for which she is famous) hot reading:

> He swung her off her feet, laid her on the rug, loomed over her, his face ablaze with the fire within, his powerful body dark and taut, rampant male

poised to take, primed to take, and a willing elation coursed though Catherine as she positioned herself to possess him.

He came into her with shocking, exhilarating swiftness, the impact of him arching her body in an instinctive and ecstatic urge to hold the deeply penetrating fullness, to have it all, the whole glorious shaft of him imbedded in the warm silky heart of her, surrounding him, enclosing him, drawing him into the ultimate togetherness.

. . .

The full moon shone on her face. The sea breeze filtered through her swaying hair. The roar of crashing waves filled her ears. But they were outside things and the vibrant inner life of this union with Zack Freeman swamped her awareness of anything else. It was like an ocean of sensation, whipped by a storm of feeling, tidal waves gathering more and more explosive power.[11]

Since the start of her writing career, Darcy has been willing to push the boundaries of romance novels in terms of her depictions of sexual content and the language that is used to describe these scenes. Much comedic mileage has been made of the euphemistic terms that are often used within romance to describe the anatomical aspects of sex, but Darcy has always striven to be more frank (but as she says, "never crude") than others; for instance, it is rare for Mills & Boon writers to use the word "clitoris" as Darcy does in her 2004 novel *The Outback Wedding Takeover* (p. 125).

It is not only at the level of the sexual, though, that Darcy emerges as a highly contemporary writer. Her novels are prepared to engage with material that can be, at times, quite disturbing. In *The Bedroom Surrender* (2003), the heroine, Rosalie James, spent part of her childhood in a Filipino child-sex brothel. This presents a twist on the standard virginal romantic heroine; Rosalie is a virgin at the outset of the book, but only because "the evil men who ran that place talked about [her] as a prize who'd fetch a very high price and they were keeping [her] for one particular client."[12] It is daring to introduce such material into a romance, as it represents an intrusion of a highly distasteful aspect of contemporary culture into the escapist world of the romance novel. For Rosalie, her past becomes the foundation of a political crusade to attempt to rescue as many children in similar circumstances as she possibly can. While *The Bedroom Surrender* concludes with the generically conventional happy ending, when Rosalie and the hero Adam are married, this does not occur until she has educated him as to how important her work is and made him understand that it is imperative that she continue. A key feature of the resolution of their romantic dilemma is Adam's willingness to do anything to help her:

> "I'll learn." He released her upper arms and cupped her face, fingers dragging at her skin, reinforcing the urgent intensity in his eyes. "All the resources at my disposal can be yours, too, Rosalie. Fly on my airline. It won't cost you anything. I'll set up another Saturn company to recruit and pay people who'd like to be involved in your mission. If saving children is your life's work, bring me into it. Share it with me."[13]

In no way, then, is Rosalie's personality or work subsumed within his; on the contrary, Adam must be educated and brought around to her way of thinking before the romantic dilemma of the plot can be resolved. One of the most enjoyable features of this book is the way in which Rosalie teaches Adam to stop being the self-centered prick he is at the start of the book. Darcy's heroines are never the spineless waifs of romantic stereotypes. As her readers point out, her heroines "refuse to compromise," but instead are women "who are not afraid of the hero just because he has power."[14] These aspects set Darcy apart from other romance writers, as she is prepared to take risks with her material, and to turn this risky element into the central feature of the books she writes. Rather than shy away from unpleasantness, Darcy transforms such material into the driver of her plot, in a manner that both conforms to the generic conventions of romance, and simultaneously pushes the boundaries of those same conventions.

Darcy has also pioneered other plot forms that are now staples of romance. Her 1997 novel *Jack's Baby* began a persistent trend of romance plots whereby the hero discovers, to his surprise and astonishment, that he has become a father. This book was extremely successful both in Australia and overseas. As Darcy explains: "Do you know, it [*Jack's Baby*] was a huge hit. . . . And what it really tapped into was the fantasy of a man as a committed father to a single mother, the guy coming and taking responsibility. . . . It was really giving the answer to all those dreams." As Darcy points out, the plot driver here is Jack's desire to convince Nina (the heroine) that he can be a good father to their child. Nina initially seeks to deny Jack any involvement with the baby, as she is convinced he does not want a child: "Jack hates babies."[15] His references to the baby as "the kid" only strengthen this impression.[16] As the novel progresses, Jack is required to demonstrate his prowess at dealing with both the minor and major problems of parenting. Jack, unlike the vast majority of romance heroes, is a manual worker – a French polisher and restorer of antique furniture, not the standard billionaire businessman. He works with his hands, and the novel insistently argues that dealing with a baby means getting one's hands dirty. The remarkable feature of *Jack's Baby*, though, is that Jack's education, which begins with a dirty nappy, is presented in a comedic manner:

> The little face suddenly assumed a belligerent expression. The tiny arms stopped waving and straightened out, hands clenching.
> "Want to fight, huh?"
> No reply. A gathering of concentration on internal matters, eyes narrowing, face going red. Several seconds passed. It dawned on Jack that the kid was pushing. Then the job was done. Relief came. Relaxation. A look of blissful peace. Jack chuckled. It was so obvious.
> . . .
> The odor started rising as Jack unfastened the plastic tabs on the nappy. It was incredibly foul. Worse than rotten egg gas. Jack's throat convulsed as he fought against gagging. Manfully he peeled down the front section of the nappy. The source of the smell revealed itself in all its slushy yellow-green horror.[17]

When the major child-rearing crisis occurs, after Nina has been hospitalized for abscesses caused by mastitis and is unable to feed the baby (which, incidentally, allows the book to provide a helpful preventative for breast soreness in lactating women – using refrigerated cabbage leaves placed in the bra to form a cold compress: when the cabbage leaves reach body temperature, replace them with fresh cold ones from the fridge), Jack must take charge. As with the nappies, the crisis of switching the baby from breast to bottle milk without female assistance is handled without the *Sturm und Drang* of high drama, but rather as a source of comedy. Jack, his two teenage apprentice French polishers, and Jack's dog Spike form a production line of a mixture of bottles, teats, and different brands of baby formula to accomplish "Operation Bottle Feed." The source of the humor here is three men and a dog, none of whom has any experience of feeding babies, trying to find the ideal combination of formula and teat flow:

She attacked the new teat like a threshing machine. For the next five minutes it looked as though formula two was a winner. Then her stomach staged a revolt. The formula came back out like a gusher. The towels took a beating. Gary removed them to the laundry. Ben brought some more. Jack did his best to soothe Charlotte, holding her up to his shoulder and patting comfort. She vomited down his back.

Nightmare alley, Jack thought, struggling to keep his anxiety under control. Spike examined the mess and decided not to lick it up.[18]

The Bedroom Surrender and *Jack's Baby* provide an insightful contrast into the variety and breadth of Darcy's style and tone. She is able to move easily between novels of high drama with disturbing content to lighter, more comedic works that are great fun to read. As Darcy says in her letter to the reader at the opening of *Jack's Baby*:

Jack came out of my wish bag. . . . I wished [my husband] could be put through the whole baby mill so he would understand and appreciate all the lows as well as the highs of having a baby. . . . I wanted him to know and understand what every woman with a baby goes through.

A substantial part of the novel's appeal, then, lies in this notion of a shared community of female experience of which men have no knowledge. First, Jack is forced to take on the child-rearing role and in doing so realizes "how a baby could reduce even the most reasonable adult to a quivering wreck." Second, Jack is "shaken into an acute realization that he was holding a miniature human being with a mind and stomach of its own, who was totally dependent on his meeting its needs. It was a highly sobering and humbling experience."[19] This is the ideal female revenge fantasy, but these scenes also have an educative function, which is evident in both novels I have discussed; Adam in *The Bedroom Surrender* and Jack in *Jack's Baby* receive a metaphorical kick in the pants to emerge from the experience as better men. This process of self-growth taps into one concern that has remained consistent throughout Darcy's career: a desire for justice, accompanied by a strong communitarian ethic.

The Outback Wedding Takeover (2004), for example, opens with the hero Mitch (a Sydney barrister) ruthlessly tearing apart a witness in a compensation case. Mitch does so in order to win compensation for his client, the witness's daughter-in-law whose husband's suicide has left her alone with a baby daughter. Mitch's motives are explained in terms of his desire for justice: "Justice would be served. And he was glad it had come to this – payment in more than dollars. People who gave pain should feel it themselves." Mitch: "never took on a case unless he believed he was fighting for right, and then he gave it everything he could bring to it."[20] This instance is not an isolated one. Characters who commit acts of betrayal are the worst of the worst in Darcy's world. Mitch's former girl-friend Harriet (also a lawyer) slept with a judge in order to try and gain a courtroom advantage; Mitch cannot get rid of her fast enough on the basis of her "win at all costs" attitude, which he despises.[21] Betrayal of this kind is the worst of sins in Darcy's books. Hannah O'Neill in *The Bridal Bargain* (2002) has suffered in a similar manner: the week before her wedding she walked in on her fiancé Flynn and putative best friend Jodie having sex. Jodie is depicted as a "user" who is the complete oppo-site of Hannah.[22]

The characters depicted with approval in Darcy's work are never users; rather, they are "givers." Adam in *The Bedroom Surrender*, Shane Courtney in *The Upstairs Lover* (1993) – whose openness and generosity are in stark contrast to the other members of his selfish, grasping family – and the completely over-the-top Sunny King in *Strike at the Heart* (1987) are only some examples. Darcy's novels incessantly posit an ethical center of their narratives, one that privileges adherence to a code of conduct. Those characters who act out of egoistic motives are given short shrift, and often end up disgraced in some way. In *The Outback Wedding Takeover*, Kathryn's former fiancé Jeremy attempts sexually to assault her in a drunken rage, but Mitch catches him in the act and gives him a beating.[23]

The ethics of the characters combines with the plots of the novels to make Darcy's works eminently readable. These are not simply narratives of heterosexual romance, but also works of popular culture that are edu-cative in the sense mentioned above: male and female characters are taught some form of lesson about themselves within ethical narratives that examine the nature of romantic love. In *The Outback Wedding Take-over*, this sense of values in symbolized by a chess set. Mitch is an avid chess player, and sees the world in the same way as he sees the chessboard. The heroine Kathryn comes to realize this during a conversation with Mitch's father-figure:

> "He cuts through all the grays and goes straight to the core of any issue."

"Black and white," the old man remarked, nodding thoughtfully. Then he asked, "Does that trouble you, Kathryn?"

She shook her head. "Not at all. I like it. He has a system of values that I feel very secure with."[24]

The novels illustrate certain modes of behavior through characters' actions, and in doing so ask the reader to consider the foundations on which romances are based. The system of values that the novels endorse is inherent to a successful romance. The texts demonstrate that romances that are not based upon principles of honesty, trust, and sharing are romances that will fail (if indeed they are romances at all). The upshot of this is that there is an ethics of romance here that is not present in the work of other authors. Yes, the endings are happy, and certainly the reader can see how the partnerships between the characters will turn out, but alongside these generic aspects is a sustained interrogation of what makes for a successful romance. It is more here than the clichéd "eyes across a crowded room"; rather, romance is a set of shared valued and principles.

This ethic of values and mutual good is evident on both a personal level and in wider, societal contexts. In Darcy's 1995 novel *Climax of Passion*, the heroine (Amanda) seeks to restore her father's reputation after he claimed to have discovered the fabled crystal caves of Xabia, but was dismissed and ridiculed. Amanda eventually proves that the caves do indeed exist, but that the Sheikh of Xabia has suppressed all information about them. His reasons for doing so, though, are expressed in terms of being for the good of Xabia and its people. The caves contain crystals that are used as a catalyst in the production of rocket fuel "and other chemical processes." The Sheikh explains that the crystals would be too tempting for Western nations:

> "Do you imagine any of the world's great powers would care what happened to Xabia and its people while they fought for their share of what is here?
>
> ". . . Xabia will not become another Kuwait," he went on remorselessly. "Neodymite crystals are more valuable than the black gold that motivates war. There would also be the price of corruption."[25]

For the Sheikh, it would be wrong to mine the crystals, no matter what extra wealth they would bring. The long-term good of the nation outweighs the short-term profit; mining the crystals would be a concession to both greed and self-interest, which Amanda realizes: "To right the injustice to her father was to wrong others."[26] Again here, the communitarian spirit infuses the novel in its conviction that acting out of purely selfish motives is antithetical to social good. These novels ask readers to step away from their own personal desires and consider not just the welfare of others, which is a key value, but the justice of a given situation. The emotional impact of Darcy's work in part rests on this sense of justice that infuses so much of her work. Ultimately, in all of Darcy's novels, it is better to be a giver than to be a taker.

One final aspect of Darcy's work that makes her the best Australian romance novelist is the awareness the texts show of themselves as being objects of popular culture. In her novels, Darcy presents her own theory of how popular culture – and how romance novels, as part of popular culture – should work, providing readers with a guide to the aesthetic judgment of these books.

The key example here is Darcy's 1987 novel *Strike at the Heart*. To summarize the plot briefly: Jackie Mulholland is a widow in her mid-30s with two sons. She is a clay artist, making a meager living selling her pottery. Her new neighbor is the filmmaker Sunny King, whom Jackie initially despises for what she sees as his ostentatious vulgarity, which is represented in the house he has built on the adjoining property:

> Only a madman could have built such a monstrosity of a house. He even had the arrogance to call it King's Folly. With all its stupid turrets it was more like Court Jester's Folly. The man had no sensitivity toward the environment, no sensitivity at all.
>
> Jackie's mouth curved in disdain at Sunny King and all he stood for. These newly rich people despoiled everything they touched. They had no manners, no civility, no sophistication.[27]

Sunny King is thus introduced as a boorish, uncultured oaf. The source of his wealth, though, is significant: he makes films featuring crime fighter Dirk Vescum that are avowedly popular, by which Jackie is mortified. "It disgusted her even further that Sunny King had gotten rich by tapping the baser instincts in people."[28] Even worse for Jackie is the appeal that Sunny's films have for her two sons, who are keen Dirk Vescum fans. Rather than products of popular culture, Jackie's tastes run to opera, which Sunny sees as fitting someone with Jackie's "high-tone class."[29] The conflict between the two characters is established immediately, but what is significant about this is that it is a conflict on a cultural level. Sunny is (newly) rich, popular, and successful in his filmmaking, whereas Jackie represents high culture in her tastes for opera, and the artistry of poverty in her limited sales of ceramic *objets d'art*.

Jackie perceives Sunny as the very avatar of what are supposedly the worst aspects of popular culture: loud, vulgar, crass, and a corrupter of young minds. He is, certainly, overpowering and occasionally annoying, to the extent that Jackie goes so far as to start shooting at him.[30] Jackie is moved to outrage and anger at everything Sunny stands for, yet it transpires that although Jackie deplores Sunny's films, *she has never seen them*. Jackie has passed sweeping and critical judgment on a cultural form that she knows nothing about. This is analogous to the way in which romance fiction is treated by its critics, just as it is analogous to many of the typical responses to popular culture in general – the notion of "I don't have to read/see/watch something like that to know that it's bad."

For *Strike at the Heart*, though, the situation is turned around when Jackie is finally persuaded to watch the first Dirk Vescum film. When she does so, her opinion is transformed. While the film's plot is described as "trite," Jackie is unprepared for "the emotional way in which Sunny King had developed it. There were moments in the love-death scenes which wrung her heart and almost moved her to tears." By the end of the film, the audience is left "on a high moment of emotional satisfaction."[31] On the strength of her response, Jackie then goes to see the second Dirk Vescum film, and is even more impressed:

> Behind the appeal of exciting action was the strong sense of rightness, of good against evil, of feeling for others, of loyalty and bravery and honor and love. . . . They were good entertainment and carried a high level of morality and humanity which won her admiration and approval.[32]

The Dirk Vescum films, then, represent exactly the same qualities as Emma Darcy's novels. Yes, the plots may well be – in one sense – trite. What distinguishes these books is, like Sunny King's films, that they convey this same "strong sense of rightness" and provide their readers with the emotionally fulfilling conclusion that Jackie admires. Darcy's fans find the same emotional fulfillment in her novels: "the climax is very touching, it brought me to tears";[33] or, "I loved the Characters, loved that they were flawed and had issues. This book was full of emotions that made you really feel for the couple."[34] *Climax of Passion* concludes with Jackie realizing that the man she has been disparaging for so long is in fact an overwhelmingly kind and generous man who at the end of the novel risks his own life to save those of her sons. In this context, it is Jackie who must be educated to be more humble and not so hasty in her judgments. This realization occurs when she helps Sunny provide the musical soundtrack for the final Dirk Vescum film. Sunny is stuck for something musically suitable, but after seeing the rushes, Jackie provides the ideal musical accompaniment: the high-culture strains of Wagner's *The Ride of the Valkyries*. Sunny plans to adapt this, however:

> "I can see it now. That's the material to use. We'll jazz it up. Make it really big. Use three orchestras. Intersperse it with a rock band. I know exactly how to do it now."
>
> A rock band! Intersperse Wagner's great music with a rock band! All Jackie's delight at providing the answer to Sunny's problem was instantly crushed by a mountain of horror, quickly followed by a tidal wave of furious indignation. Her mouth opened. Her brain tossed around venomous words. Her voice lifted to shrilling pitch.
>
> "You phil . . ."
>
> Sunny turned to her, his face still alight with happy triumph. Her mouth bit down on her tongue, cutting off the word, philistine, in mid-shrill. Her brain abruptly changed gears and whirled again. Hadn't she wanted to make him happy? And what right did she have to be so arrogant in her judgments?
>
> You need a bit of humility, Jackie Mulholland, she warned herself. You're not always right. Sunny King had proved time and time again that he knew what he was doing when he was making movies for the market. Horses for courses, she reminded herself fiercely.[35]

Jackie is therefore forced to re-examine her somewhat snooty values to discover that her judgments have indeed, as she says, been arrogant. She has denounced Sunny's films without seeing them, as well as initially forming a strong dislike for Sunny without knowing him. The question the text poses, by implication, is what right do critics of romance fiction have to make their judgments? Jackie represents critics who will disparage and mock that with which they are not familiar. *Strike at the Heart* demonstrates that exposure to these derided cultural forms, accompanied by a process of evaluating them *on their merits*, may well produce a change of attitude, or at least a diminution in the insults hurled at popular culture.

As I argued above, Darcy's books contain within them an unambiguous moral center, just as her hero's films do. Darcy's novels also give their audience emotional satisfaction, be it in a comedic or more serious mode. This emotional satisfaction is the product of the reader's sense of the appropriate conclusion of the romance plot, as well as the knowledge that the more disreputable characters have been punished in some way. Darcy argues for ethical values to underpin romance, rather than merely sexual passion or physical attractiveness. Characters in her novels must undergo some form of educational transformation before the romantic plot can be fully resolved, yet at the same time, it should be stressed that these are not overtly didactic plots. The reader is not bombarded with finger-waving lessons, but is instead shown how short-sightedness, hasty judgments, and willful blindness need to be overcome. Emma Darcy's novels conclude with her protagonists demonstrably better people than they were at the outset. And that is, ultimately, what makes Emma Darcy Australia's best romance novelist.

Notes

1   Deyan Sudjic, "Where William Morris meets Mills & Boon . . . And Loses," *Observer*, August 4, 2002, p. 10.

2   Mark Hodgkinson, "Leicester Miss Chance," *Telegraph*, August 27, 2003, p. 3.

3   Valerie Parv, *The Art of Romance Writing: Practical Advice from an International Bestselling Romance Writer* (Crow's Nest, NSW: Allen & Unwin, 2004), p. x.

4   Julie Beard, *The Complete Idiot's Guide to Getting Your Romance Published* (Indianapolis, IN: Alpha Books, 2000); see also Parv, *The Art of Romance Writing*; Kate Walker, *Kate Walker's 12-Point Guide to Writing Romances* (Bishops Lydeard, Somerset: Studymates, 2004).

5   Juliet Flesch, *From Australia with Love: A History of Modern Australian Popular Romance Novels* (Fremantle, WA: Curtin University Books-Fremantle Arts Centre Press, 2004), p. 249.

6   Marcie, "Review of *Craving Jamie*," April 16, 2001, <http://www.amazon.com/exec/obidos/tg/detail/-/0373118813/qid=1109385123/sr=1-1/ref=sr_1_1/103-6859298-1426248?v=glance&s=books> (accessed on February 26, 2005).

7   Quoted in Flesch, *From Australia with Love*, p. 250.

8   Ibid., 251.

9   Susanna Carr, "What I'm reading," <http://www.susannacarr.com/archives/arc_rec-reading_main.htm> (accessed on February 26, 2005).

10   All Emma Darcy quotations from personal interview, January 2004.

11   Emma Darcy, *The Blind-Date Bride* (Chatswood: Harlequin-Mills & Boon, 2003), pp. 51–2.

12   Emma Darcy, *The Bedroom Surrender* (Chatswood: Harlequin-Mills & Boon, 2003), p. 130.

13   Ibid., p. 171.

14   "A reader," "Review of *Wedding*," July 29, 1997, <http://www.amazon. com/exec/obidos/tg/detail/-/037311463X/qid=1109386337/sr=1-78/ ref=sr_1_78/103-6859298-1426248?v=glance&s=books> (accessed on February 26, 2005).

15   Emma Darcy, *Jack's Baby* (Chatswood, NSW: Harlequin-Mills & Boon, 1997), p. 32.

16   Ibid., pp. 29, 33.

17   Ibid., pp. 96, 98.

18   Ibid., p. 158.

19   Ibid., pp. 158, 160.

20   Emma Darcy, *The Outback Wedding Takeover* (Chatswood: Harlequin-Mills & Boon, 2004), p. 13.

21   Ibid., p. 16.

22   Emma Darcy, *The Bridal Bargain* (Chatswood: Harlequin-Mills & Boon, 2002), pp. 128, 95.

23   Darcy, *The Outback Wedding Takeover*, p. 105.

24   Ibid., p. 180.

25   Emma Darcy, *Climax of Passion* (Chatswood: Harlequin-Mills & Boon, 1996), p. 110.

26   Ibid., pp. 113–14.

27   Emma Darcy, *Strike at the Heart* (Chatswood: Harlequin-Mills & Boon, 1987), p. 9.

28   Ibid., p. 8.

29   Ibid., pp. 110, 112.

30   Ibid., pp. 80–1.

31   Ibid., pp. 93–4.

32   Ibid., p. 104.

33   "A reader," "Review of *Claiming His Mistress*," December 18, 2003, <http://www.amazon.com/exec/obidos/ASIN/0373122063/ qid=1109463711/sr=2-1/ref=pd_bbs_b_2_1/103-6859298-1426248> (accessed February 27, 2005).

34   Elspeth M. Mcclanahan, "Review of *The Blind-Date Bride*," February 14, 2005, <[http://www.amazon.com/exec/obidos/tg/detail/-/0373123086 /qid=1109464098/sr=1-50/ref=sr_1_50/103-6859298-1426248?v=glanc e&s=books> (accessed on February 27, 2005).

35   Darcy, *Strike at the Heart*, pp. 161–2.

5

The Best Website For Men Who Have Sex With Men: cruisingforsex.com

Mark McLelland

I think all this hype about one day the world being hit by a stray mete-orite and the entire human race getting killed off is a total load of crap. I think the world would more likely come to end if suddenly every computer on this planet was inundated with pictures of cock. There would be pandemonium and uproar from all quarters. Millions starv-ing, thousands getting bombed, who gives a shit, but oh my god, show a bit of cock and there's hell to pay. Yeah, I want that cock, cock pouring into every lab, on to every bank machine, cock splashed across the neon lights of Times Square, Tokyo, Piccadilly. Flashing cock. Pul-sating cock. Adverts of cock. Heaps of cock. Mountains and mountains of endless cock.[1]

All the Dick and Ass You Can Eat

Cruisingforsex.com (CFS) is the Internet's most visited website for men who have sex with men (MSM) whether in real life, on screen, or simply in their heads. It was the winner of the 2003 Cybersocket "Best Free Adult Site" Award; was recently named "the holy grail for many gay men who go online" (*Los Angeles* magazine); and was acclaimed the number one cruising website in the world (*Cybersocket* magazine). It will also appeal to women who like to fantasize about men who have sex with men as well as women who have sex with men who have sex with men, often in the same bed and at the same time (there is a thread for bisexual swingers). It also appeals to the "bi-curious" – that is, men who suspect that other men will be more willing (and better able) to perform certain sexual acts than their girlfriends or wives. As multiple cruisers on the site are more than happy to point out, the women in their lives aren't always in the mood, expect a lot of preliminary courting and post-coital pampering, and anyway, they simply don't give good head – after all "nobody (even your girlfriend) knows a man's body better than another man."[2]

CFS is not a "gay" website. In fact it is one of a growing number of "post-gay" cultural formations – like Calvin Klein underwear (which even straight men can gaze at and admire, on themselves or on the models plastered on advertising placards) or boy bands (who, while crooning love songs to ostensibly female listeners, are clearly more interested in making eye contact with each other).[3] The website is not about sexual *identity*, but about sexual *acts* and sexual *pleasures*. CFS is not even about complete people; rather, it is a celebration of body parts (mainly penises and anuses but also nipples, mouths, feet, hands, and other bits) as well as a celebration of the pleasures that these body parts can receive and confer.

Furthermore, the website offers suprapersonal pleasures through a celebration of uniforms and a fetishization of clothing. Viewers are able to seek for, describe, fantasize, reminisce about, or otherwise depict sex with soldiers, marines, airmen, state troopers, policemen, firemen, border-security guards, prisoners, prison guards, security personnel, postal workers, and a variety of delivery and maintenance men – all of whom are invoked (and enjoyed) as archetypes. Nobody cares if these avatars of the supreme sex god are nice guys – usually they are not. Indeed, the sex is often forced (or coerced), violent, and humiliating. In other words, it's great fantasy and makes having your electricity meter read worth staying home for.

CFS encourages, facilitates, and celebrates casual, anonymous sex between men. Often the sexual encounters described take place between men who are in different rooms, separated by a thin partition, in which various "glory" holes have been driven and through which sexual acts take place. Other venues include parks, rest areas, beaches, and forests. The acts which take place in these Arcadian venues usually do so after hours – that is, when daytime users have retreated to suburbia. They take place in the dark and usually in silence.

Needless to point out, CFS is not about relationships, peer support, community building, or political lobbying. Nor is it a place for the insecure to ponder the complexities of "sexual identity." Discussion *does* take place, but only on such topics as the relative virtues of cumming in a mouth or in an ass, giving or receiving head (see the thread "Why do they suck" for a paean of penis worship), or on the relative intensity of orgasms with male or female partners (better with men since the sex is usually nastier). In other words, CFS is not politically correct. As one cruiser put it:

> If anyone's taking a vote . . . Cruising for Sex and Talking Politics should be constitutionally banned from coexistence! The moral superiority of the male hard-on (over the male opinion) should become a point of federal law. Discussing politics is a known erosion to the essence, the motivation (and certainly the continuation) of a good erection.[4]

The site opens with a home page that offers the browser four main options – to "connect," "read," "look," or "buy." Click on each of these icons and you are taken to a list of other hyperlinks. CONNECT will take you to a country by country, city by city, and venue by venue listing of public places where men meet for sex with men; these most commonly include rest rooms, parks, and parking lots (and even several venues on this writer's campus). It also links to a live chat room where assignations may be made instantaneously, a message board where advertisers offer or request a variety of sexual services, and a list of escort services. READ (my favorite, being a bookish type), takes you to a list of blogs where regular cruisers narrate recent sexual escapades or, I think more interestingly, reminisce about past times – accounts of "action" in the forces in WWII are particularly fascinating. READ will also take you to a series of notice boards where cruisers post reviews of porn videos, male escorts, and sex venues and clubs, and a range of separate threads for gays, bis, straights, crossdressers, and leather and kink practitioners. LOOK leads to a cruiser gallery where members post their own pictures (this is a free service) and to a series of porn galleries supplied by CFS's sponsors (you have to pay to get beyond the opening page of these sites). CFS also produces its own porn starring amateur actors recruited via the site. A team travels around the country staging orgies, bukakkes (jerk-off parties where a group of standing men ejaculate onto a man or small group of men sitting in the center), and other events which are filmed and then sold as amateur pornography. Stills and a few minutes of video from these productions are provided free, but you have to pay to see more. BUY links to commercial porn sites and online sex merchandise stores.

Curiously, one might suppose, given the "abject" nature of the acts described, the site is well managed, gorgeously designed, upbeat, sassy, easy to use, and, most importantly, *free*. It is, among other things, an extremely *professional* venture managed by experienced cruisers who take pride in the public service they offer. Gabe, one of the site's full-time staff members, puts it this way:

> I'm grateful for this job. I believe it has saved me in a great many ways. It's demanding but it is so wonderful to care about something, to feel productive and proud of what we do. I know a lot of people wouldn't understand the pride thing. I mean, we produce porn, keep meticulous track of cruisy bathrooms the world over and give guys a way to find all the dick and ass they can eat. But to me that's just it – our sole purpose is to facilitate pleasure. There are worse things to do with your life.[5]

Quite, like campaign *against* public immorality or *for* gay marriage.

Originally started "as a lark" by Cruisemaster Keith in 1995, the site now has between 30,000 and 50,000 visitors a day, averaging well over one million a month. Although the site was set up as a hobby, by June of 1997 it had become self-financing and it now boasts a full time staff of three. While the vast majority of the users are based in the US and it is consequently American cruising sites which are the best represented, there are also substantial numbers of visitors hailing from Canada, the UK, Germany, and, curiously, Japan. However, most of the world's major holiday and business destinations are well served by the site (check out the listings for cruisy airports – just in case you have a couple of hours stop-over to fill). For men with defective "gay-dars" (gay versions of radars), it is also full of tips on how to spot potentially cruisy environments. Just as useful are its constantly updated tips on who, what, and where to avoid.

The Pleasures of the Post-Gay

I do not enjoy CFS primarily because I use it to find and engage in public sex. I find the idea that I *could* use it in this manner if I wanted to more satisfying than actually doing so. I don't really have the time to go trawling around the city for sex, and when all said and done I really do prefer a cup of tea and a good biography. I am a genuine intellectual – someone much more at home in their head than their body. The last time I was pushed against a slimy wall in a dark, dank sauna by an indistinct body groping me in the gloom, I spent the whole time thinking about how *ritualistic* sex between men can become and how the admiration, indeed, love, that pours out of a "passive" partner for the male member resembles a kind of religious awe. I'm not making this up: research has been done into the psychology of cruising which documents a range of altered states not dissimilar to the "disorientation of the senses" experienced during religious ecstasy.[6]

I enjoy CFS primarily as a discursive space – it offers me visual, but more importantly, narrative pleasure. It is a subversive space – as insulting to mainstream heterosexual norms as it is to a new homonormative gay orthodoxy that sees gay "liberation" in assimilating those very norms.[7] In other words, CFS is *fully sick*.

Let me just spell out some of the ways that I think CFS has developed an important counter-discourse both to moral-majority opinion which sees cruisers as immoral (and probably sick and criminal) and gay assimilationists who try to distance themselves from those who seek public sex (i.e. "We're not all like *them*"). First, I like the way that CFS is not a *gay* website. In the popular imagination MSM are all gay. Of course, with our "local knowledge"[8] we know that self-defining gay men are just one of the categories of men who enjoy sex with other men, but there are also bisexuals and men who identify as straight (not to mention transgenders and intersexuals). Not only does CFS supply different spaces on the site (different message boards, for instance) for gays, bisexuals, straights, crossdressers, sex workers, etc. to communicate, but it also serves as a portal for men to access a range of pornographies featuring models with a range of identities and personae.

This leads me to my second point. "Gay" culture has often been criticized for being too conformist, white, and middle class. What is interesting about CFS is that it is not a "gay" project, but might be better defined as a civil libertarian project aimed at facilitating sex between men irrespective of identification. While participation in the "gay scene" often relies on being able to create a certain "look," all you need to participate in the CFS world is Internet access. One of the great strengths of the site is that, because of its successful sponsorship from commercial porn sites and gay businesses, it is able to offer a variety of services for free, and although there are pay areas of the site, the free public access material is among the best and most extensive I have encountered on the Net.

To an extent then, CFS is a pluralizing force. What we find on CFS is the proliferation of "lifestyle sectors"[9] based not on sexual identity (like the tired old labels "gay" or "bisexual"), but on sexual *acts*. The site has helped men who enjoy very specific sexual acts (like getting blown anonymously through glory holes) to network with partners who like to blow. Of course, before the Internet it was always possible if you were living in the right city and knew the right places to go to, that you could get what you wanted, *eventually*. But CFS enables men to plan and negotiate in advance, arrange meetings either that day or later in the week, in the cities they live in or that they will be traveling to. It is this *proliferation* of opportunity and its implications that are so interesting about the site – particularly the manner in which it enables multiple users to engage with it in multiple ways without having to self-define. To this extent it is post-gay and helps us to move beyond what is becoming an increasingly moribund and redundant term. I mean, gay is really so, well, '70s.

I asked Keith, the site's co-founder and cruisemaster, to comment on my ramblings above. I pointed out that I see this brief chapter as a contribution to the ongoing development of a model where academics and popular knowledge producers don't see themselves in opposition (the website is an object to be deconstructed by academics), but as taking part in a dialogue (the website and its producers/users constitute a subject to be written with). Importantly, too, I wanted to show that public sex is a sassy subject that needs to be taken seriously as much by academics as by town planners. We should write about it, make films about it, poeticize it, and depict it in artwork.[10] Moreover, we should campaign *for* it. Indeed, we should have a cabinet minister devoted to it (after all, politicians are as likely as anyone else to be doing it). Below are Keith's comments:

> Mark, I've had a chance to read your preliminary thoughts. I'd have to say you are right on the money. This is rewarding to me, personally, since you figured out some fundamentals about CFS without any serious input from me. I made a decision way back when this site started that CFS would never be a "gay" website. We don't have a rainbow flag anywhere, and aren't likely! I wanted a space that would be welcoming to all horny men.
>
> A good friend of mine who is able to relocate for extended periods due to his work tells me he always avoids cities with gay community centers which he views as the kiss of death for his sexual purposes! Once a "community" develops enough to afford a meeting space, that pretty much

means that an identity has arrived, an identity that forces everyone – gay, straight, bi – to declare themselves. Not far behind this development is a profound change in the cruising dynamics of a locale. Straight, bi or so-called questioning men are far less likely to make use of a warm hole – any warm hole – once the community comes to believe that having sex with men is equal to being gay. Perhaps the saddest contribution the gay rights movement has made to cultures around the world is how it forces people to fit, yet again, into another box. Ironic, for sure, given the movement started as an attempt by revolutionary thinkers to challenge conformity. Now gay = conformity. Indeed, I maintain that gay people are the dullest people around these days. That cutting edge that seemed so abundant not long ago has been stifled by a strong push to be "normal."

Adding to the irony is that the larger culture doesn't want us to be normal. Oh, they may say they do, but I maintain every group must have someone who is different from them, either good or bad. So many straight people have viewed gay men as in the vanguard of pushing sexual liberties (which ultimately benefits them, too), but even these people have come to realize this is no longer the way things are, at least in North America. I no longer consider myself a gay rights activist. No, these days I'm a sex activist, pushing for sexual liberation from oppressive forces including those assimilationists you write about.

You're also right on the money about a major goal of CFS: to give a voice to "local knowledge." To give it respect and attention. To encourage the sharing of local knowledge. Presumably, this process eventually has profound social dynamics for the larger culture, plus the guys who visit CFS.

So there we are. Academics aren't completely out of touch in their towers of ivory and my meditations of the politics of public groping have not gone to waste.

Coming on a Screen Near You

Can you keep such a good idea a secret? Not in today's wired world. The site's detractors do as much, or more, to promote it than do its biggest fans. If you really wanted to publicize the site and its services, all you'd need to do is drop an anonymous email to a group of preachy Christians and the site would be denounced worldwide within hours. It may even give local Catholic clergy some new ideas and give those poor choirboys a break. It has been quoted in the *New Yorker*, *Newsweek*, *Unzipped*, and

countless other publications. Indeed it has even been featured on
FOX TV:

> How I found this site is a big chuckle . . .
>
> A few years ago, Channel 5 (FOX) here in NYC was doing some sweeps-
> week, proclamations of doom, do-you-know-what-is-going-on-in *your*-
> town sort of salacious bullshit report about men using the internet to find
> places to have sex with each other . . .
>
> WELL, they showed a shot of this site with the URL clearly visible.
> Thanks Rupert!

No doubt, information about CFS will be coming on a screen
near you. In the meantime, you can log onto Cruisingforsex.com at
<http://www.cruisingforsex.com>.

You know you want to.

Notes

1   Bodies-in-Motion's blog (October 29, 2004). All web references are within
    <cruisingforsex.com> and do not display separate URLs; however, the site
    has a useful search function, which allows for this material to be easily
    found.
2   Cockslut94539 (December 1, 2004). Special Interest Forums and Discus-
    sion Groups > Dirty Stories: Instant Jack-off Material.
3   Eve Sedgwick, *Between Men: English Literature and Male Homosocial Desire*
    (New York: Colombia University Press, 1985).
4   Reply to my online posting "What do you like about CFS" by Cock-
    slut94539 (December 1, 2004). Special Interest Forums and Discussion
    Groups > Sex Advice: Ask and Give Advice.
5   From Gabe's blog (October 23, 2003).
6   Vittorio Lingiardi, *Men in Love: Male Homosexualities from Ganymede to
    Batman* (Chicago: Open Court, 2002).
7   Lisa Duggan, *The Twilight of Equality? Neoliberalism, Cultural Politics, and
    the Attack on Democracy* (Boston: Beacon Press, 2003).
8   Michel Foucault, *"Society Must Be Defended," Lectures at the Collège de
    France, 1975–76* (New York: Picador, 2003).
9   Anthony Giddens, *The Transformation of Intimacy: Sexuality, Love and
    Eroticism in Modern Societies* (Cambridge: Polity, 1992).
10 David Wojnarowicz, *Close to the Knives: A Memoir of Disintegration* (New
    York: Vintage, 1991).

6

The Best Basketball Player: Michael Jordan

Thomas McLaughlin

The best basketball player? That's an easy one – Michael Jordan. I don't have to tell you that. You already know. Even if you don't know basketball, you know it's Michael Jordan. He is a global icon of excellence – not just the best basketball player ever, but a virtually universal symbol of excellence itself. His game made him a great player, and then Nike and Gatorade made him that global icon. The image of Michael Jordan, "Air Jordan," permeates the global village. In China he stands for individual aspiration and achievement in the emerging capitalist economy. Throughout the world he stands for American cool – specifically *African American* cool – and is the great champion who never lost his street cred, his image in the head of every player who takes the ball strong to the hoop.

Michael Jordan is a complex case study in globalization. A kid from Wilmington, North Carolina comes to excel at a game that in his lifetime goes from an American to a global fascination, riding the waves of worldwide broadcasting and marketing, transforming himself into an image that shapes the intimate identities of untold millions, all in an effort to sell more shoes. If you see that global media system as a pernicious threat to local cultures and economies, as an extension of American capitalist hegemony into every corner of the world and every level of the psyche, you might be tempted to dismiss Michael as one more calculating master of the universe, one more shill in the global market. I share that worry and that critique. But under the advertising image, behind the global icon, the fact remains that Jordan is the best ever to play the game. His image may have escaped into the machine of marketing hype, but about his excellence at the game there is no doubt. Look at the record, and more important, ask anyone who has played. In terms of the players' own definitions of greatness, in terms of the aesthetic of the game itself, Jordan really does embody the excellence he came to represent.

The record is unparalleled in the history of the game: six NBA titles, five time league Most Valuable Player, highest scoring average of all time, thirteen years in the all-star game, highest play-off scoring average, nine years on the all-defensive team, second all-time in steals. His record shows a mastery of every aspect of the game. He excelled as an individual and as the leader of championship teams; he set records as an offensive player and did the dirty work of defense; he was at his best at pressure moments in championship games.

But it's not the statistics alone that made him remarkable or marketable, it's the sheer physical beauty of his game. His playing style was powerful but classic and restrained – no move was made in order to draw attention to itself. Every move was integral to the game, the right move for the situation. Form followed function. But what perfect form. In mid-air his body reached iconic perfection, like a dancer at the height of a leap, but even in the most ordinary moments, running down the court, dribbling the ball, the beauty of his movement and his body were striking. Even people who didn't know the game at all could see it. Certainly the marketing geniuses at Nike and at their advertising agency, Weiden and Kennedy, could see it. They also saw that the formal beauty of his airborne game was perfectly suited for still photography, which allows the eye to linger on the form, detaching it from its context in the game. Of course his game was also perfect for the highlight reel, where his physical power and kinetic energy were electrifying, but still photos captured his beauty most perfectly. The classic simplicity of his photographic image then allowed it to be transformed into an abstract shape, as in the famous Nike icon – "Air Jordan," arms and legs fully extended, as close to flight as humans can get. And it is in this form that Jordan enters the global image stream, embodying our desire to fly above all obstacles, all of life's restrictions. Nike had in Jordan a visual image that could be decontextualized and translated across languages and cultures, even to people who knew nothing about basketball and would never see anything other than the abstract image. And yet this global image was never hollowed out; it was founded on the authenticity of Jordan's game. For once it seemed that the global imaginary had seized on a symbol worthy of the attention. Michael was better than the hype. He was an icon of excellence not only to that huge and uninformed global market, but also to the millions of knowledgeable people who play the game, the people who produce the vernacular aesthetic of basketball.

Basketball players operate inside a rich culture, one that they create in every moment of play. As they negotiate calls in a pickup game, they create the ethic of basketball. As they solve the strategic problems posed by unfolding game situations, they create a distinct cognitive style. As they move together through the improvised patterns that emerge from their cooperative play, their bodies take on the movement habits demanded by the tactics of the game. As they compete and cooperate in the contest, they create an emotional climate, a set of relationships that derive from the interactions encouraged by moving and thinking together. And if basketball has a discernable ethic, a distinctive way of thinking and feeling and moving, a characteristic style of emotion, relationship, and community – a culture – it also has an aesthetic, a way of recognizing excellence, as any culture would.

The place where this culture is created is in "pickup ball," in the informal games organized by the players themselves, in schoolyards and driveways, church basements and housing projects, health clubs and public parks. Serious pickup players engage in the practice so regularly and with such passion that the culture of the game becomes part of their personal identity. The aesthetic of basketball is produced in this vernacular practice, explicitly articulated in the language of the game at the moment of play. Fans and observers of the game then internalize that aesthetic, judging the game in the terms that the culture mandates. And in these terms, among the players themselves, Jordan the global icon is also Jordan the model of excellence.

In sociologist Pierre Bourdieu's terms, the aesthetic of basketball is part of the *"habitus"* – the loose structure of implicit assumptions, habits of mind, and emotion that make the practice possible. For Bourdieu the *habitus* is not a system of abstract ideas but a set of habits and tendencies put into play unconsciously in the ongoing give and take of daily life.[1] Basketball culture is created "on the fly," in precisely the terms Bourdieu uses to describe all practices – its *habitus* is not a pre-existing structure but a tendency of mind and emotion that emerges from the contingencies of specific events and can in turn be applied unselfconsciously in complex and fluid situations. The practice of basketball has an "aesthetic" in the sense that its players have developed rough standards of judgment about what constitutes excellence in the practice. They have an eye for the great play, the superior player. In this sense, every practice produces an aesthetic, a discourse in which practitioners can define and recognize excellence. This is not to say that all participants in a given practice will agree on specific judgments or on every aesthetic principle – they need only share a loose set of criteria without an established hierarchy, a discourse in which they can agree or disagree meaningfully in arguments about aesthetic judgment. Wherever two basketball players or fans gather, they will argue about the game, proving by their very disagreements the fact that they share an unspoken aesthetic, and proving by their emotion that their disagreements have a moral dimension. The standards of basketball excellence can be defined in official and goal-oriented terms – final scores of games, personal statistics, league standings, championships, all-star teams, etc. But players develop their own informal standards, defined in terms of values intrinsic to the practice, expressed in the routine, on-court chatter of the game even if they don't count in the official standings.

Basketball players talk as they play. The most volatile and theatrical element in that talk is "woofing," or "trash talking," attempts to tear down the ego of opponents by bragging about your domination and their weaknesses. But most of the talk is operational and strategic, the communication necessary among individuals trying to function cooperatively. "Watch the pick." "Move, move." "D up." "Box out." And much of this operational talk is explicitly evaluative, an instantaneous feedback loop by which players encourage and discourage specific behaviors from teammates and opponents. For example, teammates will often say "Good shot" to a player who has just *missed* a shot, if the player was open and took the shot in the flow of the game. In this context "Good shot" means "Take that kind of shot again, next time you get the chance. You may have missed, but you made a good decision which benefits all of us. Keep up your confidence." To say "Good shot" is to act on the conviction that excellence in basketball involves intelligent decision-making, not just physical ability, and that excellent decision-making will, in the long run, lead to success. This casual comment, in the flow of the action, articulates an aesthetic standard implicit in the *habitus* of the game. Players and fans of basketball have a whole vocabulary of praise and critique, a discourse of distinction put to use at the very moment of engagement. Players evaluate each other all the time, and in these routine verbal exchanges we can see the aesthetic values of basketball culture. I want to look now at a fairly random series of examples of this explicitly evaluative talk; in each case I will attempt to articulate the aesthetic expressed by the shop talk, by the vernacular of the game.

Tough shot. This phrase is used when a player succeeds at a difficult or even unlikely play. Maybe a shooter will take the ball up in traffic, against tenacious defense, and in order to avoid having the shot blocked he will readjust in the air, keeping his eye on the basket in spite of every defensive distraction. If he hits the shot, his teammates and maybe even his opponents will say "tough shot," their voices expressing a quiet mix of surprise and respect, their faces adding a wince of pain, as though they can't quite believe what they just saw, as though they are *forced* to recognize an improbable achievement. In that phrase players express one of the central values of basketball culture, a respect for the player who rises above the routine, who has so much self-confidence that he can risk failure, and who has the skill to pull off the play. As used by opponents, "Tough shot" says: "We did our best to stop you, we forced you into a difficult situation, and you beat us anyway." Excellence in basketball requires audacity at times, a defiance of the game's own logic.

Good look. Let's say the offensive action is on the left side of the court, with one player established in the post, another in the corner ready for an outside shot, and a player with the ball on the left wing – the deadly triangle of even the most basic basketball. The player with the ball can feed the post, pass to the corner, or drive right down the middle. And there are infinite variations of those basic choices. Because the action is all on the left, the offensive players on the right are often neglected by their defenders, who, if they are alert, are ready and eager to help on the left. So one of the players on the "off side" can slip down under the basket on the right. If the wing player on the left sees that move, he can pass the ball across court for an easy score. That's a "good look," and players on both sides will say so. The phrase expresses their admiration for the ingenuity of the play, the alertness to a development away from the action, the imagination to look and act instantaneously. Basketball players admire that alertness, a readiness to act in unexpected ways, to devise a novel strategy on the run. There are of course players who survive purely by physical skill, but most need to think creatively in order to succeed, like a chess player who can improvise off a familiar gambit.

Nice pass. This phrase sounds similar to "good look," but it has a different implication. "Good look" is about intelligence, creativity in the midst of the flow. "Nice pass" is more about physical skill, beauty rather than ingenuity. Sometimes a pass has to be threaded through a narrow opening between two defenders, or bounced with just the right spin past the defender's reach and into the teammate's shooting hand, just at the right moment for the shot, all of this on the run. A "nice pass" is a thing of visual and kinetic beauty, a perfect collaboration between the keen eye and the adroit hand. The verbal performance of "nice pass" is important, with an emphasis on the second word, louder and held longer, as though to express the surprise of it, the experience of gratuitous beauty in the midst of ordinary experience. "Nice pass" speaks to the value in the basketball community of playing the game with a flourish, with *finish*. Certainly players admire efficiency, but they also admire excellence beyond the technical requirements of the game, beauty for its own sake. "Pretty shot," we will say, or just exhale a startled "whoa" at the sight of a beautiful crossover dribble, even if it's our own ankles being broken.

That guy is a horse. Basketball can be played successfully by all kinds of physical types, from short and quick to big and lumbering. But players recognize and value pure physical strength and fluid power when they see it. Big players who can run all day and who can use their strength to augment their skill are always valued highly. Watch a tall, strong player pull down a defensive rebound in traffic, dribble the length of the court while holding off a determined defender, and then push the ball to the basket, take the hit from the help, and still make the shot. And do it all day. "That guy is a horse." Basketball players acknowledge the reality of sheer physical gifts. Sometimes you are just outmatched by a bigger, faster player, and none of your intelligence and skill matter. As with all sports, the aesthetic of basketball encourages a cult of the body, a respect for the facts of the physical matter.

Automatic. Some shooters are so excellent that, even as they prepare to shoot, someone on the court will say "automatic." They have perfected their form to such an extent that the shot *ought* to go in, and if it doesn't, you explain it as an anomaly. "Automatic" is a tribute to repetition, to the endless practice required in order to hone the jumpshot into a beautiful and effective gesture. The key is to make every release of the ball the same – effortless and precise – no matter where the shot is taken, no matter what the defense does to distract. Players understand that formal perfection leads to practical excellence. There are no formally perfect shooters who are not *great* shooters. Form precedes and ensures function. From teammates, "automatic" is a secure statement of faith and a mild taunt at the opposition, to let them know their fate just before it happens. In basketball, beauty creates an inexorable fate.

Good hustle. If some basketball language seems to value the apparent effortlessness of the graceful player, "good hustle" praises the excess of effort, the sheer will that drives some players. Basketball culture loves the fact that players will throw themselves around, risking injury and pain, in order to keep the ball from going out of bounds or to win the loose ball out of a scrum on the floor. It's the gratuitousness of that effort, the excess of expenditure over profit, that mark the great hustle athlete. After all, in a pickup game there is almost nothing at stake, and yet players will risk their bodies in the name of an ideal of total effort, on the conviction that the beauty of the game requires and deserves this fullness of self-sacrifice. It's what anthropologist Clifford Geertz calls "deep play," betting extravagantly on trivial contests, and that depth of commitment is what makes the game holy for those who practice it.

Let the game come to you. Basketball is a game of hustle and purposeful effort, but it is also a game of flow. Players make frequent decisions, interact with each other in complex ways, and move creatively in reaction to the moves of all the other players. In such a complex movement environment, it is counter-productive to impose your imperial will on the game. There are too many factors beyond your control. The complement of "let the game come to you" is "don't force it," which is to say that you can't make something happen that isn't potential in the flow of the game. The great players have the ability to sense the direction of the flow, the pace of the game, the opportune moment, and take advantage of what is available. This is not to say that great players cannot take over the game and direct the flow, but it does mean that no one can dominate every minute. You have to acknowledge the existence of the other players, all of them independent decision- makers, all of whom – teammates and opponents alike – can get in the way of your domination. In this sense basketball is a profoundly democratic sport in which all the players, even the great ones, must interact with others, take them into account. At certain privileged moments all the players take part in the same flow, and the great player will "let the game come to you" and succeed spectacularly within and through that flow.

Way to get back. One way that a close game can turn into a rout is that one team will be able to create a series of fast breaks that will crush the spirit of their opponents. So it is important for a team that misses a shot or loses the ball to hustle back on defense in order to stop the break. "Getting back on defense" requires conditioning and willpower. You have to commit yourself to this defensive effort, sprinting the length of the court, not to have the glory of scoring but to attain the quieter goal of frustrating the other team, making them set up in a halfcourt offense rather than scoring quickly and easily off the break. Basketball players see defense as a matter of ethics, doing the right thing, even if it would go unnoticed by casual fans. Teams that do not "get back" usually lose big, and they frustrate other players and serious fans who know that even an unskilled player can put out the effort to run to the other end and to develop the fitness necessary for the commitment. Basketball excellence requires a specific skill set, but it also requires a specific set of ethical commitments, and the failure to "get back" is a mortal sin.

Gotta talk out there. Basketball requires and values communication among players. In addition to the aphorisms and phrases of praise and blame that I have focused on here, there are practical and strategic discourses that go on throughout any game. Players need to communicate about the position of opponents and teammates on the court, about the score and time left, about mistakes and solutions, complaints and congratulations, etc. On defense, for example, it is necessary for teammates' well-being to "call the pick" – that is, to let the teammate know if he is about to be blocked away from the offensive player he is trying to keep up with. If you get "picked" without seeing it coming, you can get knocked to the floor or get the breath knocked out of you. So players know that they need to talk to one another, to augment their kinesthetic awareness with verbal clues. This verbal communication is also an outward sign of the unspoken connection that players feel on the court. When the flow is right, all the players share a single consciousness, a common awareness of the emerging situation in the unfolding of the game. "Gotta talk" in order to keep that consciousness alive.

My list of examples is intentionally random, in order to emphasize the fact that there is no set hierarchy in this aesthetic *habitus.* These standards of excellence – and many others – are common throughout basketball culture, but the standards that matter most in any given game are a function of local traditions and personal inclinations. Some games value beauty and formal perfection so much that players don't play aggressive defense, allowing opponents to make their beautiful moves unimpeded, on the premise that the same favor will be accorded them when they have the ball. In other games an intense competitive atmosphere dominates, so that form matters less than grit, less than the willingness to hustle back on defense or fight for a loose ball. Some players value intelligence in their own game and in others', so that for them the ability to see the "good look," to make the right decision in the right situation, becomes the epitome of the aesthetic. Any given basketball game is a function of the histories and habits that all of the players bring to it. Players who play together regularly develop a distinctive local aesthetic, almost instantly recognizable to a knowledgeable outside observer, even if it is largely unconscious to the players themselves. These personal and local idiosyncrasies insure that the aesthetic of basketball is neither universal nor timeless. The culture of the game is constantly being created and recreated by the actions and judgments of players and fans, acting in local circumstances, following individual inclinations.

Nevertheless, it is possible to sum up the complex aesthetic of basketball, not in a system of concepts but in a state of mind and body. In basketball, the phrase that describes the highest form of excellence is for a player or a team to be "in the zone" – to feel a sense of effortless mastery. As a player you can feel it, as a fan you can see it. The game slows down, becomes simple. The player "in the zone" is totally in the moment, creating on the run, connecting with all the other players, aware of the ever changing situation, moving with precision in the traffic, focused on the shifting points of orientation, connected to the ball, playing off what's open, knowing exactly what to do, anticipating the movements and decisions of all the others, making it all up on the fly. You can be "in the zone" in any endeavor, but in basketball the experience is the purpose of the practice. As an improvised and creative practice of the body and the mind, basketball at its best requires a focused presence in the moment, an openness to the emerging future, a rare combination of physical skill and mental acuteness that is satisfying in itself, not just for its contribution to the outcome of the contest. This state of mind is what the great hippie-coach Phil Jackson has in mind when he speaks of the zen of basketball, especially when an entire team is in the same zone.[2] To be "in the zone" is to embody the excellence of the game. It's why players play and fans watch.

Michael Jordan is a global icon precisely because he has so frequently given us a vivid image of that exalted state. He is, to speak in a measured hyperbole, a sacrament – an outward sign of inner grace. His play, his physical power, his bearing make that inner state, that feeling of being "in the zone," embodied and visible. There is a famous image of Jordan, from a game in which he hit five or six three-point shots, each one more improbable than the last. As he ran back downcourt after one of the shots, he turned to the courtside analysts (and to the camera) with a theatrical shrug and a wry smile, as if to say that his excellence was out of his own control, as though the game was playing itself through him.

To be "in the zone" is to feel that even as you battle for the ball or throw yourself around the court, you do so with no conscious effort or intention, participating in and taking advantage of a kinetic and cognitive flow produced by the energy and movement of all the players. That flow is literally greater than you, but if you let it come through you, you can direct it with ease, without resistance. Michael Jordan seemed almost always in the zone, especially when a game or a championship was on the line. Being "in the zone" at all the crucial moments, over years of competition, made Jordan the best player ever and a symbol of excellence that transcends the game.

The paradox of being "in the zone" is that it is, of course, not effortless at all. It requires all the elements of the basketball aesthetic, all the virtues named by its on-court language, not just the fluidity and grace that first catch the eye. And it can only happen when years of practice and intentional effort have trained the body and mind to transcend their training. The formal beauty of Jordan's game can only have been produced by endless and dedicated repetition, honing every move down to the simplest, purest gesture. He also had the game intelligence that the aesthetic values so highly. When defenders double and triple teamed him, he was always able to find the right teammate for the open shot. He had the tenacity and intensity of the classic hustle player. He understood the ethic of defense. He was physically prepared and took full advantage of his athletic gifts. He needed excellence in all of these qualities in order to get into the zone whenever the situation demanded.

The great thing about basketball, though, is that you don't have to be Michael Jordan in order to attain, at least for a moment, the state that epitomizes the aesthetic of the game. Anyone – or anyone with at least the basic skills – can get into the zone. This is particularly true in terms of shooting the ball. Even a mediocre shooter can at times be incapable of missing, no matter what the defense does, no matter how unlikely the shot. But it's not just shooting – sometimes the entire game will open up. You can anticipate where rebounds will go, see passing lanes that no one else sees, anticipate your opponents' and teammates' every move, and feel immune to defensive pressure. At these moments the excellence of the practice lives in you, despite your limitations and weaknesses, no matter how ordinary your usual game. This experience of excellence, not as some external standard by which you judge yourself, but as an internal state of mind and body, redeems the game, keeps you coming back in search of it.

The pleasure of being "in the zone" is strongest when it happens to an entire team at the same time. Suddenly even the most rag-tag pickup team can seem possessed by the gods, capable of communication and interaction that baffles the conscious mind – "how did we do that?" Pickup basketball is a team game played in real time, with no pre-set strategies, no game plans. All decisions must be made instantaneously, on the move, sharing a finite space with many other fast-moving bodies, all following their intentions as independent decision agents. The potential for physical and cognitive chaos is high. Yet it is routine even in pickup games with total strangers for players to achieve almost magical communication, all making independent decisions and moves that somehow cohere and achieve grace. And at rare and privileged times an entire team can be so "in the zone" that they can collaborate and improvise like jazz musicians or freestyle rappers. When a team is "in the zone" they *are* the excellence of the game. Their state of mind and body is the point of the entire practice.

For players and fans this experience of basketball excellence has profound effects. Players who have experienced being "in the zone" come to want the same kind of experience in the other practices of their life. Basketball creates a sense of heightened experience, so that being "in the zone" is accompanied by a sense of privilege and even holiness. More pragmatic activities, which do not have the heightened affect of play, may make it more difficult to recognize this heightened state of consciousness, even when it occurs. Is it possible to get "in the zone" when mowing the lawn or doing the dishes? Yes, but there is almost no cultural support for recognizing the experience. Playing basketball and learning so viscerally what "in the zone" means can allow players to recognize it in other areas of their life. I certainly now know when I'm "in the zone" as a teacher. Some classes are so effortless they seem spontaneous, even if they have been preceded by rigorous preparation. Having the experience of excellence in an embodied practice like basketball creates the urge to experience it in every practice of daily life.

For fans, it is the powerful visibility of basketball excellence that makes it so useful. Because basketball players *embody* "being in the zone," they also make the experience visible to others. Being "in the zone" is a state of consciousness, but it is most compelling to spectators when it is made visible in a physical practice. You can't exactly *see* when a chess master is "in the zone," or a doctor or a quilt-maker. This dramatic visibility explains part of the appeal of all spectator sports. We need to see this excellence at work in order to recognize the ways we can gain access to it ourselves. It is vain to wish to "be like Mike" in basketball, but it is possible to use his excellence as a model for the pursuit of excellence in whatever practice is our own. We do our jobs, our daily chores, because we need what they produce for us – money or prestige or power – but we can *love* to do them because they are challenging and engaging in themselves, worthy of our most serious attention. To play basketball or to watch Michael Jordan play is to participate in a life-enhancing practice that produces at its best a spiritual state that no one can do without. The aesthetic of basketball is about naming that state and affirming its worth.

Notes

1   Pierre Bourdieu, *The Logic of Practice*, trans. Richard Nice (Stanford, CA: Stanford University Press, 1990); Pierre Bourdieu, *Outline of a Theory of Practice*, trans. Richard Nice (Cambridge: Cambridge University Press, 1977).
2   Phil Jackson, *Sacred Hoops* (New York: Hyperion Press, 1995).

7

The Best Sneakers: The Nike Air Max Classic TW

Claire Gould

Sneaker [sni:kers] americ., plural – the sports shoe

Sneakers, trainers, running shoes, pumps, plimsolls, runners, chucks, sports shoes, athletics shoes, hi-tops, lo-tops, joggers, shell-toes, three-stripes, skate shoes, gutties, tackies . . . call them what you like, they're all the same thing.

Comfortable, casual footwear for the masses, these shoes – available in a spectrum of colors, shapes, and sizes – not only cushion and protect feet; they become a strange yet common fetish for some people.

The best pair of trainers: The Adidas Superstar shoe. White with three stripes on each side, and with a "shell toe," these were originally worn by rappers Run DMC in the mid-1980s and made a comeback in late 1999. They had an appeal that reached all corners of the globe, with different colors and styles of laces available from country to country. They may not be the most comfortable shoe at first, but they are the only trainer that trainer freaks would make concessions for, and buy in addition to their latest trainer conquests. They just look so damn good . . .

To date I've had five pairs of Adidas Superstars – with light blue, metallic blue, khaki green, red, and currently navy blue stripes.

They look awesome. But they're not the "best trainers" in the title of this chapter. They're not the Nike Air Max Classic TW . . . Because to understand the appeal of trainers, the passion they create in sneaker freaks, you have to understand how trainers become a part of you . . .

You're The One That I Want

I was 7 years old when I fell in love for the very first time. Not with Agnetha, the blonde one from ABBA. Not with John Travolta, the current heartthrob of the time. The object of my affection was green and gold, measured seven inches in length, cost two pounds from Woolworth's in Stockport, England, and was the most beautiful thing I had ever owned.

It was a training shoe – well a pair, to be precise. The most wonderfully comfortable things I had ever been blessed to put on my feet, they had three Velcro straps instead of laces or buckles (very high tech for 1978, let me assure you), four "go faster" stripes on each side, and looked tremendous with my Mr Men trousers. They were Gymtracks – a Woolworth's own brand, and I was smitten. I spent the remainder of the day staring at my feet. My brother had opted for the traditional lace-up variety, but my sister and I spent that evening fastening and unfastening our trainers, just to hear that unique Velcro sound.

I took extra special care of my trainers, even, on occasion, wearing them to bed. I was in absolute awe at how beautiful my feet looked clothed in something so amazing. (It was just one year later, in 1979, that Nike introduced the Nike Air running shoe – the first trainer in the world to incorporate an air bubble into the heel of the shoe.[1])

In the years between 1978 and 1998, I developed a bit of an obsession with trainers. Buying them, looking at them, trying them on (which is dangerous because they become part of you and you have to take them home), but very rarely putting them to the use for which they were intended. Why would I want to muddy my beautiful trainers when I could walk on paths, keep them clean, and adore them?

Culture Club

I blame it on my youth.

A teenager in Thatcher's Britain in the 1980s, I was very aware of spiraling unemployment, the miners' strike, and the country's dazzling efforts at the 1984 Olympic Games in Los Angeles. And believe me, these are linked. In the glory days of British athletics (from the golden days of the Moscow Olympic Games in 1980 onwards) our success set a trend. Cue lots of Sebastian Coe and Steve Ovett wannabes running around parks, going for gold.

From the first release of a keep fit aerobic video in 1982, sports clothing became high fashion items with shoes to complete the outfit. Both media and cosmetic industries reinforced their belief in new health exercise and youth movement by promoting it as a marketing opportunity. Outfits were not complete unless worn with expensive sport shoes, usually endorsed by celebrities from professional sports.[2] Couple that with the UK's fanatical following of all things soccer, and as a sports company, you have a captive audience.

The influence of youth culture on athletic shoes has been around for a long time. The 1981 movie *Fast Times at Ridgemont High*, with Sean Penn wearing Vans checkboard-print slip-ons, created a considerable demand for these skate shoes.[3] Actually *having* the money and being able to *find* the money were not the same – but in a pretty depressed UK, people were able to clothe themselves with the latest from Bukta, Puma, Adidas, and Hi-Tec. Trainers were the main draw card – and it was a global feeling.

The driving force of new athletic shoe design is not merely performance. The use of athletic shoes for casual wear and fashion plays a large role in shaping their appearance. Today, the US athletic shoe market is a $13 billion per year industry that sells more than 350 million pairs of shoes each year. These shoes have penetrated into all facets of mainstream America, and have become a fashion statement.[4]

Japanese cultural critic Zeshu Takamura argues: "In the last century, trainers have gone from rubber soled plimsolls to air-cushioned, gel-filled capsules worn as much for their looks as their sporting performance."[5] The UK has the same ethos today – the leisure industry is a multi-million pound extravaganza, but that's nothing compared to the sheer volume of trainers that are worn there. White is the current color *de jour*, and having the "right" running shoe can often define your social class, or help give you a leg-up into the next one – in a superficial sense, at least, for "Shoes contain a wealth of social messages both literally as well as symbolically."[6] Indeed, journalist Rick Reilly claims that: "It is my assertion that Nike's power to sell comes from deep-rooted yearnings for cultural inclusiveness."[7]

Swooshification of the World

If you're looking for an early example of a running show, dig out an old pair of plimsolls. They were created from a newly developed process called vulcanization – still in use today – which uses heat to meld rubber and cloth together: "Not only were plimsolls comfortable, but unlike other shoes, they allowed the wearer to move around without making a noise. Because of this, they became known as 'sneakers'."[8] The sneaker is perhaps the most lasting design of all sport shoes. The word sneaker was first used in 1875 and referred to an early croquet shoe which was developed in the US. During the 1950s sneakers became associated with the emerging teenage leisure market. Canvas topped shoes were the "in" style, with Keds for girls and Chucks for boys. Both brands (Chucks are Converse) are still available today, though the Converse shoes retail at a much higher price – and with a larger kudos tag – than Keds ever have.

Meanwhile, Nike, or Blue Ribbon Sports, was born out of the boot of founder Phil Knight's car in 1963. In a collaboration between Knight and college runner Bill "Jay" Bowerman, the duo cited their own personal dissatisfaction with niche sports shoes as the driving force for their business enterprise. The Nike name and the trademark Swoosh were devised in 1971, and the company had a breakthrough in 1972 when Bowerman famously used his domestic waffle maker to forge outsoles with traction. Subsequently, by the late 1970s Blue Ribbon Sports had officially begun trading as Nike and had notched up US$270 million in sales. Nike, the winged goddess of victory according to Greek mythology, has been responsible for the "Swooshification of the world."[9] Nike was named as 1996 Marketer of the Year, and it was said that the Swoosh was more recognized and coveted by consumers than any other sports brand – arguably, than any brand. In Rick Reilly's enthusiastic account:

> Woe to you who underestimate the Swoosh. Tiger Woods, the coolest athlete on Planet Swoosh, has the Swoosh on the front, side and back of his hat, on his shirts and sweaters, and on his socks and shoes . . . But when Woods turned up in Thailand to play in a tournament, and his luggage had gone missing, he had to play pro-am without his usual compliment of Swooshes. He lasted just thirteen holes before heat and exhaustion got to him. Clearly, the Swoosh is the source of all his power.[10]

As a trainer fanatic in training, I first became aware of Nike in the 1980s – the "Swoosh" started appearing all over the place, most notably on the feet and shirts of US sporting figures. Nike was initially as popular in the UK for its windcheater jackets and bags as it was for its footwear.

I Knew You Were Waiting

By this time, I had done four years of university and tried a variety of trainers. Converse skate shoes and Simple were my personal favorites, but I refused to wear Reebok and had yet to be seduced by the charms of Adidas Superstars. By 1998, it was widely believed that the Nike Swoosh was better recognized globally than McDonald's golden arches logo. From humble beginnings indeed. And it was also in 1998 that I had my first glimpse of true perfection and greatness in the form of footwear. How my life was about to change . . .

Now in my first year of university lecturing in regional UK, I needed a certain trainer. One that would stop the rain and snow from soaking my toes, that would be comfortable, but more than anything would convey faux coolness to my students on my behalf. Rummaging in the bargain bin of a faceless sports superstore in South Wales, I came across the most beautiful trainers I had ever seen. Now remember, I was a real trainers fan. So I wasn't in the market for new ones – in a practical sense. But I had also learned that playing off need against want was always a great way of persuading myself to part with cash where trainers were concerned.

The shoe of my dreams was a khaki- and clay-colored Nike Air Max Classic TW, size 6.5, just waiting to be taken to a good home. (This particular shoe was known as both BW and TW, depending on which part of the world you lived in. Both pairs that I have been fortunate enough to own have been TWs, but much of the research for this chapter refers to the BW. They are one and the same.) It had been dumped in a pile of orange and black Nike boxes, in the bargain shoe section of the store. From the moment I picked it up, I was in awe. This shoe looked beautiful. Light yet sturdy, it was comfortable to wear, and unlike anything I had ever seen before.

The fact they had been consigned to the bargain basement scrapheap meant they had not been a particularly big seller – and so I wasn't going to come across many other pairs gracing the feet of others. I really hate seeing the same shoes on the hooves of the rest of the public. And I'm not alone in this:

> The most aggravating trainer-related incident is when you are the first to get a really nice pair, everyone sees them and gets them, and then you just look like another Johnny-regular-feet! It happened to me with a pair of Etnies – they were lovely and comfy and I got them four years ago, then a year later everyone had a pair. Now I'm just waiting for my current trainers to be picked up by every Tom, Dick, and Harry.[11]

This is a very real issue for the hard-core trainer lover. While the fact that we have something so aesthetically pleasing on our feet is important, the real challenge and appeal is to find a shoe that is reasonably unique and not particularly commercial. This may sound a little odd, since shoe manufacturers produce trainers as a business, in the hopes of making a huge mark-up – but you only have to visit the millions of discount outlets around the globe to know that what tickles the fancy of the shoe-buying public can be worlds apart from what the shoe company expects. Thus, when trainer freaks find that "special" shoe, the fact that it lacks mass appeal makes it all the more alluring. There's a real sense of elitism within the trainer community – with some freaks refusing to divulge the brand and style of their latest acquisition for fear of losing the kudos and credit for the shoe find.

But I digress. Back to my beautiful trainers.

Due to their languishing in the discounted section, they were a steal at fifty pounds. I always look for these shoes when I visit any shoe store or new country, and they currently retail for 125 pounds (A$230). So they were sold, to the woman with a trainer fetish. And a grin that would make Michael Jordan jump through hoops in his Air Jordans.

Let me try to explain the appeal of this shoe.

1998 was the year of cargo pants. All-girl group All Saints and Natalie Imbruglia had done their bit for the army surplus stores, and cities and towns were filled with weekend-warrior-looking people, ready to do battle at the supermarket check-outs. The more pockets the better. Whether you were draped in khaki green, racing green, or stone brown, cargo and combat were the buzzwords. But this shift in fashion posed quite a problem for fashion fans. What shoes go with cargo pants? Other than jack boots? And can you really get into pubs and clubs with jack boots on? Er, no.

My beautiful trainers – in khaki and clay – went perfectly with cargoes. And jeans. And just about everything I owned. But more importantly, because they were part of the Nike Air range, they had an air pocket in each heel. The aim of this was to offer cushioned support whilst exercising. This would have been of tremendous benefit to the hardcore exercise junkie. The benefit of this for me was that it made me look 1.5 inches taller, and stopped my cargoes from dragging along the floor. GENIUS!!!! I had an instant spring in my step.

The Nike Air Max Classic TW was marketed as a "cross trainer" – a basic all in one training shoe, and since I was due to head off on a back-packing expedition to Australia later that month, they were ideal. A no-fuss shoe, this trainer did not need silver swooshes, air-conditioning pockets or re-pumpable air pockets. Oh no, the beauty of this shoe was its sheer simplicity. And the fact that I had found it! As I gaze at people's chosen footwear from time to time, I am amazed and often horrified at the sheer girth and décor of the trainers they favor. But each to their own . . .

I wore my new finds religiously. With everything. Everywhere. They traveled with me on my first trip to Australia, saw me through some tough trekking times, helped me find my sea legs while sailing, and kept me walking just that little bit taller. They were great to dance in, and although their talents seemed to know no bounds, even they couldn't stop me from pulling all the ligaments in my ankle while bouncing around to the 1998 English Soccer World Cup anthem "Vindaloo." While I was sitting in casualty feeling very sorry for myself, my main concern was not for my very black, swollen, and aching left ankle, but for my relatively new trainers, the left one of which was dirty as a result of my tumble. Luckily they were not damaged (unlike my ankle) and it was 14 full months before they were retired to the back of my wardrobe, due to excessive wear. I still loved them, but no amount of scrubbing and watching them spin around in the washing machine could get them looking anywhere near respectable. And, oh, how they smelled.

Subsequently, I have spent the last six years looking for a new pair to replace them. Other brands and styles have tried and failed. The Nike Air Max Classic TW is in a class of its own. I did manage to find a pair in a different color in Perth, Western Australia in 2000, but they didn't have the same stamina. The air in their air pockets didn't seem as sweet.

And their baby-blue coloring meant they couldn't withstand too much dirt, or the typical Australia red earth. They didn't last long. Once safely back in London and approaching my thirtieth birthday, I decided to go to visit the Mecca of all things Swoosh – Nike World on Oxford Street. Surely they would have an Air Max Classic TW in the right color?

I was disappointed – with the rise of Hip Hop, the variety of Nike Air Max Classics in inner London ranged from black to white, with little in between. How Michael Jackson would have loved them. My little brother certainly did and adopted them as his own. Meanwhile, I learned through my fruitless search that the Footlocker chain has the exclusive global rights to some Nike shoes. It's true – and they do have the Air Max Classic TW. But not in pretty colors.

I was persuaded by an Oxford Street Footlocker sales assistant to take a pair of the regular Air Max trainers, favored by then Spice Girl Mel C – Sporty Spice. They had the air pockets, for heightened comfort (or in my case, just height) and were comfortable enough. But they weren't the ones I really wanted. I bought them regardless, which was a real waste of £125 as I have only ever worn them twice: once to play five-aside soccer and the second to go for a drink with a friend, who lampooned me for wearing "lesbian football boots." Game over. They were on the transfer list to the back of my wardrobe, and now live on the feet of my flat mate.

So my hunt continues. Tragically, Nike only releases a limited version of the Air Max Classic TW each year, and as recent styles and fashion trends have dictated, the bulk of these are in black and (or) white or luminous colors. The luminous colors I blame on tennis sensation Serena Williams. Sponsored by Nike, she has assisted in taking the Swooshification of the world to a whole new level – almost another planet it would seem – with her custom-made Nikes that would look more at home on Princess Leia's feet or the set of *Barbarella* than they do on centre court at the US Open. But God bless her, she's flying the Nike flag. Perhaps I should have a word in her ear about commissioning MY shoes in MY colors . . .

Freaks Like Me

In desperation, I have been forced onto the Internet in the hunt for my shoe – and have been heartened to find there are other trainer freaks like me. True, the shoe they covet is not my own, but this makes me happy. To know that other people out there are this concerned/obsessed about their own favorite brands and styles of sports shoe makes me realize I am not alone, and probably not as mad as I suspect you think I am. They know about and respect the Adidas Superstar – but each is passionate for their own particular trainers. And how cool they are!

Actor Samuel L. Jackson is a sneaker freak who claims to own 275 pairs of sports shoes – all in the original boxes. Not so much *Pulp Fiction* as *Pump Fiction*, it seems Jackson's footwear fetish originates with his upbringing. He told contact music.com:

> I have a sneaker obsession, because my mom never bought me a pair of Converse All Stars when I was growing up 'cause they cost too much. So once I reached the point that I could have any pair of sneakers I wanted, I just kept getting sneakers . . . I label all the boxes. They have names on them, what color they are, what style they are, all that. I love sneakers. I just couldn't imagine not having lots of sneakers anymore.[12]

Other sneaker freaks were happy to tell me about their relationship with their trainers. Sam Draper, an English teacher from London, seems to have had a similar epiphany with shoes. In his account of his own love for sneakers, he notes that:

> My love of footwear, and more specifically trainers, came late in life, and despite an addiction to Converse baseball boots and Doc Martens. The Reef trainer has changed my life forever. Wide-fitting, brown suede, they looked and felt fantastic. Seven years on, they're a little battered and bruised, but I love them just the same. There IS a God, and he's wearing brown Reef trainers.[13]

Thankfully, Sam and I are not alone in our absolute adoration of sporting footwear. There is even a magazine published in the US all about trainers. *Sole Collector* looks at the hottest styles, reviews the latest show releases, takes a retro look at vintage shoes and reader favorites, as well as articles and a forum to buy, sell, and swap trainers. But it's not always as broad as "just trainers." Brand loyalty is an important theme in the discussion of sneaker freaks. Ian Wilson, a regular web-logger to the BBC Collective site, told me about his strong brand loyalty to his favorite shoes: "Currently, Puma seems to rule the trainer world (I like the suede ones with the badge on the front), closely followed by Adidas. But Nike? Forget it!"[14]

Another common theme is the necessity of compromise. Bliss told me: "I got new trainers last nite. A pair of KLX's. I don't love them, but the shape is the best I have seen in ages, they sit beautifully under your jeans!!! I also saw a pair of Vans I want that I might have to go back and buy."[15] Another contributor to online trainer discussions shares my problems with the colors currently available for runners:

> I currently have a pair of navy blue Fila's with orange soles and detailing, with black "sharks teeth" attached to the side of the orange sole at the front. They are in a hiking/mountaineering style and are very comfy. But men are being let down badly in trainer design at the moment. The makers need to supply many of the women's ranges in larger sizes. They seem to think color is effeminate – and that black and white is masculine.[16]

A problem that trainer lovers in the twenty-first century are encountering more and more is a lack of fit between style on the one hand and practicality on the other. Apprentice Rock Star told me that:

> I went to the lengths of buying Asics tiger touch rugby trainers, they have like a turf sole and are deadly on slippery surfaces, I've lost count the number of times I've nearly eaten dirt on some ravekid's talcum powder. But I'd have countless pairs of trainers, if only I could find decent styles . . . Lacoste trainers are really nice and soooo comfy, I just bought a pair. Not as preppy as they sound and not so overdone like all the other brands.[17]

As I'm sure you'll have noted, no two people mentioned here cite the same shoe as their personal best. There is a difference between the recognition of the importance of the Adidas Superstar and the passionate love for particular trainers. I've yet to find another person other than my brother – trainer freak or otherwise – who can wax lyrical about the Nike Air Max Classic TW. This doesn't detract from the benefits of the shoe – merely that, as I mentioned earlier, the appeal of trainers is as much about their uniqueness and lack of popularity on a global scale, as it is about their comfort.

As the trainer crosses over from pure sports shoe to an acceptable all-weather, all-day shoe, it seems trainer lovers are looking more and more toward retro-styles, and away from the all-singing, all-dancing sports master shoe – although it is important to emphasize that there are two types of trainer buyer. In the broadest sense, there are those who use them to play sports, and those who use them to play.

Runners are for the gym. Trainers are to wear out.

I'm not sure which umbrella I fall under, as on the one hand I'm not the most unsporty person you'll ever meet; but on the other, when I wear my trainers out I am very careful not get them trampled, dirtied, or marked. But that's just my way. And I am a trainer freak. And as far as I'm concerned and in terms of who has the throne in the urban-footwear jungle, the Nike Air Max Classic TW comes out on top.

Further Reading

<www.sneakerinfoarchieve.sneakercommunity.com>
<www.sneakerfreak.com>
<www.niketalk.com>
<www.podiatry.curtin.eu.au/sport.html>
<www.thescene.com.au>
<www.solecollector.com>
<www.kicksology.net>
<www.nike.com>

Notes

1 Donald Katz, *Just Do It: The Nike Spirit in the Corporate World* (New York: Random House Inc., 1984).

2 Stephen M. Pribut and Douglas H Richie, "A sneaker odyssey," *Dr Stephen M Pribut's Sports Pages*, 2002, <http://www.drpribut.com/sports/sneaker_odyssey.html> (accessed September 11, 2005).

3 Ibid.

4 William A Rossi, *The Sex Life of the Foot and Shoe* (Melbourne, Fl: Kreiger Press, 1993), p. 47.

5 Zeshu Takamura, *Roots of Street Style* (Tokyo: Graphic-sha Publishing, 1997), p. 51.

6 Ibid., p. 11.

7 Rick Reilly, "The swooshification of the world," *Sports Illustrated* 86/8 (Feburary 24, 1997): 78.

8 Katz, *Just Do It*, p. 194.

9 Reilly, "The swooshification of the world," p. 78.

10   Ibid.

11   Jack Allan, personal interview, conducted through <www.bbc.co.uk/collective>.

12   "Jackson's huge shoe collection," April 11, 2004, <http://www.contactmusic.com/new/xmlfeed.nsf/mndwebpages/jackson.s%20huge%20shoe%20collection> (accessed September 11, 2005).

13   Sam Draper, personal interview, conducted through <www.bbc.co.uk/collective>.

14   Ian Wilson, personal interview, conducted through <www.bbc.co.uk/collective>.

15   Bliss, personal interview, conducted through <www.thescene.com.au/forum>.

16   Alex Barker, personal interview, conducted through <www.bbc.co.uk/collective>.

17   Apprentice Rock Star, personal interview, conducted through <www.thescene.com.au/forum>.

8

The Best Action Console Game: *Grand Theft Auto: San Andreas*

John Banks

—— **Just What Is It About *Grand Theft Auto*?** ——

Gaming matters a lot to me. It is just as significant a part of my cultural life as watching films, listening to music, and reading novels. A high point of my videogaming has been the many hours I've recently spent playing the action game *Grand Theft Auto: San Andreas* on my PlayStation 2 console.[1] It provides many high-quality gaming moments packed into a massive 3D play environment. With *San Andreas* you get to explore your very own 1990s gangsta-themed world that spans three carefully detailed, vibrant cities. But why claim that this controversial and rather violent game is the *best* action console game?

What about other titles, such as Bungie's 2004 release of *Halo 2* on the Xbox, or another of my favorites, *The Legend of Zelda: Ocarina of Time*, released back in 1998 for the Nintendo 64 console? How can I defend the assertion that *San Andreas* is the best? I could point to the forum debates among fans on game review sites such as Gamerankings. com or IGN.com in which the comparative merit of titles such as Bungie's *Halo 2* and Rockstar's *San Andreas* is vigorously debated. Gamers have developed a sophisticated language with which to compare the quality of videogames. They refer to elements such as narrative, graphics, sound- and voice-acting, interface design and game play (the sense of how the game feels to play). My proposition that *San Andreas* is an outstanding game, and perhaps even the best action console game, is therefore not just grounded in my personal tastes. In making this evaluation I am drawing on categories of judgment, distinction, and discrimination that are in the process of being developed and refined by a community of gamers. In fact, one of the reasons that I so highly value *San Andreas* is that the game's design, and the debate and discussion about its value and merits, have contributed to our understanding of what videogames are and do as cultural practices. This adds an additional dimension to my valuing of *San Andreas*. In making this evaluation I am also drawing on my membership in another community: I am an academic researcher in the emerging field of games studies. In writing about *San Andreas*, my identities as a gamer fan and academic researcher intersect in ways that can be challenging and at times discomforting.

But while all this is true, it is important to emphasize the bottom line: *Grand Theft Auto: San Andreas* is an amazing game play experience. After spending upwards of 80 hours playing the game's central character of CJ and advancing his rise through the crime world of San Andreas by completing a complex, interlinked series of missions, I find myself playing through a spectacular chase sequence. In this final mission I hijack a SWAT tank and then use it to bulldoze my way into a crack fortress. An exhilarating action sequence then follows in which I chase down a corrupt cop, Tenpenny, who has escaped in a fire-truck. I'm driving a Stinger convertible. To successfully complete this mission I need to carefully maneuver the vehicle, keeping in touch with the fleeing Tenpenny, while avoiding collisions with pursuing police vehicles and Molotov Cocktails being thrown by rival gang members. CJ's brother Sweet manages to clamber aboard the fire engine, but is eventually thrown clear, and I must avoid running him over as he falls onto the convertible. A brief cut-scene then plays in which Sweet switches with me (CJ) to take on the task of driving while I open fire on the fleeing fire-truck, rival gang cars, and police cars. Eventually, motorcycles join the chase as well. The chase ends when Tenpenny loses control of the fire-truck in a spectacular crash from an overpass bridge. It took me a number of attempts to successfully complete this mission, using the Play Station controller to drive the car and then aim and shoot. After playing for so many hours I had a strong intuitive sense of the controls, to the point that the analog stick and buttons seemed to disappear. I was on the streets of Las Venturas, driving that convertible as CJ. I had a sense of inhabiting a richly interactive action world in which there is so much to do. But completing the game story wasn't the end of the *San Andreas* experience for me. There was still so much left to do and explore that I found myself regularly returning for another gaming session. I still needed to compete in tournament car races and I still wanted to improve my score in a series of BMX bike challenges. *San Andreas* is a big place that offers many richly interactive game experiences.

Rockstar games' *Grand Theft Auto* series has been one of the more commercially successful and critically acclaimed action videogames of the past few years. First appearing on the Sony PlayStation 2, the games have also been ported to both the Xbox and PC gaming platforms. Praised by game industry press and gamer fans as offering innovative designs that creatively explore the interactive potential of games, the series has also been the target of moral panics concerning their adult-orientated violent content. Senator Hillary Clinton recently commented:

> [P]robably one of the biggest complaints I've heard is about some of the video games, particularly *Grand Theft Auto*, which has so many demeaning messages about women and so encourages violent imagination and activities and it scares parents. I mean, if your child, and in the case of the video games, it's still predominantly boys, but you know, they're playing a game that encourages them to have sex with prostitutes and then murder them, you know, that's kind of hard to digest and to figure out what to say, and even to understand how you can shield your particular child from a media environment where all their peers are doing this.[2]

The recent controversy surrounding explicit sexual content that can be unlocked for *San Andreas* by downloading the "Hot Coffee" hack has reignited these debates. The Entertainment Software Ratings Board (ESRB) in the US responded by changing the game's rating from "M" to "AO." In Australia, in the absence of an AO rating for videogames, the title has been removed from retail shelves. The game review press on the other hand tends to be unanimous in its praise for the quality and excellence of the *Grand Theft Auto* series. The games have been among the most favorably reviewed titles to be released over the past few years. It is up there on the list with such must-have, must-play games as the Microsoft Game Studios-published and Bungie-developed *Halo* and *Halo 2*. The influential online site gamespot.com, after awarding *Grand Theft Auto: San Andreas* a score of 9.6/10 (superb) and bestowing it with an editor's choice award, commented that "*Grand Theft Auto: San Andreas* is a stupendous thrill ride that shouldn't be missed."[3] In reviewing the game for IGN, Jeremy Dunham writes:

I'm not going to beat around the bush. *Grand Theft Auto: San Andreas* is the single best PlayStation 2 title I have ever played ... In short, it's a terrific unending masterpiece of a game – and one that will never fall victim to an over-exaggeration of its lofty status. It's the defining piece of software for Sony's successful sophomore system, and it's almost impossible to imagine a PlayStation 2 library without it.[4]

The *Grand Theft Auto* series, culminating with the recent large-scale 3D environment of San Andreas, has legendary status among gamers. Indeed, games studies researcher Gonzalo Frasca argues that the game is one of those important titles that changes our idea of what games are meant to be. It provides the player with the freedom to explore an immense and open playground:

GTA3 allows you to perform a lot of actions in an immense playground. To mention just a few: you can hit and kill people, carjack and drive an enormous variety of vehicles, use several cool weapons, play vigilante, be a taxi driver, repair and paint your car, listen to several radio stations, have sex with prostitutes and burn people alive. And these are just some of the possibilities.[5]

It is this sense of open-ended game play freedom generated by *Grand Theft Auto: San Andreas* that I suggest defines it as the best action console game. Other games may arguably have better quality graphics, sound, scenario, and mission or level design. But I can think of very few that provide the compelling game play experience of occupying or in-habiting a richly interactive game world.

With the *Grand Theft Auto* series, developer Rockstar has been pushing the boundaries of this emerging mode of entertainment that we call video-games. The unashamedly edgy, violent, mature content also gives the series "cred" with adult gamers. Rockstar is not making games for kids. However, this chapter will not address in any detail the debate about violent gaming content. Instead, I consider why *Grand Theft Auto: San Andreas* can be so highly valued as the best console action game. Why do gamers such as myself find ourselves investing so much time playing *San Andreas*? I have now spent upwards of 100 hours exploring the 1990s gangsta-themed play environment that the Rockstar development team has crafted. So what is it about this game that keeps us playing? What is it about these violent action titles that Senator Clinton and others concerned with the violent representational content of these games fail to get? What does *Grand Theft Auto* do so well to garner the praise and accolades of game review press and gamers? Does it unfold a compelling and carefully crafted narrative, or is it the visceral thrill of using your controller to successfully guide a motor-vehicle through a drive-by shooting scenario while being pursued by police cars, motorcycles, and rival gangs all the while with your favorite '90s rap blasting from one of the in-game radio stations? What is it about this game that earns accolades such as:

> There really is no other game like it, despite there being many imitators, and this is precisely the kind of experience that reminds why, exactly, we play games: to be liberated from the constraints of reality, and explore living, breathing worlds. Few games have come this close to realizing that promise.[6]

Narrative Meets Free-Form Play

San Andreas builds on the successful action-environment formula of the previous titles in the series. It offers the gamer a carefully crafted and open 3D environment in which to play. In the earlier *Grand Theft Auto III* (2000) the player starts out as a low-level criminal who rises through the Mafia ranks in the 3D cityscape of Liberty City.[7] The game offers a *Godfather* or *Goodfellas* type experience. Players advance their small-time crime character by progressing through a series of missions that involve delivering items for crime bosses and killing rivals. However, much of the fun in the *Grand Theft Auto* series is not simply tied to the player's progression through a linear story-driven mission structure. Players are invited to explore the open-ended 3D-rendered city environments, in effect creating their own free-form action sequences involving elaborate car jacking and car chases. This play includes performing stunts by leaping vehicles from ramps that are cleverly hidden throughout the city for the gamer to discover. Much of the fun for me involved sharing stories with friends about the spectacular stunts and action sequences we were able to orchestrate and string-together in our crime rampages through Liberty City. This freestyle mode of game play has continued to be the defining feature in both *Grand Theft Auto: Vice City* and *Grand Theft Auto: San Andreas*.[8]

The strength of these games then is the combination of narrative and genre cues (for example, references to crime-action and mafia films such as *Goodfellas, Scarface,* and *The Godfather*) with a more open-ended and free-form play environment. The game designs rely on referencing and connecting with players' wider popular cultural experience and tastes in the forms of filmic narrative, music, and clothing styles to assist with successfully positioning the player within the game-world space. In making this evaluation, I am drawing on references in academic game studies that consider and debate what games are, and the complex relation between games as spaces or environments and narrative. For example, in "Game Design as Narrative Architecture," Henry Jenkins argues that videogame consoles generate "compelling spaces" that can be structured to facilitate "different kinds of narrative experiences." I suggest that this is precisely what the *Grand Theft Auto* games do so well – in Jenkins' terms they provide an evocative space by building on stories and genre traditions that we already know.[9]

They successfully shape our imaginings of crime and gangsta-themed stories, and create a richly textured environment filled with interactive opportunities that we can explore as players.

Grand Theft Auto: Vice City expanded on this game play experience by providing a bigger city with even more possibilities for fun action sequences. *Vice City* plays out in a 1980s Miami-themed crime spree playground that playfully references television series such as *Miami Vice.* The in-game radio stations tune in to appropriate 1980s rock and pop. *Grand Theft Auto: San Andreas,* the latest addition to the series, has expanded this design approach still further with an even larger play environment that encompasses a West Coast US-styled State of San Andreas set in the 1990s. Completing the game requires the player to explore three cities and their surrounding countryside. Starting out in Los Santos, an LA-styled city that includes gangland ghettos where much of the action is played out, players eventually progress to San Fierro (based on San Francisco) and the glitzy Las Venturas (based on Las Vegas). The game's setting and style draw extensively on 1990s gangsta films such as *Boyz N the Hood.* In-game radio stations contribute to this gritty gang-war feel by playing rap songs from Dr Dre, Compton's Most Wanted, and Tupac Shakur. Public Enemy's Chuck D provides the voice for the Radio DJ on the classic-rap station that you can tune into as you're driving.

A significant factor contributing to this sense of world-scale in *San Andreas* is the technical achievement that load-screens are kept to a minimum. As players move from one area of the game world to another, their sense of involvement and engagement is not interrupted by waiting for the content to load. The transitions between areas are generally seamless. There is a lot happening on the screen in *San Andreas* and graphical glitches such as frame-rate slow-downs, although present from time to time, are kept to a minimum. The game world of *San Andreas* is staggering in scale – it is huge. But it is not just the scale of the game world that is impressive. More importantly, it is the interactive potential for play that fills this carefully designed space. It would be a relatively easy game design and production task to build a large world, but then fill it with the same boring textures, art content, and encounters. The achievement of the Rockstar development team is embedding throughout the game world a series of engaging and challenging interactive opportunities, including mini-game encounters.

The game mission structure centers on the character of Carl Johnson (CJ), a young man who has returned to his neighborhood in Los Santos after learning that his mother has died. His arrival home is interrupted by events involving corrupt police. CJ's local gang is the Grove Street Families, and its control of the local area has been usurped by rivals – the Ballas. Early missions involve riding pushbikes to familiarize the player with the layout of the streets, and taking back control of the area from the Ballas by spray-painting over their graffiti tags. For example, one mission requires the player to drive a car around the neighborhood accompanied by CJ's brother Sweet, locating the Ballas tags and replacing them with the Grove Street colors. Follow-up mission goals include disrupting the Ballas crack-dealing operation by beating up a group of dealers with baseball bats and intercepting a car-load of Ballas gang members then destroying the vehicle by running it off the road or alternatively shooting it up. As I managed to drive the vehicle up beside the rival gang members, Sweet and gang member Ryder leant out of the car windows to shoot at the rival vehicle. After completing the mission, your "wanted level" with the local police increases and if you encounter any patrols, they give chase. To reduce this level you are required to visit a "Pay 'n' Spray" location, where your vehicle is repainted.

After completing the drive-by mission, a new series opens that involves traveling to Ryder's house and then assisting him to steal weapons from the home of a retired military veteran. Follow-up missions in the series challenge the player to rob a train of ammunition, and then break into a National Guard warehouse for yet more ammunition. Other missions link back to the corrupt police officers Frank Tenpenny and Eddie Pulaski, assassinating gang members at their direction. The final sequence of Los Santos missions involves tasks that aim to reunite the Grove Street Families gang. This effort is interrupted by a raid from a police SWAT team. After escaping from this, during which the player navigates through a chase sequence with police helicopters, cruisers, and motorcycles, CJ discovers that his brother and he may have been set up and ambushed through some kind of arrangement between fellow gang members Big Smoke and Ryder, with Tenpenny and the rival Ballas gang. At this point CJ is directed by Tenpenny to leave the city, then to find and assassinate an ex-police officer in a witness protection program who is providing evidence against Tenpenny. More mission sequences follow. These open up the city areas of San Fierro and finally Las Venturas. A significant six-mission strand in the Las Venturas area involves CJ seeking to disrupt the local Mafia's bottom line by robbing Caligula's Palace, the mob-run casino. Completing these missions include successfully controlling the character CJ in a parachute drop onto a hydroelectric dam with the aim of laying explosive charges that will be detonated during the heist to disrupt power to the casino. Controlling the parachute descent in order to land within a designated marker area provides challenging fun. Completing the heist also requires you to steal police motorbikes and hide them in a packer truck. Another mission goal is to sneak into a military base, evading or shooting well-armed guards, and then steal a sky-crane helicopter. The narrative progresses through a chain of missions, eventually directing you back to Los Santos. As riots erupt on the streets of Los Santos, CJ decides it is finally time to confront and defeat the enemies of the Grove Street Families. These overlapping mission sequences are more complex and lengthy than the previous games in the *Grand Theft Auto* series.

The strength of *San Andreas* is the relationship between this unfolding narrative and the free-form, open exploration of the game environment. For example, just cruising around the neighborhood of Los Santos, exploring the gang territories, ordering pizza at a local shop, and visiting the gym for a workout to buff up CJ's body and improve his physical statistics or combat skills all contribute directly to the player's immersion in the gang culture environment. Buying clothing in the gang colors and getting haircuts from barbers that improve your "cred" or respect rating with the local gang also contribute to this sense of immersion. Locating the barber in Los Santos and getting a flat-top style added 25 per cent to CJ's respect rating and 25 per cent to his sex appeal rating, although it cost

$500. One of my earlier aims in the game was to purchase green jeans and a pair of green high-top sneakers; this color of the Grove Street Families gang adds significantly to CJ's respect rating. None of these activities – which I spent a reasonable amount of time completing – contributed directly to advancing the narrative. But they all contributed to the sense that I was occupying and participating in a game world environment.

Game reviewers and players often comment on the quality of the non-player character voice-acting in *San Andreas*. In particular Samuel L. Jackson as officer Tenpenny and James Woods as the mafia boss character of Mike Toreno provide strong performances. Here again, the presence of these voice actors links gamers' experience of playing *Grand Theft Auto: San Andreas* with their wider consumption of popular culture. Our familiarity with the roles Jackson has played in films such as *Pulp Fiction* contributes to the gritty credibility of the game. Here the point is not to justify or defend the quality of *San Andreas* by comparison to other cultural forms such as film. *San Andreas* is not a film and it is not seeking to create a filmic experience. Nor is it a gangsta rap CD. However, the references to the broader terrain of popular culture contribute to the sense of occupying and moving through a fleshed-out world. What *San Andreas* does better than perhaps any other action game is provide us with a well-designed space that gamers want to hang out in and explore. The episodes and encounters that are the missions of *San Andreas* also provide the gamer with a path for moving through and experiencing the game world. Completing particular missions directs the player to travel to new game areas. And the design of *San Andreas* provides a compelling framework for the player's free-form exploratory play. It is packed with interactive possibility. And it is this rich diversity of interactive opportunity and potential that keeps bringing me back to San Andreas for yet another session of play.

There's Just So Much to Do in San Andreas

Much of the fun in playing *Grand Theft Auto: San Andreas* is simply cruising around the enormous world in a motor vehicle that the player has probably stolen, then finding and unlocking the cool things there are to do. On top of the overarching narrative described above, the setting is full of mini-games.

For example, after entering a bar I noticed a pool table, and then discovered that it isn't just eye candy setting the scene. You can rack the balls up and play a game of pool with a well-modeled physics system. You can also wager on the outcome of the game. In other areas players encounter arcade machines on which they can play through some classic video-game action, attempting to beat their previous high score. Other mini-games include a series of BMX challenges in which CJ rides a bike through a BMX park, passing through checkpoints within a set time. The player can return to the park and replay the challenge as often as they like, attempting to beat their previous high score. There are also street races with a variety of cars in which the player competes against other computer-controlled drivers around a check-point course. Cash rewards are awarded if you win the race. In the San Fierro city region there are six different race tournaments available, including Dirtbiking and Go Karting. Each race tournament offers a different game play experience. For example, the Karts in the Go Karting challenge are low to the ground and therefore capable of sharp turns. However, the steering with the controller is very sensitive and therefore missing other traffic and pedestrians encountered as you navigate through the course becomes quite a test. It is also a lot of fun speeding through narrow alleyways while avoiding hitting dumpsters. Longer tournament events involve sports cars racing from San Fierro to Las Venturas. However, in order to unlock many of the race tournament events the player is first required to complete a series of different vehicle training schools, covering motor vehicles, bikes, boats, and planes. Completing the courses unlocks various mission types and increases your driving skill ratings, thereby improving your chance of successfully completing the race tournament and other vehicular-themed missions. Another vehicle-based mission is the taxi driver series. The player enters a taxi and then presses a button on the controller for a customer location to show up as a blue blip on the radar and game world map. The passenger must be picked up and then dropped off at their destination within a time limit in order to earn tips.

Among my favorite series of mini-games is the opportunity for gambling that can be found throughout *San Andreas*. It quickly became a convenient way to raise the funds needed for upgrading CJ's clothing, motor vehicles, and hair styles. In Los Santos I regularly participated in off-track betting and wagering against the computer in pool games. However, when the Las Vegas-themed city area of Las Venturas unlocked for me to explore, the gambling opportunities also expanded, with the casinos providing blackjack and roulette tables. As CJ's gambling skill rating improved I was able to play on tables with higher betting limits and borrow increasing amounts against the house. Players can improve their gambling rating by finding horseshoes that can be located throughout Las Venturas. If you manage to collect all 50 horseshoes, then your gambling luck improves significantly. In one memorable session of gambling at the casino, I over-borrowed and ended up owing money. Shortly after leaving I received a phone call from the casino owner reminding me that I owed him money. I elected not to repay and received a second call in which the owner informed me that his associates were going to pay me a visit. Not long after the call I had a shoot-out with a carload of his associates who were seeking to collect on the debt. It is moments like these that deliver an outstanding gaming experience. Here I wasn't just playing out a sequence of mini-games, thereby seeking to maximize my character's gambling rating, but rather participating in an expansive interactive environment that regularly provided surprising and challenging play opportunities. This episode contributed to my sense of immersion in a gangsta world in which I had taken on the role of a high-stakes gambler.

Opportunities to Create those Memorable Gaming Moments

It is the many unexpected gaming moments in which players discover ways of creating play opportunities in an open-ended environment that distinguish *San Andreas* as an outstanding action title. When discussing *San Andreas* with fellow gamers, they generally comment on the high production values in terms of graphics, sound, and music; the massive and detailed 1990s gangsta-themed world; the character dialogue and clothing; the diversity and control of motor vehicles; the intricate narrative with multiple plot-threads in which the player takes on the role of CJ and experiences his rise through the gang ranks; and the staggering number of mini-games. But more often than not the discussion generally comes around to those unexpected gaming moments when the gamer relates one of *their* favorite *Grand Theft: Auto San Andreas* moments. It may be the particular way in which they managed to win a tournament race (the customized car they were driving, etc.). It may be their strategy for completing a game scenario that advanced the story. The brilliance of *San Andreas* is that the well-crafted design combination of narrative, genre, and a free-form mode of play provides a compelling place where many gamers want to spend a lot of time and explore. As Jeremy Dunham comments in his IGN review: "The number one reason that *Grand Theft Auto: San Andreas* is so amazing to begin with: it's the first game I can ever remember that asks its players to wonder 'What can't you do?' as opposed to 'What can you?'."[10]

The design of *San Andreas* provides a brilliantly conceived adult-themed playground for players to explore the interactive potential of those compelling 3D entertainment spaces that we call videogames. In reaching this judgment I am playing across the boundaries of my belonging to the taste communities of gamer fans and academic game researchers. My approach to this cultural object that is *San Andreas* is informed by my participation in *both* of these communities – communities in which we are still exploring and debating how to discuss, evaluate, and understand precisely what the cultural practice of videogaming is.

Notes

1   *Grand Theft Auto: San Andreas*, PlayStation 2 CD-ROM, Rockstar Games, 2004.

2   Hillary Rodham Clinton, Senator Clinton's speech to Kaiser Family Foundation upon release of "Generation M: Media in the Lives of Kids 8 to 18," Senator Hillary Rodham Clinton Speeches, March 8, 2005, <http://clinton. senate.gov/~clinton/speeches/2005314533.html> (accessed June 7, 2005).

3   Jeff Gerstmann, "Review of *Grand Theft Auto: San Andreas*," Gamespot. com, October 26, 2004, <www.gamespot.com/ps2/action/gta4/review. html> (accessed August 30, 2005).

4   Jeremy Dunham, "*Grand Theft Auto: San Andreas* – The best PlayStation 2 Game ever?," *IGN.com*, October 25, 2004, <http://ps2.ign.com/articles/ 559/559560p1.html> (accessed August 30, 2005).

5   Gonzalo Frasca, "Sim Sin City: some thoughts about *Grand Theft Auto III*," *Game Studies* 3/2 (December 2003), <http://www.gamestudies. org/0302/frasca/> (accessed June 7, 2005).

6   Miguel Lopez, "*Grand Theft Auto: San Andreas* Review," *GameSpy.com*, October 25, 2004, <http://ps2.gamespy.com/playstation-2/grand-theft-auto-san-andreas/561830p1.html> (accessed August 30, 2005).

7   *Grand Theft Auto 3*, PlayStation 2 CD-ROM, Rockstar Games, 2001.

8   *Grand Theft Auto: Vice City*, PlayStation 2 CD-ROM, Rockstar Games, 2002.

9   Henry Jenkins, "Game design as narrative architecture," in Noah Wardrip-Fruin and Pat Harrigan, eds., *First Person: New Media as Story, Performance and Game* (Cambridge, MA: MIT Press, 2004), pp. 118–30: 122, 123–4.

10 Dunham, *"Grand Theft Auto."*

9

The Best Motorbike: The Ducati 916 Superbike

Margaret Henderson

What remains as the permanent contribution of the machine . . . is the technique of cooperative thought and action it has fostered, the esthetic excellence of the machine forms, the delicate logic of materials and forces, which has added a new canon – the machine canon – to the arts . . .

Lewis Mumford, *Technics and Civilization*[1]

The cultural logic of modernity is not merely that of rationality as expressed in the activities of calculation and experiment; it is also that of passion, and the creative dreaming born of longing.

Colin Campbell, *The Romantic Ethic and the Spirit of Modern Consumerism*[2]

Considering the practical and symbolic importance of speed to motorcycle design and riding, it is unsurprising that the motorcycle industry exemplifies the general tendencies and rhythms of late capitalist commodity production. Each year sees a new batch of models released, differentiated from previous models by various forms of technical innovation (and with a resultant drop in resale values), and catering for more and more specialized factions of the motorbike community. Last year's incredible, perfect superbike is supplanted by a better, even faster model, while its engine may be transplanted into the more comfortable geometry of a sports tourer model bike, hence broadening the appeal of that particular marque. This year's most gorgeous bike gets quickly replaced by another in twelve months' time. Yet one particular bike arguably stands above this procession, holding its place as a truly great motorbike – the Ducati

916 superbike. Although motorcyclists are well aware of the vagaries and impossibility of objective judgments about the "best" motorbike, from its release in 1994 onwards the 916 was seen by the motorbike press, fans, riders, and the art-design world as something extraordinary: it "became an icon without really trying."[3] More than ten years later (a long time in bike industry terms), the 916 still elicits the same powerful response. This chapter explores just why the 916 can be defined as the best (or at least an iconic) motorbike for many motorcyclists, myself included, which in turn allows me to outline a system of motorbike aesthetics – that is, the categories or values used by riders to discuss, order, and evaluate bikes in general.

I will provide only a brief sketch here of the 916, preferring to let the riders' voices and photographs give a fuller picture of its characteristics. The 916 was first displayed at the Milan Bike Show in October 1993, "where it caused a sensation," and was released in 1994 to much acclaim.[4] Indeed, "the 916 won every 'Bike of the Year' award [given by motorcycle magazines] in 1994."[5] It was designed by Massimo Tamburini, who had previously designed for the motorcycle companies Bimota and Cagiva. The 916 is a race bike for the Superbike class, and was a replacement for the Ducati 851/888, designed by Massimo Bordi, another beautiful and brilliant bike that performed well in the World Superbike series, and which re-established Ducati as a manufacturer of high-performance sports bikes using advanced technology.[6]

According to Tamburini:

[T]he design brief that we received from Castiglioni [then one of Ducati's owners] was to create a highly distinctive bike from front and rear, one that had to have its own distinctive personality. Our work on the design, front and rear, including the underseat exhausts, gave it this personality. One which an observer would know, even from behind, was a 916 and not a Japanese bike.[7]

The 916 uses the Ducati trademark tubular steel trestle frame and desmodromic valves, a single-sided swingarm (for ease of tire removal and because it looks so good), dual headlights, and twin underseat exhausts ("where most engines use a camshaft lobe to open a valve and a spring to slam it closed, desmodromics calls on camshaft lobes to both push a valve open and to pull it closed." This avoids the problem of broken springs.)[8] It is fully faired, initially was available only in a single seat model and in one color – red. The bike's engine is a liquid-cooled, fuel-injected, four-stroke, ninety-degree twin cylinder, using four valves per cylinder, with a total engine displacement of 916 cc (increased in later models). The gear box is six speed, operated by a dry clutch. The bike uses top-quality components, such as Brembo brakes, Showa upside-down forks, and an Ohlins rear shock. And it is fitted with a massively wide rear tire: a 190/50. In 1994 the road version would have cost you A$24,995 (plus on-road costs) if you were lucky enough to be able to buy one. Production could never keep up with demand.[9]

Figure 9.1 Utopia comes in yellow as well (front view)

Figure 9.2   Utopia comes in yellow as well (rear view)

Figure 9.3 Utopia comes in yellow as well (side view)

This list of specifications only hints at why the 916 is such a great bike. With my background in road cycling and its strong Italian heritage, I was a prime candidate to fall for the 916. I had always liked sports bikes, and had owned a few Japanese ones, but when the 916 came along, that all changed. Its stunning looks and innovative design caused a continental shift in my motorcycle loyalties. The 916 seemed the perfection of the sports bike form: lean, slim, technologically advanced, a design breakthrough, but still classical; elegant, but noisy and awesomely powerful. It was not an in-line four cylinder, it didn't have a fluoro paint job, it was just a red, svelte v-twin from Italy, with all the history and mystique that identity suggests. And it was exotic: price and availability kept it special. Here was a bike that could put a stop to restless desire.

But what do other riders think of the 916? I canvassed readers of the Australian motorcycling magazines *Two Wheels, Rapid Bikes*, and *Australian Road Rider*, and I approached the on-line discussion groupswww.netrider.net.au, Ducati.net, and Ducatiexperience.com (respondents will be denoted by the relevant discussion list). In this research, and in bike reviews and articles, there is no shortage of riders who think that the 916 is the best bike. Indeed, this bike seems to generate superlatives, poetry, and love. And it wasn't just Ducati riders who argued that the 916 was the best – almost half the respondents didn't own Ducatis (of those who identified their brand of bike). Nearly all respondents were men, which is understandable given that women are still a small minority of riders, and that the 916 is a large capacity, relatively expensive, and specialized sports bike.

As the riders' responses show, motorbike aesthetics is a system that comprises a rider's faculty of appreciation, properties of the bike, and the experience of the bike itself. Nine recurrent themes and categories of value emerged, which I explain in detail below. The overwhelmingly prevalent criterion was the bike's looks, second was the bike's sound, followed by its design. Then, in no order of priority, came the qualities of performance, racing results, the ride experience, the bike's heritage, its exotic nature, and its sex appeal. These categories suggest the values and discourses underlying motorbike aesthetics, which draws upon the obvious fields of technology and technics, racing, sexuality, masculinity, and physical prowess; as well as those discourses derived from high culture, sociocultural mythologies, and a metaphysics of the self. This broad network of meanings seems to bear out John Alt's claim that the motorbike as "commodity is always something other than the thing itself: it is buried under, and inseparable from, cultural representation."[10]

Considering that motorcycles are such powerful symbols, always "something other than the thing itself," and have even been described as a "perfect metaphor for the 20th century," I would like to suggest one interpretation of the 916's beauty and iconic nature.[11] For when I thought about why the 916 represented motorcycling perfection, and as I worked through my own and other's opinions and theories, it became apparent that this particular motorbike seemed able to resolve some of the fundamental dichotomies structuring modernity, namely:

innovation / tradition
technology / the human
high culture / popular culture
artisanal production / mass production
artistic / technical
reason / emotion
form / function
· aesthetics / everyday life
the individual / collective identity

Just maybe, then, the Ducati 916 is not only the best motorbike, but also is a version of Utopia Now. That is, the 916 represents a brief realization of a particular longing underlying modernity, finally achieved after a century or so of the industrial revolution, and on the cusp of the next millennium. (And just as symptomatically for this epoch, Utopia was concretized in the commodity form, and was all too soon updated and replaced.)

Visual Appearance

> Championship winning bikes weren't meant to be so pretty. (netrider respondent)

The 916's looks are an overwhelming factor in making the bike so great, with nearly every respondent and reviewer commenting upon them. Tamburini seemed to perfect the shape and lines – clean, simple, uncluttered – creating the template for the ur-superbike. And then there were those radical looking exhaust pipes, headlights, mirrors, and swingarm. The shape and fittings seemed to update the classical style of Italian racing bikes with more futuristic lines and shapes, hence managing to be both classic and modern. Or, as Paul Rutherford notes, "the 916 defined the contemporary form of the sports bike."[12] Understandably, its looks invite love at first sight, as one rider from Ducati.net explains:

> In the early 70s I thought the Norton Commando was the most beautiful bike made. Everything just fit together so nice. And then in the early 90s the 916 hit the shores. I was mesmerized by this bike. The look of the bike is functional. It is so compact and looks so sleek for the size of its motor. It is a work of art. The dual headlights and lines of the fairing blend so well with the tank and then the tail. And the double pipes out the back, tucked away! No one had thought of that, and now everyone is copying it. The single sided swingarm keeps it so simple.

Doug Abadie describes a similar conversion:

> I've owned Triumphs, Nortons, and built a Rickman/Kawasaki in my livingroom . . . However, in 1993, I saw a picture of the Ducati 916 and fell in love immediately. When I bought one of the first ones to arrive in the US I was overwhelmed by the looks: Sleek fairing w/exhausts under

the seat, "cat's eye" headlights, singlesided swingarm, RED with gold highlights (frame, wheels, headlight bucket, decals etc.).[13]

The 916's successful integration of classical elements with modern forms seems to insure that such a beautiful bike is, however, more than a bike. Respondent after respondent described the 916 as a work of art, "classic," "timeless," "simplicity of form," and "purity of form" being the typical phrases used to define its looks. Some referred to the bike as "mobile sculpture" or noted the sculpted bodywork (netrider). Not surprisingly, the 916 found its way into art galleries and private collections, into a film and even a poem.[14] In effect, the 916's merged identity as machine and art object challenges modern Western culture's separation of high and popular cultural forms, and the aesthetic realm from everyday life.[15]

Sound

> There is no need for your bike to sound like a vitamizer/blender when it can quite easily sound like a thunderstorm. (netrider respondent)

The distinctive sound of the 916 was the second most frequent quality listed by respondents, and functions almost like a master signifier of Ducatis in general, a sound "definately [*sic*] well loved by all" (netrider). Sounds can tell you a lot about a bike: the type of engine, how the bike is being ridden, whether it is maintained, and the type of exhaust pipes used. For instance, because of their high-revving engine, two-stroke bikes whine like mosquitoes, while mid- and large-bore four-cylinder Japanese sports bikes sound like jets – smooth yet awesome. For Ducatis, with their v-twin engines and usually Italian pipes (Contis or Termignonis), their sound is a deep, throbbing, growling rumble that turns into a roar at higher revs, but is also "mellow and exotic," full of unique character and understated power (Ducati.net). Even Japanese v-twin bikes can't emulate this bassissimo note. As one rider comments, "I tell many folks it's the Italian symphony."[16]

Apart from the engine and exhaust, the 916 has another distinctive sound. Most bikes use a wet clutch; however, because it is designed for racing, the 916 has a dry clutch which eliminates oil viscosity drag on the engine. This makes for clunkier and noisier gear shifts: "[W]hether you love it or hate it, that wonderful dry clutch rattle can never be replaced by the common sound of drowning mosquitoes created by many bikes" (netrider).

But what is the appeal of noisy pipes, clutch, and engine, apart from the fact they have become so strongly associated with Ducati and the 916? Perhaps it is because the pipes and the clutch draw attention to the essence of the bike. What the 916 is about – namely, churning out great whacks of power and carving up roads – is not toned down or "civilized" by technological smoothness. Rather, its rawness and machine identity are accentuated. Maybe this is what riders mean when they say a bike has "character": deep down, under the beautiful bodywork and technical innovation, it is still a mechanical beast, like all its predecessors. And as Ducati riders know, the throb of the engine and rumble of the pipes translate into the physical experience of riding the bike, hence the aural becomes tactile. Perhaps there is something about being close to that rhythm, whether it's felt as sexual or even as a pre-Oedipal return to being near the mother's heartbeat. (Remember, the mother is your first love object.) Thus the 916's aural quality collapses the distinction between machine and human.

Design

> Design is emotion brought to form: this is the significance of Ducati's story.[17]

The 916's excellence in design is another major factor in making it the best motorbike, and reiterates its status as a work of art. Further, the bike's design is a key signifier of its Italianness, and locates it within a unique tradition of industrial design "which depends, only minimally, upon models borrowed from elsewhere."[18] Certain motorbikes, and particularly Ducati bikes, are identified by their designer's signature, reinforcing the notion of the bike as a work of art made by artists rather than simply engineers, and adding to its aura of exclusivity and identity as an aesthetic object. This is particularly so in more experimental bike design, for example, Erik Buell's bikes or Philippe Starck's Aprilia Moto 6.5. In the case of Ducati (as in Italian design history more generally),[19] its history is narrated through a succession of major models and designers. For instance, Fabio Taglioni invented Ducati's trademark and revolutionary desmodromic valve system in the 1950s (still in use today); Bordi designed the 851; Miguel Galluzzi created the monster in the early 1990s. And Tamburini, of the exotic Bimota and Cagiva bikes, designed the 916. When a rider chooses a 916, it is also choosing the "high cultural" Italian design tradition.[20]

But what made the design so good? For many, it is attention to detail, and innovation. Ian Falloon notes: "Everywhere there was the most spectacular attention to detail, from the machining of the top triple clamp with its steering damper, to the levers and controls."[21] You can "take one part off and that part is still beautiful" (netrider). Such quality of design did much to counter Ducati's sometimes inconsistent approach to finish. And the bike incorporated a number of innovations – "state-of-the-art motorcycle thinking" – which marked a new era for Ducati.[22] These included a single-sided swingarm that has greater rigidity, a frame designed so that servicing is easier, an engine that can be removed quickly from the bike, a fuel tank which forms part of the enlarged air box, adjustable steering geometry, and aerodynamic under-the-seat pipes.[23]

But what the 916 design really represented was a perfect example of functionalism, meaning that form should follow function.[24] Respondent after respondent noted that the bike was a totally integrated package. "Each detail was considered for aesthetic and function and combined into a form (aggressive and yet feminine) that was pure."[25] Or, as Carugati explains:

> It has no kin among faired motorbikes, since in sport bikes the fairing is an addition, cladding to reduce air resistance, protecting the mechanicals that establish their identity . . . But the shell of the 916 interprets the totality of the machine, enhances it, heightens it, optimizes its performance, and is therefore inseparable from the mechanicals, is born conjoined with them.[26]

Although "[w]hen the 9's first came out after the 851/88 it shocked the world!" the design of the bike still managed to be a Ducati. "At heart she remained true to the philosophy and drive that has inspired so many riders over the decades. This kind of dedication of evolving an engineering principle to it's [*sic*] limits as the 'time's technology' dictates commands a type of respect."[27] Hence the 916 was radical and traditional, artistic and technical, functional and beautiful, and classic while astoundingly modern.

————————————— **Performance** —————————————

> We affirm that the world's magnificence has been enriched by a new
> beauty: the beauty of speed.[28]

As its functionalist ethos suggests, the 916 didn't just look good, it also
had the performance to match, a key quality when judging motorbikes,
particularly in the sports bike category. The street model weighs 198
kilos dry (more for the biposto version) and puts out 109 horsepower
at 9000 rpm. The 1995 race version weighs 157 kilos dry, puts out 144
horsepower at 12,000 rpm, and the manufacturers claim a top speed of
over 300 kilometers per hour (though various motorcycle tests managed
to get around 250 kilometers per hour). The street version accelerates
from 0 to 60 mph in 2.9 seconds, and it can pull up from this same
speed within 27 feet.[29] Whichever way you look at it, that's a lot of
going fast (and a pretty good ability to stop) with not much weight
under you. And as I explain later, such performance translates into
racing success.

This is not to say that the 916 was the fastest or most powerful superbike of the mid- to late 1990s. Rather, it was how those raw figures
translated into street and track performance, and this is where the bike
reveals that it is a total package, pulling together the engine, body work,
ergonomics, chassis, and componentry into magical handling. Among
many others, the British publication, *Motor Cycle News*, waxed lyrical
about what the bike could do. The bike has "brutally quick acceleration,"
"massive mid-range torque," "[h]andling is quite stunning, yet so easy
to take full advantage of." "It feels as if you can charge up to a bend, lay
the bike flat on its side . . . spin it round the turn then stand it up straight
just by twisting the throttle."[30] Or, as one of the respondents explains,
in more real world terms

> I told my wife that the reason I loved that bike was that it had saved my
> life when I had blown a turn or gotten out of shape on a rough road. The
> bike would correct itself as long as I didn't do something stupid. Besides
> the confidence-inspiring handling, the massive power of those Ducati
> Horses would pull out of corners and leave the rest behind.[31]

To put the 916's performance in the most simplest terms: "At any speed
the Ducati feels fast."[32]

The Ride Experience

[W]e must prepare for the imminent, inevitable identification of man with motor, facilitating and perfecting a constant interchange of intuition, rhythm, instinct, and metallic discipline of which the majority are wholly ignorant, which is guessed at by the most lucid spirits.[33]

As suggested by the title of Carugati's history of Ducati, *Design in the Sign of Emotion*, Ducatis (and bikes in general) are about emotions and physical sensations. Some bikes just feel good from the minute you get on. Others you get used to, and some are never right. With its performance characteristics and design, the experience of riding a 916 is another quality that inspires poetry in riders. "It's a work of art to look at, but also to ride. The way it seems fall into corners, the sprawled ergonomic caress of the rider aboard, the mechanical intimacy of the engine . . . can be an intoxicating experience" (netrider). For another rider:

Riding . . . my Ducati 916 . . . is a sublime experience – the sound, the smell . . . the gracefulness, the trust one can have in its ability to go where you want that I have never experienced in a Jap bike for instance . . . It is also the exhilaration of speed, but not as a mechanical instrument that at any moment could fail you and catapult you into oblivion. That can of course happen – but the rider, and not the machine fail [*sic*], if it does . . . [Y]ou are always aware that the bike is coaxing you to do better . . . to live closer to the edge. But you trust the bike.[34]

The bike isn't just about exploring limits of machine and rider, however, but simple pleasure as well: "[T]he 916 makes each ride a special experience . . . Be it just bouncing the sound of the v-twin off city walls, pretending you are foggy [Carl Fogarty, who won the World Superbike championship on a 916] on your favourite road."[35]

One of my greatest pleasures . . . is to go for a ride with my brother, which only happens a few times a year, and look over at him [on a Ducati 748] and think to myself "man, this is sooo cool, me and Corbin ridin' together down the highway on a couple of absolutely gorgeous Ducati Superbikes!"[36]

From how the body sits into the bike's shape, to the precise feedback from the chassis and bars, to the way the 916 makes the rider ride harder: all these suggest that the pleasure of the 916 derives from a brief surmounting of the barriers between human and machine, and a temporary equilibrium between *eros* and *thanatos*.

──────────────── **Racing** ────────────────

> [P]lease do not forget an other [*sic*] obvious element of this Ducati's beauty. Since 1994 the 916/996/998 series has won more races and championships, from the local to the world stage, than any other motorcycle. Now that's beautiful! (Ducati.net respondent)

From their earliest beginnings motorcycles have been raced, whether to promote a particular brand, to aid technological development, or for sheer pleasure. Charles M. Falco argues that "the impact of racing on the evolution of motorcycles cannot be understated."[37] Even for a rider who will never break the speed limit or ride on a race track, the racing legacy is there somewhere in the bike's technics or the rider's psyche. From its first foray into motorcycle production with the 48 cc Cucciolo ("Puppy") engine of 1946, Ducati has recognized the importance of racing to its sales and development.[38] And because of its premier designer Fabio Taglioni's interest in racing, most of its models have been high-performance sports bikes, that is, built for racing. This purity of purpose and its long list of racing triumphs is a major factor in the Ducati's appeal, a tradition that continued with the 916, and another facet of its allure.[39]

For those stunning looks have a serious and uncompromising purpose: to win races in the Superbike category which pits v-twin engines against smaller capacity and heavier four-cylinder bikes (with the rules ensuring technical parity). And the 916 did so. In its first year of racing, it won 12 of the 22 races; after further development in 1995 it won 13 of the 24 races, hence easily winning the overall title and the constructor's title.[40] By the end of its racing career it had won eight World Superbike Manufacturers' Titles and six Riders' Titles.[41] As riders noted, this domination of Superbike racing is proof of the bike's superiority, and, for not a great amount of money, the street motorcyclist can purchase a model quite close to the racetrack version – something unthinkable for a Formula One fan. Ironically, for such an elite machine, it is, to an extent, relatively democratic, and harks back to the original purpose of Italian scooters and bikes as being cheap transport for the people.

Heritage

Ducati, with passion / always in search of perfection / goes straight ahead on its way. / Since it honors the city, / give it ten out of ten / and sing its praises.[42]

Many riders referred to the bike as having character, as being a Ducati. That is, the brand represents a particular form of motorcycling – namely, Italian – and hence one defined by a historical and cultural lineage that provides this character. I term this the heritage factor, one closely aligned with the categories of design and racing. By a mixture of marketing, race results, longevity, styling, and design, Ducati has become metonymic of Italian motorcycling, and thereby also draws upon cultural mythologies of "Italianness" in general. And like Harley-Davidson, Ducati has become synonymous with motorbikes. For the general population and many riders, Ducatis represent the essence of motorcycling.

One of the founding brothers of Ducati described the company's story as "a fable"; we can extend this to say that the Ducati heritage is very much structured by fables about Italian culture and history.[43] Hence we have a repeated association of the bike with style over technology, design excellence, sexiness, beauty, exoticism, classicism, passion, high culture, and grace. Such terms mark the 916 as the essence of Italianness: "Italian motorcycles – unlike any others, to me they suggest a Mediterranean sense of enjoyment of life. They are not just machines, not just race winning implements, not statements of alienation ([like] HDs! [Harley Davidsons])."[44] When you ride a Ducati, you are riding an entire cultural mythology.

And then there is the Ducati heritage (overlapping at certain points with this Italianness), which makes it the essence of motorcycling: "[T]here is something more to Ducati than the bike . . . Ducati represented all the best things about motorcycling" (netrider). For instance, Ducati signifies a long history of precision engineering (how many other motorbikes can be denoted by their factory's suburb – Borgo Panigale, a suburb of Bologna), an equally long racing history (compared to Japanese bikes), a concentration on hardcore racing bikes, the closeness between the racing and street-bike models, and "brilliant engineering overseen by Marx Brothers management."[45] Further, Ducati is a tiny Italian company specializing only in bikes (although this has not always been the case), up against the might of Japanese industrial conglomerates like Yamaha and Honda. Finally, there is a mystique surrounding the design and the production methods, which in turn has made Ducatis comparatively uncommon commodities. As a rider explains:

> Even if Italy is considered a highly industrialized country, the roots of Italian economy and culture are agricultural and artisan in nature. Artisans are those who have the exceptional capability (and cultural heritage) to produce very high quality artifacts (but in small numbers). . . . All Italian motorcycle makers started as artisans, DUCATI in my view is still producing "artisan like products" . . . Here the 916 . . . an artisan artifact, elegant and efficient, not made by the 1000's.[46]

Perhaps the power of the Ducati heritage is best summed up by the same rider: "you can reproduce a Honda factory in the USA or Volkswagen in Mexico but you will never be able to have a DUCATI in New Jersey or North Carolina." The Ducati heritage thus signifies a balance between innovation and tradition, and mass production and an artisanal mode.

Exotica-Uniqueness

> Like all good forms of art [Ducatis] are often emulated but never equalled.[47]

> Who wants to be common and ride a bike they see many times over on the road? (netrider respondent)

This type of heritage is a major contributor to the 916's identity, one that, like all identities, is defined by what it is not, as well as by what it is. As the earlier comment by Tamburini makes clear, Ducatis are *not* Japanese bikes. In motorcycling terms, Japanese bikes signify cutting-edge high technology, relentless innovation, reliability, a capacity to copy and improve upon others' work, the efficiencies of mass production, and hence a cheaper price tag for the rider. In contrast, Ducatis have "soul," attributed to a uniqueness in design and production and their exotic origins, which in turn makes them symbols of high culture, good taste, and rarity.[48] In an era of the mass production of a dizzying array of bikes, inbuilt obsolescence, and globalizing mass culture, these qualities are a considerable part of the 916's appeal. Moreover, as a number of riders note, these qualities transfer to the rider. Motorbikes denote individualism and nonconformism, and with its exotic aura, the 916 becomes a symbol of intensified individualism.[49] John Orchard suggests that "the 916/998 conjures up recognizable [*sic*] images of unique styling for people that do not want to be seen as everyday people."[50]

While the marque is a status symbol and marker of individuality, it also guarantees a collective identity. Once you ride Ducatis, you become a Ducatisti, or Ducati fan, part of a loyal clan who put up with the good and bad models, the idiosyncracies and the magic, the expense and the joy. For example:

> I also usually enjoy being unique and many people in Alaska have never even heard of Ducati. I feel like I'm doing my best to enlighten them tho. I even put big DUCATI decals on the side panels so folks could see what the name of the beautiful machine they were looking at was.[51]

One gets to stand apart from the masses, but also to become part of a passionate subculture (demonstrated by the riders' generous replies for this chapter) amidst the anomie of modernity.

The Bleedingly Obvious – Sex Appeal

> If you want to come with me / I'll take you on my Cucciolo / the motorcycle's tiny / but it throbs just like my heart.[52]

> Ducati – SEX ON WHEELS. (netrider respondent)

The throbbing engine positioned near the rider's crotch, ecstatic thrills gained at the limits of experience, and the phallic shape of a beautiful machine make for a close association between motorcycles and sex – an image that the motorbike industry and mass media have been careful to cultivate. I've left the quality that most obviously makes the 916 such a good bike until last because, as response after response pointed out the 916's sexual appeal, or theorized its aesthetics in highly sexualized terms, it seemed that the "sexiness" of the 916 could not be isolated from one or more of the categories already discussed. As the "Ducati – SEX ON WHEELS" comment suggests, the 916's sex appeal tells us not only about the bike's desirability, but what we think about sex as well. Perhaps then the 916 is a fable about late twentieth-century sexuality, something suggested by one rider's comment that these machines "provoke the closest thing to lust that a human can feel for a machine."[53] And for another, "these bikes stimulate 4 of the 5 senses, simultaneously – and maybe then some which haven't been discovered yet."[54]

Desire for the bike is based primarily on its visual appearance, with its form being coded as either feminine or as beast-like. "The feminine lines of the gas tank and seat along with the aggressive front fairing grabs the onlooker by the scruff and demands a good stare."[55] But as this comment makes clear, this is not a conventional passive femininity, but a powerful, aggressive one, and intrinsic to its allure. The 916 thus suggest a particular ideal of beauty and desire, embodied in a machinic femme fatale.

The 916's sexiness arises not only from its looks, but also from its sound (that stirs "deep primeval viscera"), and from the sensation of riding.[56] "But the real knockout punch is delivered when the key is inserted and the hart [*sic*] of the machine comes alive. This is no one night stand. She will reward the skillful rider with all the passion promised with the alluring bodywork."[57] Ducati character, design, and performance combine to make a sensual riding experience, delivering ecstasy and danger. The 916 rattles, throbs, glides, roars, it tips outrageously, it blasts through space and time to physical and emotional freedom. What more could you want from a partner? And the Italian mystique imbues the bike with another layer of desire, adding images of passion and exoticism. (I confess that I called my 750 monster "Sofia" in honor of Sofia Loren.) Indeed, when Carugati describes Ducati design as emotion brought to form, or when riders describe lust for a motorbike or its incredible beauty, they point not only to the imaginary contours of desire, but to a longing to overcome the subject/object, human/machine, human/"beast," and reason/emotion dichotomies that have structured and limited the Western psyche. And it seems that the 916 is the right desire machine for the job.

———— Requiem for the 916 ————

In 1998 two Ducati models, diametrically opposed in the significance of their projects, the Monster and the 916, together crowned the summit of the spiral that forms the gallery circuit at Frank Lloyd Wright's celebrated New York museum [in "The Art of the Motorcycle" exhibition].[58]

How fitting that the bike which seems to symbolize so much of modernity takes its place, in best modernist fashion, nearly at the summit of a canonical exhibition of motorbikes.[59] Yet equally significant is that two years earlier an American company, Texas Pacific Group, bought a major stake in the cash-strapped Ducati company. Major changes occurred: a new logo and corporate identity were constructed, production was increased, and a broader range of models was introduced. The Ducati-Performance line of accessories was launched, and marketing efforts aimed at maximizing the Ducati image were stepped up, with a number of cross-merchandising arrangements being entered into (for example, with Donna Karan!).[60] In 1998 Texas Pacific Group completed the buy-out of Ducati from the Castiglioni brothers, and Ducati was publicly listed on the stock exchange in 1999.[61] For Ducati to survive, such a repositioning and rebranding was necessary.

Although the 916 continued to win races and sell well, it was replaced in 2002 by the 999 model. Ironically, a bike that epitomized motorcycling perfection has been outmoded by one marketed as "Ducati 999: the best twin ever."[62] Thus the beautiful 916 tells us two "big" stories about the contemporary West. As the best motorbike, the 916 represents a utopia beyond the tensions between form and function, innovation and tradition, art and life, artisanal and mass production, human and machine, the individual and the collective, and high and popular culture. Its fate, however, suggests a "bigger" story about economic power and commodity production, technology, and marketing that seems virtually unstoppable.

Acknowledgments

Many thanks to all the respondents for their generosity and insight; the editors of *Two Wheels*, *Rapid Bikes*, and *Australian Road Rider*; and Ducati Brisbane for providing a 996 for the illustrations.

Notes

1   Lewis Mumford, *Technics and Civilization* (London: Routledge & Kegan Paul, 1934).

2   Colin Campbell, *The Romantic Ethic and the Spirit of Modern Consumerism* (Oxford, New York: Blackwell, 1987).

3 Aidan Walker, "Icons for the foolish few," *Blueprint* 175 (September 2000): 119.

4 Ian Falloon, *The Ducati Story: Racing and Production Models from 1945 to the Present Day*, 3rd edn. (Sparkford, Somerset: Haynes, 2000), p. 142.

5 Ibid., p. 144.

6 Decio Giulio Riccardo Carugati, *Ducati: Design in the Sign of Emotion*, trans. Richard Sadleir (St Paul, MN: MBI Publishing, 2001), p. 102.

7 Dean Adams, "The man behind the MV Agusta F4 . . . and the Ducati 916: Interview: Massimo Tamburini," trans. Jonathan Maizel, May 16, 2005, <www.superbikeplanet.com/tambo.htm>.

8 Jon F. Thompson and Joe Bonnello, *Ducati* (Osceola, WI: MBI Publishing, 1998), p. 15.

9 *The Art of the Motorcycle* (New York: Guggenheim Museum, 1998), p. 379.

10 John Alt, "Popular culture and mass consumption: the motorcycle as cultural commodity," *Journal of Popular Culture* 15/4 (1982): 129–41: 136.

11 Thomas Krens, "Preface," *The Art of The Motorcycle* (New York: Guggenheim Museum), p. 16.

12 Paul Rutherford, personal correspondence, March 30, 2005.

13 Doug Abadie, personal correspondence, March 30, 2005.

14 For example, "The Art of the Motorcycle" exhibition at the Guggenheim museum, and "Ducati 2000 – An Icon for the Century" exhibition at the University of Northumbria, Newcastle upon Tyne; see Walker, "Icons for the foolish few," p. 119. The poem is "Milan," by Frederick Seidel, quoted in Carugati, *Ducati*, p. 129.

15 John Dewey, *Art as Experience* (New York: Capricorn Books, 1958).

16 Mark Haldane, personal correspondence, April 7, 2005.

17 Carugati, *Ducati*, front cover.

18 Penny Sparke, *Italian Design: 1870 to the Present* (London: Thames and Hudson, 1988), p. 7.

19 Ibid., p. 8.

20 Ibid., p. 10.

21 Falloon, *The Ducati Story*, p. 143.

22 "Ducati 916," *Cycle World* (July 1994): 30–4: 34.

23 Ibid., pp. 30–2.

24 Barry Brummett, *Rhetoric of Machine Aesthetics* (Westport, CT: Praeger, 1999), p. 16.

25 Albert Gregori, personal correspondence, May 12, 2005.

26 Carugati, *Ducati*, p. 139.

27 Ducatiexperience.com.

28 F. T. Marinetti, "The founding and manifesto of futurism 1909," in Umbro Apollonio, ed., *Futurist Manistos*, trans. R. W. Flint, J. C. Higgitt, and Caroline Tisdall (London: Thames and Hudson, 1973), p. 21.

29 "Ducati 916," *Cycle World* (July 1994): 35.

30 Kevin Ash, "Soul-ed Out!," *Motor Cycle News* (February 2, 1994): 12.

31 Abadie, personal correspondence.

32 Andrew Kruger, personal correspondence, May 12, 2005.

33 F. T. Marinetti, "Multiplied man and the reign of the machines," in R. W. Flint, ed., *Marinetti: Selected Writings*, trans. R. W. Flint and Arthur A. Coppotelli (New York: Farrar, Straus and Girous, 1972), p. 91.

34 Rutherford, personal correspondence.

35 Gregori, personal correspondence.

36 Haldane, personal correspondence.

37 Charles M. Falco, "Issues in the evolution of the motorcycle," *The Art of the Motorcycle* (New York: Guggenheim Museum, 1998), p. 26.

38 Carugati, *Ducati*, pp. 33, 35–7.

39 Thompson and Bonnello, *Ducati*, p. 7.

40 Falloon, *The Ducati Story*, p. 144.

41 See <www.ducati.com/racing/00_home_racing/corse/index.jhtml?family =duccorse#> for a full list of racing results.

42 Jingle by Dino Berti, translated and quoted in Carugati, *Ducati*, p. 17.

43 Carugati, *Ducati*, p. 20.

44 Rutherford, personal correspondence.

45 Thompson and Bonnello, *Ducati*, pp. 7, 9.

46 Ducati.net

47 Tony McGillvery, personal correspondence, April 1, 2005.

48 Gregori, personal correspondence.

49 Alt, "Popular culture and mass consumption," pp. 130–1.

50 John Orchard, personal correspondence, March 17, 2005.

51 Haldane, personal correspondence.

52 Radio jingle, quoted in Carugati, *Ducati*, p. 23.

53 Kruger, personal correspondence.

54 netrider.

55 Ducati.net.

56 Abadie, personal correspondence.

57 netrider.

58 Carugati, *Ducati*, p. 139.

59 See Jeremy Packer and Mary K. Coffey "Hogging the road: cultural governance and the citizen cyclist," *Cultural Studies* 18/5 (2004): 641–74.

60 Falloon, *The Ducati Story*, p. 161.

61 Ibid., p. 167.

62 Advertisement, *Rapid Bikes* (February/March 2005): 11.

10

The Best Propaganda: Humphrey Jennings, *The Silent Village* (1943)

John Hartley

The story of the men of Lidice,
who lit in Fascist darkness a lamp that shall never be put out.[1]

All art is propaganda . . . however, not all propaganda is art.
                                        George Orwell[2]

It may not immediately be obvious why propaganda should feature at all in a collection about "beautiful things" in popular culture. Unlike most of the other items selected for inclusion in the book, propaganda is typically not chosen or purchased by its consumers; rather, it is foisted upon them. Propaganda is hardly "in" popular culture; or if so it's like a virus – something that infests an environment for its own purposes, which may be harmful to the host organism. And no one, at least those of us drilled in modern Western democratic-process ideologies, is supposed to *like* propaganda.

But I love Humphrey Jennings's 1943 wartime propaganda film, *The Silent Village*. More than that, I nominate it as the *best* propaganda, of which there has been a lot, and I've seen a lot, some of it much more famous than this two-reel black-and-white Anglo-Czechoslovak-Welsh film from 1943, including several other Jennings films. So, before discussing *The Silent Village* itself, it is necessary to consider why propaganda has such a bad press in the West, and why some of it might be considered beautiful anyway, even when as in this case its subject is total war.[3]

———————— **Propaganda and Democracy** ————————

The default definition of propaganda in English bears all the traces of political history going back to the Reformation and the French Revolution: hatred of (a) the Catholics and (b) the French – foreign religion and foreign ideology. Witness these quotations from the *OED*:

> 1842 BRANDE *Dict. Sci.* Derived from this celebrated society [Congregatio de Propaganda Fide], the name *propaganda* is applied in modern political language as a term of reproach to secret associations for the spread of opinions and principles which are viewed by most governments with horror and aversion.

And:

> 1807 *Weekly Inspector* (N.Y.) 28 Mar. 75/1 We have ever been disposed to attribute the wonderful success of the French, since their revolutionary era, to *Propagandism* or, in other words, to the poison of their principles, circulated by their emissaries; and corrupting the *mind* of the nations they proposed to attack.

Since the very idea of propaganda is to subvert a given country's religion, its government or even its "mind," and to put that nation in jeopardy of attack, it would seem to follow that "the best" propaganda is that which succeeds in producing, from the point of view of the "home" nation, the worst possible outcomes. Recommending "the best" of such a weapon is surely perverse or worse – tantamount to trying to name "the best Fenian outrage" or "the best suicide bombing." It is in provocative bad taste.

Propaganda appears to strike at the heart of a basic proposition of Western-style democracies. Political theory requires that the sovereign citizen-voter is the *source* not the destination of both political legitimacy and government actions, so nothing is more important to democracy than that the citizen is informed. Michael Schudson has argued that in the USA the conception of the citizen has evolved since the early days of the Republic, from a democracy of trust (in prominent families), via a democracy of partisanship with the ascendancy of political parties, to "a democracy of information," and finally (currently) a "democracy of rights." He says that the *information* democracy was established between 1880 and 1910 and featured the "elevation of the individual, educated, rational voter as the model citizen": "Politics came to be organized and narrated in a way more accessible to rational reflection. Presidents made promises, crafted programs, offered comprehensive federal budgets, and championed policies. Newspapers covered politics with a degree of dispassion."[4]

Schudson points out, however, that just as this rational model of citizenship gained ground at the turn of the twentieth century, emphasizing the exercise of individual choice, so individual participation in voting drastically fell. It was the earlier carnivalesque ritual of expressing public loyalty to a partisan cause that brought voters to the ballot box, not the private calculus of rational information. And so, perversely, the elevation of the "informed citizen" produced an equal but opposite need for new devices to persuade the voter to vote at all. In short, reason and emotion learnt to coexist, not least in the form of spectacular party conventions and presidential campaigns.

Political campaigning using propaganda techniques became an internal necessity for democracies, while foreign propaganda remained an external threat. The "horror and aversion" of those who were at the receiving end of propaganda soon turned to imitation and reciprocation. Propaganda necessarily became indigenized. Thenceforth, a distinction had to be made between "our" propaganda and "theirs." One goal of "our" propaganda in times of emergency was to drum up *enmity* (not rational calculus) to the point where citizens would be willing to kill for their country, a feat that required "carefully concerted propaganda" (such as war movies) to overcome self-restraint and "legitimize . . . the joy of killing and destruction that have been repressed from everyday civilized life."[5]

Propaganda and Publicity

Meanwhile, in everyday civilized life, what may be called "informed consumption" prospered too. Consumers needed to be persuaded to choose wisely just as citizens did. Soon the term began to be applied to commercial as well as political campaigns, although the term (as opposed to the practice) remained stigmatized in the US. The *OED* again:

> 1929 G. SELDES *You can't print That!* 427 The term propaganda has not the sinister meaning in Europe which it has acquired in America . . .

In European business offices the word means advertising or boosting
generally

And:

1938 R. G. COLLINGWOOD *Princ. Art* ii. 32 Where a certain practical
activity is stimulated as expedient, that which stimulates it is advertisement
or (in the current modern sense, not the old sense) propaganda.

Expert elites in politics and commerce became skilled in propaganda
techniques while seeking to persuade their own citizen-consumers to
resist propaganda from disapproved sources. A fundamental contradiction
entered the life of commercial democracies: consumers and voters *must*
be influenced by persuasive campaigns (to buy this, vote for that, go to
war); whereas the notion of the "informed citizen" required that they
must not succumb to propaganda.

The contradiction had to be resolved at the point of reception, because
popular culture was thoroughly suffused with propaganda, which soon
became part of the everyday fabric of modernity. As the familiar cliché
about the media has it, citizen-consumers are "constantly bombarded"
(as if by the French) with advertising, PR, spin, and party political publicity. The skills of daily life soon included navigating such stuff, much as
everyone had to learn how to navigate crowded streets, where some
attempts to attract one's attention would be far from welcome, while
others were part of the pleasure of being out in public. Propaganda was
not a national matter, but something that the general population had to
deal with personally every day. Just as most people pick up the skills
required to get by unmolested in the city, so they soon learn how to avoid
commercial democracy's many blandishments. And since familiarity does
breed contempt, propaganda could not escape it.

Naturally a propensity to aversion among the target population spurred
the experts and professionals to greater efforts in their attempt to get the
blasé commuter to make eye contact with their proffered delights. Propagandists learnt the tricks of popular entertainment, including the use
of mass psychology and marketing. Over time, the semiotic intensity of
modern life became self-generating; people expected more from those
who presumed to address them. Audiences and consumers took their
reading competencies and avoidance strategies with them from street to
screen, and propaganda followed them there.

Politics is not only a matter of rational calculation but also a source of affiliative passions and an object of personal desires. Some propaganda was able to hit the emotional, aesthetic, or spectacular mark. Advertising professionals, psychological experts, and visual artists occasionally excelled themselves, producing work that long outlived its instrumental purpose. It could be thrilling at the time and actually provoke those actions desired by the propagandist. Later on it might achieve timeless status. For instance, inaugurating the age of YOU – direct address to the citizen in order to provoke individual action – was Alfred Leete's "Your Country Needs You" (1914, British) and James Flagg's Uncle Sam version of it (1916, US).[6]

Documentary realism could serve as propaganda too, as could the "decisive moment" of photojournalism. This was the fate that awaited Joe Rosenthal's 1945 photograph of Marines raising the US flag over Mt Suribachi. While "Iwo Jima" started life as a news photo for AP (and remains under copyright to them), it was immediately converted to US propaganda use on 3.5 million posters for the Seventh War Loan Drive. Since then it has become "the most reproduced photograph of all time"[7] – literally the picture that "won" WW2 for the American century.

Propaganda and Reality

Propaganda was visibly present in the form of commercials and sponsorship in the mass media, but its techniques also pervaded modernity's two great realisms, drama and journalism. It turned up in – and *as* – movies and news. This is not to say that propagandists deliberately subverted the purpose of the information media, although that certainly did happen on all sides from time to time. The point is almost the opposite; i.e., that propaganda and the techniques used to reveal the real were the same. Both propaganda and news turned social or political problems into conflict-narratives; both traded in negatives; both cast ordinary people as the victim; both used eyewitness techniques and documentary reportage to establish authenticity; both used expert commentary (the omniscient male voice-over) to invoke a preferred solution; both resolved the plot by showing happy or grateful citizens, or where the plot was not resolved by showing their ongoing misery.[8]

Where they differed was in the attribution of agency to the solution. News reported on the agency of expert institutions that acted on behalf

Table 10.1 Propaganda and news: differential audience positioning[10]

Realism (news, novel)	Propaganda
attention drawn into text	attention directed beyond text
conflict resolved diegetically (in story)	conflict provoked dialogically (in audience)
aligned to past (completed action)	aligned to present/future (action to come)
judgmental omniscient spectator	engaged active participant
truth in objects	truth in faithfulness to cause
mimetic representation	techniques on display
fix the future with the present	challenge the present with the future

of the citizen-viewer. It sought narrative transparency, following a realist aesthetic where truth can be seen to arise from facts, evidence, and the properties of the real as observed and reported by accurate techniques. But propaganda was not a spectacle about the drama of the real; it was a call to arms. The agency required to solve problems was not a representative body but YOU.[9]

Propaganda is much less respectful of current realities than is realism, because it is primarily interested in what may become true in the future. It can therefore be much more open about how it seeks to achieve its effects, including the fact that it intends to have those effects upon "YOU," the viewer. So propaganda differs from realism in this crucial respect, that it positions the audience quite differently (see table 10.1).

Propaganda and Art

Realism and propaganda have been kept separate in Western political rhetoric in order to preserve the idea of the informed citizen. But there was no such need to distinguish propaganda from art. The Old Masters were propagandists for their patrons, both religious and political, like Michelangelo for successive popes and Vasari for the Medicis. Two of the most admired modern oil paintings were conceived and received as anti-war propaganda: Goya's *Third of May 1808*,[11] and Picasso's *Guernica*.[12] Robert Hughes has written about Goya's "great propaganda pieces":

> The content of [Goya's] utterance, the perception that war is a despicable and monstrous injustice, an impartial machine that kills men like cattle and, most of the time, leaves no residue of glory behind it, is the prototype of all modern views of war. What the common people of Europe discovered in their millions in the twentieth century . . . Goya foreshadowed [and] gave monumental form to in the *Third of May*.[13]

Hughes claims this propaganda artwork as the prototype of "all modern views of war" – the focus on common people rather than leaders, on suffering and death rather than on glory, on faceless mechanized militarism against human values, on documenting events rather than portraying idealized dynasts. He compares the key figure in the painting not with art but with contemporary journalism:

> Goya's stocky little martyr-of-the-people is one of the most vivid human "presences" in all art. . . . He is a two-hundred-year-old equivalent of those few photo images that leaked out of Vietnam into long, emblematic life: the screaming naked girl running away from a napalm strike, toward the camera, the chinless police chief blowing out the brains of a plaid-shirted suspect at point-blank range with his kicking .38 on a Saigon street.[14]

The industrial age produced art out of its own political and commercial enthusiasms, shifting from oil painting to distributional arts like the promotional poster and cinema. El Lissitzky's 1919 poster *Beat the Whites with the Red Wedge* has become a design classic,[15] and the anti-Nazi photomontage of John Heartfield (Helmut Herzfelde)[16] has inspired successive art/politics movements and leftist agit-prop from Dadaism right up to Rock Against Racism.[17] The most famous prototypes of propaganda in cinema are Sergei Eisenstein's 1925 *Battleship Potemkin*, and Leni Riefenstahl and Walter Ruttmann's 1934 *Triumph of the Will*.[18] Both attempted to show the energy and power, to say nothing of the inevitability, of modernization from below; the replacement of old order with a dream of proletarian supremacy, socialism, and national socialism respectively, before the ideal turned to totalitarian nightmare on both sides. Their reputation rests on their status as cinema, on artistic grounds; they are emptied of the very meanings for the communication of which they were originally commissioned. Indeed, perhaps because the USSR and the Third Reich have themselves collapsed, these two films seem to cause less contemporary offence than the prototype of cinema itself and the first American feature film, D. W. Griffith's 1915 *Birth of a Nation*. For many, its merits as a movie are still overshadowed by the story of a US founded in racism, a nation "born" in the actions of the Ku Klux Klan.[19]

Why then, given a crowded field, is Humphrey Jennings' *The Silent Village* the best propaganda?

Silent Villages

The village was the mining community of Lidice in the Czech Republic. In 1942 it was in the occupied German "protectorate" of Bohemia and Moravia, whose governor (Reichsprotektor) was SS Obergruppenführer Reinhard Heydrich (*The Butcher of Prague* or *Der Henker – the Hangman*). Heydrich was one of the architects of the Holocaust, chairing the January 1942 Wannsee "Final Solution" conference that laid out the plans for the extermination of all European Jews. He was assassinated in Prague by RAF-assisted Czech partisans, dying on June 4, 1942.[20] Nazi reprisals included the murder of more than 1,300 Czechs, among them the destruction of two villages:

* Lidice (June 10): out of a total population of 500, 340 died. The entire male population of 173 men was shot, the women and children deported. Estimates suggest that 143 women survived the war and 85 died; 17 children survived the war and 82 died. The village was razed. It was rebuilt after the war.[21]
* Ležáky (June 24): 32 or 33 men were shot; 11 women and children deported, two infants survived the war.[22] Ležáky was razed and has not been rebuilt.

The destruction of Lidice was reported in Britain, causing a great stir. A Czech poet and diplomat called Viktor Fischl (a.k.a. Dagan Avigdor), exiled in London with the Czech government, interested Humphrey Jennings of the Crown Film Unit in the idea of making a film about the atrocity. Jennings scouted South Wales – a mountainous mining area comparable to the Czech landscape – for suitable locations. He found the small village of Cwmgiedd [pronounced koom-geethe], near Ystalyfera in the upper Swansea valley, under the glowering bulk of Mynydd Ddu (the Black Mountain).

Jennings virtually took it over. He lived there for several months, giving lectures at the local Miners' Institute, making notes toward his book *Pandaemonium*,[23] and coaching the population of Cwmgiedd to take the collective role of the people of Lidice (by playing themselves) in his film. *The Silent Village* is an early version of a "re-enactment" documentary – it depicts the events of Lidice by having the villagers of Cwmgiedd re-enact them; but at the same time it is straightforward documentary, since the people, the life they live, and the issues they deal with all belong to Cwmgiedd itself and to the South Wales mining community, in time of war. In this respect it is also an early version of "reality" programming – like *Big Brother*, it puts ordinary people in a difficult situation and lets us observe their humanity as they cope with it; except of course that "Big Brother" in this case was the real one – not Humphrey Jennings, but a totalitarian state.

The Silent Village and Reality

Watching the film, it helps, although it is not essential, if you know something about Jennings and his other films. There's a language and grammar at work which is part documentary convention, part Jennings's own poetic idiom. You'd know from *Listen to Britain*, for instance, that shots of the countryside, especially stands of elms and flowing streams, signify the natural continuities underlying his particular vision of British-ness. You might know that Jennings was fascinated by "the coming of the machine" to Britain – the world's first industrialized country – and that locomotives, mines, and factories figured prominently in his imagery. You'd have remembered his charismatic use of sound from the "sym-phonic" *Listen to Britain*; his ability to carry meanings and moods without words, by the skilful editing and layering of sync, effects, and music. You might even recognize his interest in surrealism and collage from some of the odd juxtapositions or symbols. Jennings also uses docu-mentary conventions that help the viewer by showing how time and seasons pass, and he associates those seasons with moods of the action (it's summer morning at the beginning; snowy winter by the end).

The Silent Village is in two parts, showing life before the coming of the Nazis and then what happens afterwards. It opens with a "day in the life" of Cwmgiedd, showing all of the important locations in the village – the big white-painted chapel, the very heart of the village, with a high wall around the graveyard, the pit with its stark chimneys and winding gear towers, the school, terraced houses, and the shop. We're introduced to the people by seeing what they do through a working day – everyone singing in the chapel, colliers working at the pit, teacher and pupils chanting in the schoolroom, women cleaning house, doing the washing, breaking coal, and scrubbing the front step, a man digging an allotment, customers in the shop getting by with an extra jar of pickle despite the rationing. There's a fair bit of talk and it is all in Welsh, without subtitles, augmented by the singing we heard at the beginning from the chapel. We see the end of a shift, the naked blackened colliers showering and showing what fine tenor voices they have, the schoolday finishing with Teacher saying "P'nawn da plant" (Good afternoon children) and their polite response before they scamper away. A wide shot reminds us of the valley, and the time of day; then the evening activities get under way. The men walk home to the strains of "Gwyr Harlech" (Men of Harlech). We see them joining their families, presided over by traditional "mam" in her apron who dispenses tea. We also see the more modern kids at the cinema enjoying a Donald Duck cartoon, men at the pub chatting, and union officials of the Miners' Federation – known as "the Fed" – holding a branch meeting to discuss silicosis. The sequence ends with a fast-cut collage of scenes under an inspiring male-voice choir, showing the mountain under which the coal lies, the stream through the center of the village, the stone bridge with a horse and cart toiling across, the pit working at night, the terraced houses – and then their interiors where we see a couple quietly at home: he's reading, she's sewing; in another house a young woman is being fitted with her wedding dress, a man plays with a toddler, a young girl dresses her teddy, mam helps a boy with his homework, nan brushes baby's hair . . . and again we see the chapel, peaceful at night.

Jennings has quietly introduced us to almost everything he needs to tell the story of Lidice. Now we are to see all these scenes and people again, but with a deepening sense of horror. Between them, Jennings and the villagers have created a socialist-utopian vision of a strong community united in language and purpose, in its associations – the Fed, chapel, school, and shop, and in the rhythms of family and neighborly life played out under the shadow of both nature and industry, season and siren. Jennings makes the vision arise from the villagers; this is a film about Wales, imagined as fully as possible in its own terms in order to stand convincingly for Czechoslovakia. We can only feel the terror of Lidice's destruction if we're convinced by the values of Cwmgiedd, and begin at once to care for its way of life.

Meanwhile, Jennings has introduced cinema-goers the world over to a neglected part of Britain, using the vehicle of government-sponsored propaganda to tell the story of the industrial working class from the inside. He allows no external reference to intrude into this vision. There are no celebrity actors, no imposition of a shaping authorial voice (a bad habit that bedeviled British documentary films from Grierson's *Night Mail* onwards), no reference to the British government (with whom both Jennings and the villagers would have had their differences despite the war effort), nor even of the war itself that villagers, crew, and audiences alike knew was on to the death.

Now an inter-title signals the shift to the second part of the film: "*Such is life at Cwmgiedd, and such too was life in Lidice until the coming of the Nazis.*" How does Jennings use his slender resources to re-enact the invasion of a country, subjugation of its people, and then tell the true story of how a brutal governor is assassinated, leading to the reprisals at the end? This is surely too much to ask of an amateur cast, too expensive to achieve on the budget of a documentary? Aided by his surrealist sensibility, Jennings is more than a match for this challenge. Militarism, Nazism, and occupation are reduced to their essence in a few simple symbols. A gleaming official car, always blaring military music or a German voice, but whose occupants are never seen, stands for German militarism. It is in fact a very English SS Jaguar, but it looks suitably alien in rural Cwmgiedd, and there's gallows humor in its name – SS. On its roof is mounted an enormous loudspeaker to stand for the alien language of the aggressor, the techniques of totalitarianism, and to convey the orders of the invader. Domestic radios carry the propaganda of the occupying force into the homes that we've come to know. Beyond a few glimpses of uniformed guards in the later action scenes we never see the enemy. This shows Nazism as dehumanized and mechanistic, and foregrounds what the war is being fought *for*, not against. In short, Jennings solved production constraints in a way that enhanced rather than limited the imaginative force of the film.

Jennings draws us in to the story of Lidice by stages, asking his village cast only to do what would have been within their everyday repertoire. The second part of *The Silent Village* begins with the stream again, now running fast; then cuts to the bridge on which we'd seen the horse and cart of the delivery man. Now it carries the intrusive alien car, harbinger of occupation with its military music, which turns into the village and passes the familiar scenes; houses, knots of women, the shopkeeper. They all turn to look. A disembodied German voice from the loudspeaker informs the villagers of the new reality.

A new scene, and already conditions have worsened. The car returns; the loudspeaker informs the population that under the authority of Reichsprotektor SS Obergruppenführer Reinhard Heydrich it is permissible to set aside existing laws, to confiscate property, hand people over to the secret police or impose the death penalty. The next scene shows the reaction of the miners, led by the officials of the Fed; they respond to the news that unions are "no longer needed" by going through an all too evidently democratic process and voting to strike.

The Jag returns to threaten "enemies of the state" with destruction. Suddenly there's small-arms fire in the hills surrounding the village. Everyone looks. We see men running, carrying a stretcher – then the chapel interior, and a home where a wounded man lies – "Mae'r wedi marw" (he has died). We see the chapel – hymns again – this time for the dead; outside the trees tremble in the wind.

Now the school. The teacher announces in English that an order has been received that there is to be "no more Welsh spoken" in school. This is a breathtaking bit of displacement, for as every Welsh viewer would know it was the English government that suppressed the speaking of Welsh in schools in the nineteenth century, using a punishment known as the "Welsh Not" to discourage its use.[24] For those among the audience who don't know the history, the brutal gesture of conquest is clear; for those who do, the pain of such an order is already felt. The teacher makes the children promise to speak Welsh at home, on the roadside, at play – "do not forget your Welsh."

We see the ruined castle above the village. A reminder of the English conquest of Wales, now it is where patriotic saboteurs gather. Next, a housewife with a printing kit, turning out copies of *LLAIS-Y-WERIN* (Voice of the People), whose heading reads "Cynnyrch Gweriniaeth yw Rhyddid" (The Product of Democracy is Liberty). The same woman now listens impassively while ironing at home, as her husband translates what it says. A voice-over in Welsh then English intones: "What is to be done? Go back to the mines. Work slow. Organize sabotage. Put sand in the machine. Pour water in the oil." Who among the audience would have recalled that "What is to be Done?" is the title of a revolutionary pamphlet by Lenin? Who would have stirred uneasily in their seats as socialist miners plotted industrial sabotage? Would any of them have remembered that less than a decade earlier in 1934 the then Home Secretary had called out the troops onto the streets of Tonypandy in South Wales to confront these same miners as if they were armed insurrectionists, or that the Home Secretary in question was none other than wartime Prime Minister Winston Churchill, head of the very government on whose behalf the people of Cwmgiedd were now enacting sabotage and insurrection?

The next scene escalates the conflict. Under a soundtrack featuring the traditional Welsh song "Ar hyd y nos" (All through the night) we see the same faces and knots of people that we've seen before, but now their words signify conspiracy. We see the ruined castle on the hill, symbol of ancient struggles for independence. Then a lyrical moment – a man in his parlor pours warmed milk into a bottle while his wife cuddles the baby – before glimpses of the mine and the chapel and graveyard under snow.

We see a dramatization of resistance – a black-faced miner shoots a uniformed guard; another is taken down by assassins; the mine-workings are dynamited. Cut to the school: the now English-speaking teacher proclaims to the children: "The conquest of Wales was a very slow process . . ." Cut to the ruined castle; to the smoking mine and a wide view of the valley.

At this point a voice introduces news of the assassination attempt on Reichsprotektor Heydrich; a German accent speaking over a hurriedly pasted-up wall-poster. We glimpse a German soldier with a rifle, standing guard in front of the village War Memorial. Cut to a domestic radio set. The voice demands information about a lady's bicycle, serial number 40363, implicated in the attempt on Heydrich, and requires all residents to report for "registration" at the state police HQ. Failure will render them liable to be shot. We see the school behind the bars of a locked iron gate.

The villagers line up to be "registered." It is done with dramatic tension and narrative economy. Each one comes to a desk. We see so much in each person's face, expression, stance, and garb. Here is a true portrait of what is valuable about individuals no matter what their station. It is already an elegy of a lost community. Each person gives their name, age and occupation:

W. H. Morgan, 40, teacher
Gwen Jones, 47, housewife
L. T. Jones, 50, collier
David Alexander, 55, collier

Myfanwy Alexander, 49, housewife
Owen Alexander, 55, milkman
Edith Williams, 22, home duties
H. C. Williams, 24, collier
Margaret Daniel, 40, teacher
Thomas Lewis, 36, collier, blacksmith

A radio inside one of the houses continues the roll-call of villagers, but these people have been "sentenced to death by shooting." Apparently they had "publicly approved" of the attempt on Heydrich. The radio-voice intones:

David Davies, born 1901
Hannah Davies, born 1903
Dai Alec Davies, born 1922
Meaghan Davies, born 1924
Glynnis Davies, born 1925

Someone listening to the radio protests, "she only just laughed at them": a capital offence, a whole family wiped out.

A cutaway to the shop then back to the radio; Heydrich is dead. The disembodied voice recites an elegy to him, then continues with sentences of death: "Ianto Evans, born 1884 . . ." A hand switches off the radio – no more!

Now the loudspeaker on the car is merciless: the village has "aided and abetted" the assassins, and will "produce" them by midnight. We see again the people, the stream, trees – and a clock ticking over to midnight.

The sky shows dawn. "Mae hen wlad fy nhadau" (the Welsh national anthem – Land of My Fathers) fades up on the soundtrack. We see the chapel wall. The menfolk are discovered, singing the anthem, shrinking slowly back against the wall. Cut to the children, sunlight bathing their silhouettes, as they are marched under armed guard across the playground to waiting lorries. The women are tramping across the bridge, clutching their bundles. One looks back. The men are lined up against the wall. They sing the anthem to the end. At that instant, we hear shots as the picture cuts to the cemetery, the language to German, the music to Wagner. We see the burning wreckage of the school, broken items from homes (a sewing machine, a portrait), lying in the stream. Gothic script proclaims the sentence:

𝕬ll the male adults of the village have been shot, the women have been sent to a concentration camp, the children have been handed over to the appropriate authorities. The buildings of the locality have been leveled to the ground and the name of the community has been obliterated —

But – a new caption tells us – "that is not the end of the story." We see the valley again, restored to here-and-now Welshness: a shepherd leads his flock down the lane, the children skip into the playground, women and members of the Fed cluster to read the proclamation. The voice of the union official insists: "the name of the community has not been obliterated. It lives in the hearts of miners the world over." The Nazis want slavery, but miners won't be slaves, "because we have the power, knowledge, and understanding to hasten the coming of victory – to liberate oppressed humanity, to make sure there are no more Lidices, and then the men of Lidice will not have died in vain." Cut to a poster advertising: "Mass Meeting: Lidice Shall Live Again," and a tumble of miners coming toward the camera as if at the end of a shift, at ease, talking and joking, while the last song swells, coal-wagons trundle past, and we withdraw from Cwmgiedd via its chimneys, coal-conveyer chutes, steam, and behind them the brightening sun.

——— *The Silent Village* and **Democracy** ———

The Silent Village is propaganda but there's nothing "governmental" or even "political" about it. It does not preach a doctrine or attempt to persuade audiences to a cause or an action beyond democracy itself and to "honor" Lidice. If anything, it seeks to inform citizens about *themselves.* In other words, at the heart of *The Silent Village* is a vision of *popular culture* – the culture of the people "as a class," as Jennings puts it in *Pandaemonium,*[25] made by the people themselves. The likelihood of that culture being "silenced" by Fascism is what motivates its passion.

The radically democratic step that Jennings takes from this threat is to show these same people taking the defense of that culture into their own hands, not delegating the use of violence to the state and bureaucratizing it in the army as was usual in war films,[26] but exercising it directly, and organizing it through associations like the Fed, which their own state, never mind that of the enemy, is known to have treated only recently as subversive and threatening to its authority.

Jennings does not assume that viewers would be aware of the details of life in working-class Wales any more than they would know much about Czechoslovakia. He expects the audience to see their own lives within those details, and so he has been at pains to get them right, letting some of the local peculiarities and difficulties of language, class, and nation poke through the idealized portrait of community and family life, in order to show that they apply everywhere. The villagers are convincing as Czech miners – and by extension suffering humanity at large – because they are authentic about themselves. Hence, and challengingly for the legitimacy of state authority anywhere, the justification the film offers for the use of violence by private individuals also applies everywhere.

Jennings's vision of "popular culture" is not just broad (i.e. humanist), it is also deep – it speaks to everyone in society, from top to toe, integrating the lives of ordinary people into the fate of nations. Others have commented on the extent to which wartime Britain really did achieve a popular egalitarian national purpose, and Jennings did it in other films too, notably *Listen to Britain*, but *The Silent Village* is unusual in making the popular source of that unity so clearly class-based and non-metropolitan – even non-English.

But the result is more Shakespeare than socialism. Jennings links the top of society with the bottom, national survival with workers' lives. The film lets ordinary people speak for themselves, but they get to speak *about* something much more important than their own conditions. There's not a word of the self-expression or identity politics that limits so much documentary about ordinary people, and there's not a whiff of the documentary tradition of the victim.[27] *The Silent Village* makes the people the protagonists of the most important drama in the people's century: their actions can change history; their humanity can move the audience. Seeing this film, we know why we're democrats and "what is to be done."

The Silent Village and Publicity[28]

Propaganda it may have been, but this "great little film" (*Daily Express*) was well received at the time by professional peers and the untutored public alike, even by the Americans. It was favorably reviewed in *Time* magazine: "all it takes to make screen fact as good as the best screen fiction is the know-how."[29] It was nominated for an Oscar as Best Documentary Feature for 1943 (won by another British propaganda movie, *Desert Victory*).[30] Jennings became a scion of film history, a favorite of scholars and filmmakers. Lindsay Anderson, Richard Attenborough, Lord Puttnam, and Mike Leigh are all professed fans, although the films they mention most are *Listen To Britain* (1942), *Fires Were Started* (1942), and *Diary for Timothy* (1945).[31]

The Silent Village and Art

Many films boast that you can see "the money on the screen." An extraordinary feature of this film is displacement. What you see on the screen is *not* the means of production. You see what Jennings called the "means of vision."[32] *The Silent Village* inherits Jennings's knowledge of and interest in high art, his views about industrialization and class, his leftism, his delight in cinema as an entertainment medium, even his role as a propagandist, heir to Goya and "Your Country Needs YOU" alike. But the film *displaces* it all. It's not even like *Listen to Britain* or *London Can Take It*. It's not about Britain, but about Czechoslovakia. It's not English, but Welsh; not about war, but community; not about enemy, but us. Its characters are actors, but play themselves. The drama they narrate is about Lidice, but it is also about issues closer to home. Anyone in the know would understand what was being said by the Fed about the power of the union, by the teacher about the language, and by a working community about how they have created their own culture. All of these matters are part of British politics, toward which the Welsh have justifiably ambivalent feelings.[33] But Jennings displaces all of this to the common cause – there's a greater threat, which miners as part of an international community are fighting for independently. At the time these gestures of displacement must have been what enabled Jennings to make the film; now they're the undertow that gives it power and resilience far beyond other examples of the genre (*Triumph of the Will* is long and dull).

This is what makes *The Silent Village* worth watching generations later. It takes popular culture seriously, and it's still an enthralling drama. Its real stars are the people in it. The Czechs and the people of Wales both still remember it, and each claims it as part of *their own* history.[34] In Cwmgiedd, they delight in seeing their forebears, and tell stories of their uncles and aunties who had to play dead in a cowshed for this charismatic Englishman.[35]

But in one respect *The Silent Village* remains very contemporary. It is an early example of "ProAm" or interactive production in the making of movies; what might now be called "consumer co-creation." The skills and passions of the filmmaker are needed of course, but they are at the service of a greater work; one which casts the consumer as actor (not behavior), turning the major mass medium of the time from a "read-only" format into a "read and write" means of communication for its own consumers to send a message of hope across the world. The result is great collaborative art imagining genuinely popular culture. Look on this work, Big Brother, and do better.

Notes

1   On-screen credits as follows: "*The Silent Village,* Produced and Directed Humphrey Jennings; Photography H. E. Fowle; Film Editor Stewart McAllister; Sound Jock May; Asst. Director Diana Pine. Produced by the Crown Film Unit with the collaboration of the Czechoslovak Ministry of Foreign Affairs, the South Wales Miners' Federation and the people of the Swansea and Dulais Valleys. The Silent Village: The story of the men of Lidice who lit in Fascist darkness a lamp that shall never be put out." *The Silent Village,* along with numerous other Jennings films, is available for sale via <www.moviemail-online.co.uk/films/9186>.

2   George Orwell, "Charles Dickens," *Inside the Whale and other Essays* (London: Victor Gollancz, 1940). See <etext.library.adelaide.edu.au/o/orwell/george/o79e/part10.html>.

3   John Hartley, "The politics of photopoetry," *Tele-ology: Studies in Television* (London: Routledge, 1992), pp. 147–57.

4   Michael Schudson, *The Good Citizen: A History of American Civic Life* (Cambridge, MA: Harvard University Press, 1999). See also <web.mit. edu/m-i-t/articles/schudson.html>.

5   Norbert Elias, *The Civilizing Process* (Oxford: Blackwell, 1939), p. 170. See J. David Slocum, "Cinema and the civilizing process: rethinking violence in the World War II combat film," *Cinema Journal* 44/3 (2005): 35–63: 51.

6   Leete and Flagg's posters can be seen at <www.pbs.org/wgbh/amex/wilson/gallery/p_war_11.html>.

7   Harold Evans, *Pictures on a Page: Photo-journalism, Graphics and Picture Editing* (London: Heinemann, 1978, pp. 145–8); Mitchell Landsberg, "Fifty years later, Iwo Jima photographer fights his own battle," Associated Press, 2005, <http://www.ap.org/pages/about/pulitzer/rosenthal.html> (accessed September 11, 2005).

8 See John Hartley, *Uses of Television* (London and New York: Routledge, 1999), pp. 92–8.

9 John Hartley, *Tele-ology: Studies in* Television (London: Routledge, 1992), p. 53.

10 Ibid.

11 Robert Hughes, *Goya* (London: Harvill Press, 2003), pp. 307–19; see also p. 265.

12 John Berger, *The Success and Failure of Picasso* (New York: Vintage International, 1989/1993; originally published by Penguin Books in 1965); see also Robert Hughes, "The powers that be," in *The Shock of the New: Art and the Century of Change* (London: Thames and Hudson, 1980/1991).

13 Hughes, *Goya*, p. 319.

14 Ibid., p. 314.

15 John Hartley, *A Short History of Cultural Studies* (London: Sage Publications, 2003), pp. 64–87.

16 David Evans, ed., *John Heartfield: AIZ/VI 1930–38* (New York: Kent Gallery, 1992).

17 Red Saunders, "My favourite books," <pubs.socialistreviewindex.org.uk/sr169/saunders.htm> (accessed September 11, 2005). Red Saunders, a founder of RAR, discusses *Photomontages of the Nazi Period – John Heartfield* as his favourite book.

18 *Triumph des Willens,* dir. Leni Riefenstahl, 1935; *Battleship Potemkin,* dir. Sergei M. Eisenstein and Grigori Aleksandrov, 1925.

19 *The Birth of a Nation*, dir. D. W. Griffith, 1915.

20 "Reinhard Heydrich," <http://en.wikipedia.org/wiki/Reinhard_Heydrich> (accessed September 11, 2005).

21 "History of Lidice Village," <www.lidice-memorial.cz/history_en.aspx> (accessed September 11, 2005); see also "The Silent Village and The Second Life of Lidice," *Radio Prague*, <www.radio.cz/en/article/28586> (accessed September 11, 2005); related stories from Czech Radio can be accessed from the portal page, <www.rozhlas.cz/english/portal>, by searching "Lidice."

22 Libor Kubik, "News," *Radio Prague*, <archiv.radio.cz/news/EN/2000/02.09.html> (accessed September 11, 2005).

23 Humphrey Jennings, *Pandaemonium, 1660–1886: The Coming of the Machine as Seen by Contemporary Observers*, ed. Mary-Lou Jennings and Charles Madge from materials compiled by Jennings, *c.* 1937–50 (London, André Deutsch 1985, 1987, 1995; Picador, 1987; Papermac, 1995).

24 "The language in education – nineteenth century," BBC Wales History, <www.bbc.co.uk/wales/storyofwelsh/content/thelanguageineducation.shtml> (accessed September 11, 2005).

25 Jennings, *Pandaemonium* (1987 edn.), p. xi.

26 Slocum, "Cinema and the civilizing process," pp. 41–5.

27   Brian Winston, *Claiming the Real* (London: BFI, 1995).

28   Poster at <digilander.libero.it/suanj/suanj/La_Grande_Illusione/_private/ 1943-The%20Silent%20Village.jpg>.

29   "Documentaries Grow Up," *Time*, September 13, 1943, <www.time.com/ time/archive/preview/0,10987,791081,00.html> (accessed September 11, 2005).

30   "1943 Academy Awards," <www.infoplease.com/ipa/A0148238.html> (accessed September 11, 2005).

31   "Humphrey Jennings: the man who listened to Britain," <www.channel4. com/culture/microsites/J/jennings/index.html> (accessed September 11, 2005); also "The Humphrey Jennings collection," <www.moviemail-online. co.uk/films/14872> (accessed September 11, 2005).

32   Jennings, *Pandaemonium* (1987 edn.), p. xxxviii.

33   *Proud Valley*, dir. Penrose Tennyson, 1940.

34   See *Silent Village*, dir. Marc Evans, 1993; "Documentaries," *National Screen and Sound Archives of Wales*, <www.movinghistory.ac.uk/archives/ wa/collection.html> (accessed September 11, 2005). See also "Wales on air," <www.bbc.co.uk/wales/walesonair/database/silent.shtml#content> (accessed September 11, 2005); "Return to the silent village," National Screen and Sound Archives of Wales, <screenandsound.llgc.org.uk/news_ 014.htm> (accessed September 11, 2005); Dita Asiedu, "The Silent Village and the second life of Lidice," Radio Prague, <www.radio.cz/en/ article/28586> (accessed September 11, 2005); David Vaughan, "Passing the legacy of Lidice on to a younger generation," Radio Prague, <radio.cz/ en/article/67494> (accessed September 11, 2005); David Vaughan, "Josef Horak, a twentieth-century Czech hero," Radio Prague, <www.radio.cz/ en/article/30570> (accessed September 11, 2005).

35   "A Tale of Two Villages," <http://archiv.radio.cz/english/lidice.phtml>.

11

The Best Villain in *Xena: Warrior Princess*: Alti

Sara Gwenllian Jones

Alti scares the crap outta me, yet I want to embrace her, even though she'd off me in a millisecond.[1]

In the fantasy adventure TV show *Xena: Warrior Princess* (*XWP*), evil has many faces. There are the myriad minor and ephemeral evil-doers who are little more than fodder for Xena's sword – a motley crew of warlords, petty tyrants, outlaws, thugs, and, sometimes, mythological creatures such as giants, Cyclops, and evil centaurs. They represent a purely physical threat, either to Xena herself or to people, places, or objects that she is called upon to protect. These minor villains appear, wreak havoc, and are dispatched with relatively little difficulty within a single episode, never to be seen again.

Then there are the more formidable foes, the arch-enemies, the clever and ambitious villains with master-plans of world domination who keep coming back: Ares, the God of War, whose diabolical goal is to plunge humanity into eternal conflict; Callisto, a crazed Nemesis hell-bent on avenging the deaths of her family years earlier in an attack by Xena's army; and Julius Caesar, cunning and ruthless, who uses Xena as a pawn in his geopolitical power games.

And then there is Alti, the evil shaman.

Alti is the best villain in *Xena: Warrior Princess*.[2]

Things Fall Apart

Xena's story begins in three episodes of the earlier TV series *Hercules: The Legendary Journeys*, where she is introduced as a ruthless warlord whose army is laying waste the countryside. A series of encounters with the wholesomely heroic Hercules makes her realize the error of her ways. She abandons her career in tyranny and sets out alone to make amends for her crimes and to find a better way of living by serving the greater good of humanity. Her subsequent adventures are related in the spin-off series *Xena: Warrior Princess*, which was in production from 1995 until 2001. *XWP* picks up Xena's story not long after she has left Hercules and begins with an episode tellingly entitled "The Sins of the Past." From the outset, then, Xena is constructed as a flawed and brutalized hero – a warrior whose violent career was initiated by catastrophe when her village was attacked by a warlord and her beloved brother killed; who has at last become sickened by war; who realizes that she has become the very thing she set out to fight; who carries within her the burden of a dark and terrible past; and whose quest from now on is driven by her need to appease her conscience and to find redemption. Yet, despite her desire to reform, she retains a capacity for hatred and violence which comes to the fore when she is pushed beyond her limits, causing her to revert back into a merciless and sometimes sadistic killer. Xena's is a conflicted soul; her worst enemy is herself.

As this bleak profile indicates, Xena is not a conventional television action hero. She is, specifically, a species of *tragic* hero. In many respects, she has more in common with a hero like Achilles than she does with most female television action heroes. Like Achilles, she is a contrary and ambiguous figure, capable of dark passions and violent rage, and on a trajectory that can lead only to doom. But the fundamentally tragic construction of her character is obscured by the series' length and variety. *XWP* consists of 134 50-minute episodes, totaling more than four and a half days' running time. Between the onset and conclusion of Xena's tragic destiny there exists a very long middle which explores her predicament from different perspectives whilst doing little to advance it. Although *XWP* includes several story arcs that continue across anything from two to six episodes, the majority of episodes consist of self-contained storylines in which Xena confronts and defeats a threat without advancing any greater narrative.

At the same time, the series is characterized by an extravagant eclecticism that plays fast and loose with genres, time, geography, mythology, history, literature, popular culture, identity, and sexuality. Around and through this playful carnival of inconsistency runs the formal narrative apparatus of tragedy: the hero compelled by calamity onto the path of destiny, and driven by her own ethical substance and imperatives toward a tragic fall. Despite the lengthy hiatus between the beginning and fulfillment of Xena's tragic destiny, the logic of her personal history and the make-up of her character leads inexorably toward her eventual downfall in the series' two-part finale – the controversial "Friends in Need" episodes in which she chooses to complete the ethical gesture of her life by going at last into a battle that she knows that she must die to win (controversial because Xena's death at the end of the series outraged many fans, who found its manner too brutal and too absolute).

Because tragedy requires the hero to, in the end, accept circumstantial defeat in order to achieve ethical supremacy, the tragic hero's greatest conflict is not an external one against a physical enemy but rather her constant interior struggle to control her own instincts and impulses, to maintain her ethical integrity in the face of unbearable pressures, and to uphold the ethical cohesion of will and deed. Tragedy's emphasis upon the hero's conflicted self thus demands a particular sort of antagonist: one that matches the hero in conviction, and whose nature and actions afford opportunities for the exterior expression of the hero's inner being. The latter function is especially important in an essentially visual medium like television, which is ill-suited to soliloquies and must instead provide insight into characters' thoughts and feelings through dialogue, action, and the actors' performances. The most effective villains, then, are those that threaten not only the hero's mission in the world but who also recognize and threaten her ethical being, throwing it into crisis and thereby testing and illuminating it.

In order for the villain to present a challenge to the hero's integrity, villain and hero must display some common characteristics. Each must mirror the other in strength, resolve, and fatefulness; each must understand and yet still oppose the other. As mythologist Joseph Campbell writes, "Slayer and Dragon, sacrificer and victim, are one mind behind the scenes, where there is no polarity of contraries, but mortal enemies on the stage where the everlasting war of Gods and Titan is displayed."[3] Like a love affair, the relationship between hero and villain is an intense choreography of seduction and resistance, a battle of wills that involves the whole substance of each. Hero and villain bring each other into being, yet each is also bent upon the other's destruction.

From these dramatic and thematic imperatives, it is possible to identify the broad characteristics that define a good villain in *XWP*. First and foremost, the villain is a catalyst for heroic action and the personification of an agenda that is in opposition to that of the hero and which thereby serves to define and test the hero's commitment. The villain's main dramatic function is to present an obstacle between the hero and her objective and to complicate and threaten the hero's quest, increasing its difficulty and rendering uncertain its outcome. Secondly, in order to present a convincing challenge, the villain must therefore be a match for the hero – equal, or perhaps superior, to her in ability, intellect, strength, and determination. Although the conventions and requirements of a long-running, single-character-centered television series like *XWP* leave the audience in little doubt that the hero will eventually prevail, the villain must nevertheless be formidable enough to cause serious setbacks and to make the audience wonder *how* the hero can triumph. The hero's eventual success may be inevitable, but the means of its achievement should not be obvious and victory must seem to take its toll, pushing the hero to her limits. Although the villain cannot in the end defeat the hero (who must survive in order to return in the next episode), her actions nevertheless must put the hero *in extremis* where, reduced almost to despair, the hero's heroic qualities come to the fore: ethical integrity, courage, cunning, and resolve. The villain thereby fulfils a third dramatic and thematic function: through her actions, she affords us insights into the hero's character, and she does this by being a headfuck as well as by presenting a physical threat. Her tactics include forms of psychological warfare; she must be able to get inside the hero's head, to plant seeds of doubt, to threaten all that the hero holds dear, to twist and confuse, to manipulate and undermine.

Finally, the villain must be an interesting and complex character in her own right. Just as the character of the hero invites the audience to consider her thoughts, feelings, and intentions, so too must that of the villain. She must have a certain allure and an apparent depth. Her project may be despicable but we must be persuaded that she believes in it every bit as strongly as the hero believes in her own, and that she matches the hero's conviction. In *XWP* – a series that likes to eroticize and fetishize its characters and their encounters – the villain should also demonstrate, and perhaps arouse in the hero, a dangerous fascination. Although the villain's major project concerns the world-at-large, her engagements with Xena must also be of a profoundly personal nature. For a while, hero and villain are everything to one another. The hero's victory in the end is not merely the result of superior physical force but is rather the consequence of her spiritual and emotional superiority. Such conclusions require that there be an emphasis throughout upon the inner workings of both hero and villain. The character of the villain must tolerate speculation about her motives and goals, her strengths and weaknesses, her limitations, and the nature of her feelings about the hero.

What then of Alti?

Slouching Toward Bethlehem

Alti appears in only six episodes of *XWP* ("Adventures in the Sin Trade," parts 1 and 2; "Between the Lines"; "Them Bones, Them Bones"; "Send in the Clones"; and "When Fates Collide") and the first of these does not occur until the fourth of the series' six seasons. Despite her late arrival in the series, she is retrospectively projected into Xena's back story as a pivotal figure in her life – initially Xena's mentor and ally, and later her adversary. Thus Alti serves a double function. First, her introduction fills in a gap in the series' piecemeal construction of Xena's personal history that helps to flesh out Xena's character and adds depth to the action taking place in the present. Secondly, Alti's re-emergence as an influential figure from Xena's dark past lends extra weight and force to the series' explorations of love and hate, guilt and redemption, loyalty and betrayal, vengeance and reconciliation, and the conflicted self. These are the aspects of the series that form the basis of its appeal to a large audience of avid viewers, as is evidenced by the fact that they are addressed over and over by the series' fans, in quasi-academic essays, in fan fiction, and in discussions in chat rooms and on mailing lists and forums, where Xena's back story is pieced together and endlessly analyzed, embellished, and reworked.

Alti is introduced in the double episode "Adventures in the Sin Trade," which relates two distinct but cross-connected stories. The "A" storyline is set in the diegetic present where, half mad with grief, Xena searches for her companion/lover Gabrielle, whom she believes to be dead. Her search begins on a battlefield where Hades, God of the Underworld, is directing the souls of the fallen toward Tartarus and the Elysian Fields.

Xena questions him about Gabrielle but Hades tells her that Gabrielle's soul has not come to him; as an initiate of the northern Amazons, Gabrielle is destined for their afterworld and not for the Elysian Fields. Xena journeys alone to the northern Amazon territories – a land of deep dark forests and wind-scoured steppes, located in the vast and wild region where Europe blurs into Asia. There, Xena dresses in shamanic garb and performs a blood ritual that enables her soul to leave her body and travel to the Amazon afterworld. On the way there, she encounters, in spirit form, a tribe of dead Amazons, together with their queen Cyane, who are trapped in a no-man's-land and are unable to complete their journey to the next world because of a curse that Alti has placed on them. Xena realizes that her own actions years earlier are partly responsible for the Amazons' predicament. She postpones her search for Gabrielle in order to help them. When she returns to her body, she finds herself among a group of young Amazons who have survived the destruction of their tribe, and she is once again embroiled in a conflict with her old enemy Alti.

The "B" storyline is set in Xena's past and is related through flashbacks to a time when she was a ruthless warlord, partnered with the barbarian Borias and living from battle to battle in pursuit of ever greater conquests. Though a skilled fighter, she has not yet become a supreme warrior, or learned to discipline herself or allowed herself to exercise compassion. During this period of her life, she is anarchic, wantonly violent, cruel, and unscrupulous. Into the smoky warmth of the yurt she shares with Borias comes the shaman Alti with Anokin, her young female apprentice, at her side. Alti has plans even more ambitious than Xena's own, and seeks a powerful ally to help her achieve them. She intends to kill Cyane and to seize the Amazons' lands. But her ambitions do not stop there: ultimately, she has her sights set upon world domination and an empire of evil – goals that she thinks that Xena shares and will help her to achieve.

Played by Claire Stansfield, Alti is of striking appearance: tall and wild-looking, with a face of raw, bony beauty, kohl-rimmed and intense grey eyes, and a wolfish smile. She wears an antler headdress and a costume of skins and furs hung with shamanic talismans and amulets. A streak of sacrificial blood is smeared across her forehead. Her voice sounds like rocks rolling along a riverbed. She is an immediately compelling figure – dynamic, charismatic, edgy, and visually interesting. Xena falls under her spell, and falls fast. Borias, pacing the floor and trying to interrupt the bond of fascination developing between Xena and Alti, is already fading into the background. Eventually he can stand it no longer and intervenes, seizing Alti and throwing her out into the night like a stray dog. But by then it is already too late.

Alti is perhaps the most enigmatic of all Xena's enemies. She tells Xena that she was herself an Amazon until "they expelled me from their number because my power was too great," but we learn nothing more about the circumstances of this expulsion or about her past. She is a solitary figure who seems to have no tribe, no family, no lover, no friends, and no allies except her apprentice Anokin and, for a while, Xena. Now she is committed to destroying Cyane and the Amazons, melding vengeance and ambition into one deadly project. A pure predator, focused and merciless, she is wholly dedicated to the fulfillment of her goals. She seems, in some respects, the embodiment of a quasi-Nietzschean will to power. Hers is an enraptured, almost philosophical, pursuit of evil for its own sake. "I want to tap into the heart of darkness," she later tells Xena, "the sheer naked will behind all craving, the hatred and the violence. I'll become the face of Death itself, capable of destroying not only a person's body but their soul. Help me, and I'll make you Destroyer of Nations." For a while, Xena is seduced – long enough to befriend, betray, and kill Cyane, and to wipe out most of the northern Amazons.

Alti's identification as a shaman puts an unusual spin on *XWP*'s frequently fetishistic eroticism, with its regular diversions away from conventional romance and into the dark and violent realms of sexual obsession, enchantment, sadomasochism, and overwhelming desires that hurtle toward doom. The series' invocation of shamanism is perhaps its most serious engagement with a spiritual tradition. There is nothing here of the camp frivolity with which it habitually treats the Greek gods, or of the hippyish New Age sentiments that inform its nods toward Eastern mystical traditions and Christianity, or of the *Rosemary's Baby* schlock-horror fest of its dalliance with the Satanic god "Dahok" in the "Rift" episodes. *XWP* presents shamanism not as doctrine but rather as a set of practices that enable the shaman to travel back and forth between the material and spiritual realms. In "Them Bones, Them Bones," the young Amazon shaman Yakut explains the shamanic worldview that "Nature is composed of several layers of reality . . . and they're all united by one thing – the mind." In *XWP*, shamanism consists of the recognition of those realities and of the methods by which they can be accessed. No particular ethical code is ascribed to it. Like nature itself, shamanism is located beyond good and evil –

concepts that reside in the human mind and heart and which here are not attributed to any external forces.

This understanding of northern shamanism suits *XWP*'s emphasis upon individual responsibility and culpability, and its focus upon the individual's personal spiritual and ethical journey. In most of the series' Alti episodes, and especially in "Adventures in the Sin Trade," Xena is pared down to an elemental self of raw instinct and emotion, a self that must find its own path and which cannot rely on any guidance or help from without. This is Xena at her most feral and most wounded, screaming her anguish into the midnight wilderness, chasing her lost love into eternity. Alti matches her for primal instinct and naked desire: equally feral, equally single-minded, and equally intent upon bending worlds to her will. The similarities between hero and villain come to the fore in their hostile but profound understanding of each other, their connectedness, their entwined fates, and the passion of their enmity. They fall like star-crossed lovers toward mutual destruction. "I can see into your soul, Xena," says Alti in "When Fates Collide," "where you've been and where you're going. I have that power, and I will destroy you." Insight and shared characteristics make Alti the most intimate of Xena's enemies. Theirs is not a straightforward conflict of good and evil but rather a long dance of advances, feints, and retreats, involving competing and shared desires. Alti is part mortal enemy, part alter-ego, part trickster, and part seducer, a whisperer of words that flatter, cajole, and tempt. In "Adventures in the Sin Trade," she appeals to Xena's dark side in the language of power and conquest, offering an unholy alliance: "Imagine what you would do if you had the spiritual force to match the power of your army. You'd be unstoppable. Anything would be in your reach."

Vast are the Shadows

Intense, erotically charged relationships between women are a characteristic feature of *XWP*. At the heart of the series is Xena's tender relationship with Gabrielle, the naive and peace-loving village girl who becomes her constant companion. The series does not offer any final definition of their relationship, beyond its paramount importance to both characters. In many episodes, it is overtly coded as lesbian; in others, lesbianism is rendered subtextual, and in still others it is sidelined altogether as either Xena or Gabrielle temporarily becomes romantically involved with a male character. No matter what happens, though, the primary Xena/Gabrielle relationship is always reasserted in the end, and throughout the series it is articulated in the overblown language of high romance: "Even in death, Gabrielle, I will never leave you," vows a distraught Xena in "Adventures in the Sin Trade." "You are the best thing that ever happened to me. You gave my life meaning and joy. You will be part of me forever."

In *XWP*, love between women is death-defying and eternal. So too is hate.

Gabrielle's role in the series fulfils a variety of functions. She is, of course, Xena's primary love interest, as well as a helper who provides emotional and moral support and who fights alongside Xena. But although she is a source of emotional strength, she is often also represented as a circumstantial weakness: she is frequently imperiled, jeopardizing Xena's missions and requiring rescue, just like a conventional princess-in-peril in a fairytale. Gabrielle also serves a thematic function; in some respects, she constitutes an embodiment of Xena's conscience. Hers is usually a civilizing influence: when Xena strays too far toward the dark side, it is Gabrielle who reels her back in. As a consequence, it is Gabrielle rather than Xena herself who is Alti's true opposite. She and Alti compete for control of Xena's soul and destiny. In the series' dualistic configurations of good and evil, Gabrielle is the light and Alti the dark, each manifesting one side of the conflict that rages within Xena. The hero is positioned as a trophy over which good and evil, lover and enemy, struggle for supremacy.

In *XWP*, hatred and love are absolutes – all-consuming forces, sometimes as dark as each other. Both threaten the hero's autonomy and both threaten erasure of the hero's self. The emotional violence and destructiveness of love is a theme that the series frequently revisits: love in *XWP* can be life-enhancing and a source of strength, but it can also be shattering, overwhelming – an emotional maelstrom that threatens to tip over into madness. Even Xena's tender and romantic relationship with Gabrielle is not immune. This fact is explored in the so-called "Rift" sequence of episodes, where Gabrielle betrays Xena. Impregnated (immaculately) by the devil-god Dahok, Gabrielle gives birth to an evil child. Unable to accept that the child is really a supernatural being of pure evil, Gabrielle disobeys Xena's orders to kill it and instead sends it off downstream, Moses-like, in a basket. Later, the child kills Xena's son. Because of this, Xena's intense love for Gabrielle becomes an equally intense hate. She lassoes Gabrielle, drags her behind her horse for miles across country, and then hurls her from a cliff, plunging with her into the churning sea below. Love and hate both inscribe annihilation of the self. But, never shy about making up its own rules as it goes along, the series gets itself, and its two major characters, out of this narrative *cul de sac* by staging a post-death reconciliation in the form of a surreal musical set in the weird metaphysical realm of Illusia. After a lot of soul-searching and bad singing, Xena and Gabrielle are washed up on a beach and resume their lives together ("The Deliverer," "Gabrielle's Hope," "The Debt" parts 1 and 2, "Maternal Instincts," and "The Bitter Suite").

No such reconciliation occurs between Xena and Alti, yet their relationship can be understood as the dark mirror image of Xena's relationship with Gabrielle. Alti's arrival in "Adventures in the Sin Trade," with her young female acolyte in tow, immediately suggests lesbianism and invites comparison with the relationship between Xena and Gabrielle (which is well established and familiar to the audience even though this part of the episode is set before Xena and Gabrielle have met in the series' diegetic timeline). But where Xena and Gabrielle's relationship is founded upon love and mutual respect, Alti's relationship with Anokin is presented as cynical and exploitative. Anokin is Alti's tool rather than her partner, and the shaman uses her as a honeytrap to seduce, enthrall, and control Xena. Alti's sexuality is displaced on to Anokin, who becomes an instrument for the expression of the shaman's fascination with Xena as well as of her quest for power. When Anokin is killed, Xena is distraught and refuses to leave the girl's body. Bewildered by the strength of her attachment, Borias comments, "You knew her for less than a moon. What spell have they thrown on you?" Alti, though, sees Anokin's death as an opportunity to further control Xena. She offers Xena the chance to see Anokin again in the afterworld, positioning herself as the sole means of access. Thus love and desire precipitate another surrender, another loss of self.

Gabrielle is not the only female character accorded a pivotal role in Xena's life. There is Lao Ma, whom the series proposes as the real author of the *Tao Te Ching* and as a much-loved mentor who taught Xena how to control and sublimate her desires. There is Callisto, a maniacal blonde warrior in black leather, who seeks revenge for the deaths of her family and whose obsessive hatred of Xena is expressed through a series of S&M inflected encounters that campily mix flirtation and lethal combat. Callisto's vengeance-fuelled psychosis obliges Xena to confront the consequences of her past actions, the human wreckage left in the wake of

her career as a warlord, and underlines the yearning for redemption that
motivates and defines Xena's quest. There is M'Lila, who dies saving
Xena's life and who, when Xena reacts to her death with customary wild
murderousness, returns in spirit form to remind her that she has a nobler
destiny to fulfill. There is Akemi, Xena's adoring Japanese acolyte, whose
circumstances and actions set in motion a chain of events that eventually
leads to Xena's tragic death in the final episode of the series. Thus relationships with women dominate and define most of the key transforma-
tional periods of Xena's life, and each one in its way contributes to the
unfolding of her tragic destiny.

Alti is another such relationship. From the outset, their bond manifests
in a shared compulsion toward power. Betrayed by Xena at the end of
their relatively short-lived partnership, Alti becomes almost literally the
stalker from hell. Her twisted, addicted pursuit of Xena extends into
alternate realities ("When Fates Collide"), other incarnations ("Between
the Lines," "Them Bones, Them Bones"), and other historical eras
("Send in the Clones"). In "Them Bones, Them Bones," Alti – dead,
but still obsessing and scheming with impressive dedication in the spiritual realm – puts into operation an extraordinary plan to steal the soul
of Xena's unborn child and replace it with her own. "I've always wanted
to be inside you, Xena," she says, making explicit the parallels between
her intended invasion of Xena's body and rape. For Alti, lack of consent
and love are no obstacles to an eternal union of destinies:

> *Alti*: It's such a pleasure to see you, Xena – or should I call you
> "mommy"?
> *Xena*: There aren't many guarantees in life, Alti, but I promise you this:
> if you harm my child I will hound you throughout all time and between
> worlds. I will be your eternal damnation.
> *Alti*: Well, at least we'll be together again. I've so missed these intimate
> little moments.

Alti's pursuits of Xena combine a grand scheme to rule the world
and unleash evil with psychosexual desires expressed through repeated
violations and attempted occupations of Xena's body and life. There
is an almost cannibalistic aspect to Alti's hatred of Xena, a desire to
possess her power by consuming the essence of Xena's being. It is not
easy to escape an obsessive shaman with superpowers. Alti's pursuit of
Xena continues across different realities and lives. The episode "Send

in the Clones" finds Alti in the twenty-first century, reincarnated as Alexis los Alamos, a sort of postmodern Dr Frankenstein. Even though two millennia have elapsed, Alti's fixation with Xena is unabated. The episode begins in a fog-shrouded cemetery at night where Alti meets up with a dodgy-looking character with bad teeth. She exchanges a wad of banknotes for a briefcase containing Xena's chakram (her lethal, Frisbee-like weapon) and two strands of ancient hair – one strand from the "historical" Xena and the other from Gabrielle. Back in her laboratory, with the comic-relief assistance of three spectacularly geeky Xena fans, Alti/Alexis uses DNA extracted from the hairs to clone Xena and Gabrielle.

"Maturation acceleration" soon results in adult clones. All that remains is to fill their blank minds with memories to awaken their dormant personalities. Alti sets about creating the Xena she always wanted but could never have – an evil Xena who is in thrall to Alti and will share her ambition to create hell on earth. For this task, Alti uses montages of clips carefully selected from old *XWP* episodes. The three geeks each contribute their own interpretations of who and what Xena is. The male geek doesn't get much beyond fantasizing that after 2000 years of oblivion, Xena and Gabrielle are bound to be hot for the nearest available man: him. Another geek (female, dark-haired, punchy, and wearing a chakram pendant) argues "We're not bringing her back to life to counsel the lovelorn. She's got to be able to kick ass." The third geek (female, blonde, wearing a Gabrielle t-shirt, and gushing romantic sentimentality) counters that "Gabrielle is more important than Xena's fighting skills." But Alti has her own plans. When the geeks have left the lab for the night, she returns and loads the mind-programming computer with a disk titled "Evil Xena."

When Xena and Gabrielle wake, Alti employs the familiar villainous tactic of using Gabrielle in order to manipulate Xena. She lures Gabrielle outside and engineers her arrest, telling the police that she "broke into the lab dressed as some kind of, uh . . . television character." With Gabrielle under lock and key in the police station, Alti unleashes Xena to wreak havoc on the city in the course of rescuing her beloved. In one of those little twists of illogic that viewers of *XWP* are regularly expected to forgive, Alti subsequently tries to persuade Xena to kill Gabrielle by reminding her of how, in their former lives, Gabrielle's weakness and betrayal resulted in the death of Solon, Xena's son. But, as ever in *XWP*, love ultimately proves stronger than hate. Instead of turning on Gabrielle,

Xena goes for Alti. The usual loony-fu fighting ensues until at last Alti is defeated and disintegrates. Xena and Gabrielle ride off into the sunset (again . . .) in the back of a taxi cab.

A variation on the same basic format is played out again in the episode "When Fates Collide." Julius Caesar – another of Xena's arch-enemies – escapes from Hades, where he has been languishing since the Ides of March. In the Cave of Fates, and still wearing the blood-stained toga he was assassinated in, Caesar chains up the Three Fates and cuts the threads on the Loom of Destiny. In the alternate reality that ensues, he is emperor again – this time, with a sophisticated, elegant, but still deadly, Xena at his side as empress. None but Caesar has any memory of a previous existence, but in *XWP* the essential self always transcends circumstance. Alti, the High Priestess of Rome, is no less than Alti – still obsessing over Xena, still scheming, still craving ever more power. And when a young playwright called Gabrielle stages a production in Rome that is attended by Caesar and Xena, she and Xena are immediately and powerfully drawn to each other, despite neither having any recollection of their past life together.

Again, Alti uses Xena's love interest to manipulate her, first implicating Gabrielle in a plot to overthrow Caesar and then using her shamanic powers to give Xena visions of the life she shared with Gabrielle before Caesar changed destiny and the world. Alti's aim is to set Xena and Caesar against each other so that she can take Xena's place at Caesar's side. Alti mockingly tells Xena of her intentions, making clear the personal and invasive nature of her plans: "Can you feel the pain and terror in your soul? Secreting inside you? Oozing its blackness? Know this, Xena: Caesar, Rome, all of it will be mine." Her plan works: Caesar has Xena crucified in the courtyard of the imperial palace. As Xena hangs dying on the cross, Alti makes another of her sexual-relations-at-a-remove moves and seduces Caesar, taking the lover of her dying enemy, sexually experiencing a body that Xena has also experienced. But Alti has no further interest in Caesar. As he lies under her, his eyes closed in ecstasy, she pulls out a wicked-looking blade and plunges it repeatedly into his chest. The destiny that Caesar has made for himself ends in the same way as his original destiny: in both, he is betrayed and murdered by those closest to him.

Again, though, love proves stronger than hate. As the crucified Xena drifts toward death, a resolute Gabrielle arrives at the Cave of the Fates. Snatching a blazing torch from the wall, she sets fire to the Loom of Destiny and the universe goes supernova. Fortunately, the magic of television is able to overcome this cosmic catastrophe. The "real" world of Xena and Gabrielle is swiftly restored. Gabrielle finds herself wandering in the greenwood. Xena comes up on horseback from behind, lifts her up into the saddle, and they ride away.

——— Surely Some Revelation Is At Hand ———

Like myth, *XWP* draws its characters and their world with broad strokes. Subtlety and nuance scarcely figure here. The themes and codas are universal, timeless, and bold: it is the lot of human beings endlessly to shake their fists at the gods; the conflict between good and evil is never over; good and evil originate and reside not "out there" as the product of overwhelming abstract forces such as the Supernatural or Society, but within the human heart; the path of an individual's life is mapped as a struggle between will and destiny; a person is ultimately the sum of her deeds; the individual must accept full responsibility for the consequences of her actions. These are, at least in some ways, distinctly unfashionable concepts, and ones that *XWP* treats sometimes with seriousness and other times with embarrassed postmodern retreats into parody and hyperbole. Yet they seem to address something fundamental about the human condition that retains its power to captivate the imagination and which is the inspiration for almost all fan engagements with the series, revisited over and over in their stories, artwork, analyses, and discussions. In the final analysis, what makes Alti a great villain is that, like all good villains, she makes us think about what makes a great hero.

Notes

1 Lord Nelson, "The Framework of Power: Them Bones, Them Bones," 1999, <www.starpoet.com/lordnelson/bones.htm> (accessed September 5, 2005).

2 See "Xena and Gabrielle," "Them Bones, Them Bones," *Xena* Episode Guide Season 5, undated, <www.warriorprincess.50megs.com/season5/> (accessed September 5, 2005); Dana Hlusko "The way: a spiritual epiphany for Xena," *Whoosh* 32 (1995; accessed September 5, 2005).

3 Joseph Campbell, *The Hero With a Thousand Faces* (London: Fontana Press, 1993 [1949]), p. 353.

12

The Best Pop Princess: Kylie Minogue

Marc Brennan

I blame Madonna.

Before Madonna, female pop stars were allowed to be spectacles. They could be looked at and adored, mimicked and honored, and their music was there to be heard and to be enjoyed. No one expected, for example, Diana Ross, Doris Day, or Dusty Springfield to be anything but masters of their craft – pop singers. Since the arrival of Madonna, and the resultant critical and academic interest, women in pop are often unfairly compared to this post-feminist juggernaut. Don't get me wrong: I love Madonna – but after all that has been attributed to her, it is difficult to consider her a pop princess. Pop princesses, unlike Madonna, do not always attempt to be subversive, they often don't write their own lyrics, they may not challenge the male gaze, and they rarely upset established institutions (although Britney is giving her best shot). In short, pop princesses give cultural critics very little to write about. Easy to denigrate, difficult to celebrate. But there are exceptions.

Kylie Minogue has been a consistent feature in the UK and Australian pop consciousness for close to 20 years. Other pop stars, especially Madonna, work hard to be extraordinary, but it is Kylie's ordinariness which is part of her ongoing appeal. She is "Our Kylie" to housewives, journalists, gay men, teenagers, and to those who sing along drunkenly to her songs at the office Christmas party. Madonna represents ambition and authority. Kylie represents good times and good choruses. There may be many things that she is not, but there is a unique combination of attributes that have kept Kylie in the spotlight since the late 1980s – her perseverance, her persona, her performances, and, of course, her music.

If Madonna is still the queen of pop, then Kylie Minogue is the best pop princess of the contemporary era.

Perseverance

Kylie Minogue turned 35 in 2004, a year in which she celebrated close to 20 years in the entertainment industry, demonstrating that "Kylie, first and foremost, is about survival."[1] Her career began with bit parts on Australian soap operas such as *Skyways* and *The Henderson Kids* before she joined the cast of *Neighbours* in 1986. Joining the show as an unknown, the popularity of her character, Charlene, grew over time to become a television phenomenon in Australia and in the UK and Europe where the soap was also televised. Minogue's popularity continued to increase as Charlene became romantically linked with another character, Scott (played by Jason Donovan). The two characters were eventually married, with that particular episode not only rating extraordinarily, but also being recalled by many as one of the greatest moments of Australian television history.[2]

It was during the phenomenal success of *Neighbours* that Kylie first ventured into the field of popular music, releasing a cover of the song "The Locomotion," which became a Number One single in Australia (and a minor hit in the US). In October 1987, Kylie flew to the UK and recorded a song with writer/producers Stock, Aitken, and Waterman, a trio who dominated the charts during the late 1980s with songs performed by, for example, Dead or Alive, Sonia, Rick Astley, and Kylie's on- and off-screen partner Jason Donovan. Kylie's song, "I Should Be So Lucky," spent five weeks at Number One on the UK charts and had similar success in Australia, Germany, Finland, Israel, and Japan. The initial success of both Kylie and *Neighbours* co-star Jason Donovan was attributed by many to the fame generated by the popularity of the soap throughout Europe, with critics assuming that both careers would be short-lived and quickly forgotten. While Donovan's musical career was indeed short-lived, Kylie's was only beginning.

Following on from the success of "I Should Be So Lucky," Kylie left *Neighbours* and continued to release singles and albums with her producers, Stock, Aitken, and Waterman. Between her first release and 1991, Kylie amassed more than ten Top Ten singles in both the UK and

Australia, demonstrating her staying power and proving many of her critics wrong. She says of this time:

> I was being given a really hard time in the press. It was not a nice time for me, but I also remember people coming up to me in the street, and rather than asking for something, they would give by saying things like, "Don't worry about what they write" or "We believe in you." It wasn't as if I was doing anything wrong, I wasn't hurting anybody or lying to them, I was being attacked for being me. For being popular and being uncool.[3]

Although they were widely recognized as the bastion of uncool, Kylie continued to record with Stock, Aitken, and Waterman until 1994. However during the early part of that decade attention was less focused on the music than on the radical transformation that had occurred on the body of Minogue herself. During a supposedly raunchy romance with INXS front man, Michael Hutchence, rumors of kinky sexual exploits abounded and Kylie's new look suggested something that was all but hidden previously – sex. Gone was the frizzy permed hair, wide brim hats, cutesy dresses, and pink shoes. In came the sheer blouses, heavily made-up eyes, slinky skirts and dresses, and one impressive pout. Fans began to say that even her music was beginning to represent the new Kylie, most famously claiming that the song "Shocked" contained the line, "I was fucked by the power of love." Regardless of the truth of this assertion, a new image was cast. Kylie appeared on the cover of the once achingly hip "style bible" *The Face* in October 1991, all pout and heavy eyes, with the headline, "Too Sexy! Kylie Remade," confirming her new status as a sex symbol. Throughout the 1990s music was secondary to the body of Minogue for both journalists and some academics.[4] Rather than label her music, it was Kylie herself who was continually labeled and relabeled. This aspect of her appeal was deliciously ridiculed by Minogue herself in the video for the song "Did It Again," which portrays a brawl between the most noted of these labels – CuteKylie, SexKylie, DanceKylie, and IndieKylie.

Reacting to the continued focus on her body, Kylie attempted a musical transformation during the mid- to late 1990s. First, she left her long-time producers and signed up to a dance label replete with a new team of songwriters and producers. The results were less immediate than previous releases and Kylie's chart presence began to wane. Following this, she then attempted to reinvent herself as a serious artist and songwriter with her next album (originally titled) "Impossible Princess." Greeted by a bewildered public, the album was a comparative failure and she was "released" by her record label. A testimony to her perseverance, Kylie undertook what was meant to be a relatively brief Australian tour during this time. Her "Live and Intimate Tour" in 1998 became the highest grossing tour for an Australian artist, with multiple concerts selling out in record time across the country. Kylie has stated that it was this experience that caused her to rethink her career trajectory. Signed up by a new record label the following year, a meeting with songwriters would reveal an artist who was beginning to appreciate her appeal. In describing what she wanted her new album to sound like, she responded in four words – "poolside, beach, cocktails, and disco."[5] Kylie was returning to pop.

Since 2000, Kylie has returned to the upper reaches of the European and Australian music charts. The albums "Light Years," "Fever," and "Body Language" have all featured Number One singles, with each album often selling more than the entire back catalogue of her music. Releasing three albums in less than three years has earned her the title of "the Hardest Working Diva in Discodom,"[6] which not only recognizes her recent output but also the effort she has put into her profession. As her one time music producer Pete Waterman said recently, "This wasn't meant to be a 20-year career."[7] The sheer longevity of Kylie's career and the hits and misses along the way are undoubtedly part of her appeal. Perseverance is a key factor in Kylie's appeal, but looking like you're enjoying yourself is another.

Performance

She's a living Barbie doll. All gay men want to play with her, dress her up, comb her hair.[8]

[Kylie's story] is one of transformation, from soap star to pop star, a narrative of re-making herself, not with the steely will-power of Madonna, but with a playful forage through the dress-up box to see what kinds of outfits she should try on for size.[9]

While the above quotes point to Kylie's broader appeal, it is her body that is still the focus of many articles appearing in the UK tabloid press and various celebrity/tabloid magazines. Her butt, the most discussed part of her body, "is perfect, according to a study by the University of Central Lancashire, which deemed her 0 : 7 waist-to-hip ratio to be the cultural ideal."[10] But there are those who look beyond the body and argue that Kylie's appeal lies in "a curious innocence that the rest of us have lost."[11] Certainly this is apparent in the "Barbie doll" comparisons, but it is made explicit in her performances. Kylie as a performer, like most pop performers, is about spectacle. What possibly makes her unique is the degree to which she is portrayed as having fun in her performances. It is this that in turn signifies a sense of innocence.

Kylie's "comeback" single "Spinning Around" was released in 2000 and immediately thrust her back into the spotlight, both musically and through the attention that was paid to the accompanying video. The video takes place in what looks like a rather hip nightclub, with Minogue popping up on the bar (literally), on the dance floor, and gyrating around guests on leather lounges. Dressed in impossibly short gold hot pants, sheer blouse, and gold stilettos, and with overtly revisionist (flicked) hair, the outfit – and, indeed, the music – presents a shameless call to the 1970s and the golden days of disco. Kylie is smiling or pouting throughout the loose choreography of the video that includes performing what looks like the "bus stop" and "the bump" on the dance floor and at the bar. Innocence and fun are connoted by the 1970s styling with the use of colors and the cinematography evoking a party atmosphere as well as a musical genre that is associated with good times. There are no hidden messages in the video, nor is there a sense of irony – it is a celebratory performance. Even staunch Indie/ Alternative music paper, the *New Musical Express* (*NME*), couldn't read it any other way. Reviewing the single, but obviously referring to the video, it says:

> And on she goes. The years may pass by but Kylie will only look younger, keep wearing smaller and smaller hotpants and continue pumping out ever more hyperactive pop music . . . Indie chancers throw away your hair slides and take note. This is the sound of someone enjoying what they do. Does it scare you?[12]

The sarcasm directed at the readership of the *NME* reveals some of the common critical discourses that imbue popular music with its meaning. Music's perceived abilities to appeal to the subconscious, incite political beliefs, or reveal social injustices result in limited ways of understanding the attraction of music which shares none of these aims. In Kylie's musical world, the music and the performance are simply about fun.

It was this aspect that was performed so succinctly as Kylie toured Europe and Australia in 2001. The "On A Night Like This" tour again broke box office records in Australia, but it was a very different tour from her previous one. Whereas her tour three years earlier had been designed to showcase her ability to sing and showed some restraint in costumes and props, her 2001 tour was an unabashed camp celebration of what Kylie was/is, reflecting the way she has always been perceived by her fans and, to some extent, her detractors. Literal interpretations of songs found the performance reveling in all of the excesses of pop that have informed its history, with one reviewer noting as a live performance that it was "more Broadway than Beatles."[13] The opening song "Loveboat," for example, finds Kylie being lowered by a giant anchor onto a deck below where she is joined by a nautically attired troupe of dancers as she sings what must be one of the campest songs to be recorded in recent times. This is unsurprising from a performance that also includes a song called "Your Disco Needs You" and a cover of Olivia Newton-John's "Physical." Ironic? Unlikely. This tour portrayed a performer who was finally at ease with the label of pop star and was positively embracing it. The tour proved that not all pop stars lip-sync (Britney), over-sing to prove their ability (Christina), or have the need to drain pop music of its fun by trying to reclassify performance as art (Madonna). In the musical world of Kylie, pop has an essential meaning – fun.

It was during this tour that Kylie performed a new song that would go on to be her biggest hit. "Can't Get You Out Of My Head" is quite simply one of the best pop songs ever written and went on to sell four million copies worldwide. Like the "Spinning Around" performance the previous year, the video for this song, despite its futuristic feel and high production values, was a performance of fun. Kylie herself appears in a number of guises: sophisticated (hair tied back, slinky back dress), futuristic (black/white jump/tracksuit, pigtail), girly (short sparkly go-go skirt, boots, and frizzy hair), and, most memorably, sexy (dressed in what the editor of this collection called, "less a dress than a strategic use of toilet paper"). Kylie flits between these guises with numerous close-ups, revealing a sly smirk that is never condescending, employing robot-style choreography that seems to be a bastardized version of moves made famous by Michael Jackson early in his career. With no apparent narrative, the video is a celebration of style, music, and dance, with the jerky and highly unnatural choreography implying a stylized homage to the 1980s. The 1980s, and in particular the music from that period, have come to represent style over substance, but pop fans will remember this as a period of unabashed great tunes provided by performers such as Wham, Duran Duran, ABC, Madonna – and, of course, Kylie Minogue. This period, for those who don't need to dress their musical criticism in restrictive frameworks, was fun, and both the song and the video performance of it revisit this period with aplomb.

Revisiting iconography from previous decades was a central aspect of Kylie's "Fever" tour, which traveled around the UK in 2002. Again, the tour was a huge hit with audiences, as well as with most critics, who were slowly starting to understand Minogue's appeal. The UK's largest selling music magazine, *Q*, said it was "a riot of pop culture references . . . deftly done, letting people in on the joke if they want to be, without insulting those who don't."[14] The British newspapers understood the joke. The *Guardian* hedged its bets, acknowledging, "this is not an artist at the cutting edge, but shameless end-of-the-pier stuff, done to perfection."[15] The *Daily Mail* argued that "few can perform with as much infectious energy and visually stunning style of Kylie,"[16] the *Sun* declared the performance "a triumph,"[17] while the *Daily Telegraph* argued that "Kylie, the self-proclaimed Princess of Pop to Madonna's Queen, has taken the throne."[18] This is certainly something *Q* magazine was happy to support on the cover of its June 2002 edition (see figure 12.1).

The triumphant discourses that accompanied the "Fever" tour offer some insight into why Kylie Minogue is the best pop princess, especially in comparison to someone like Madonna. Madonna, live, is a performer who likes to keep a steely distance from her audience, via strictly choreographed performances, the use of often political and sexual imagery, and her sinewy, hyper-masculine frame. Kylie's performances are about celebration and, in comparison to her rivals, they celebrate the ordinary and the achievable. Kylie isn't as toned and fit as Madonna, cannot sing as well as Christina Aguilera, and cannot dance with as much detail and speed as Britney or Janet. This is part of her appeal. Like her ability to maintain a career against the odds and her celebratory performances, giving the impression of being ordinary and the girl next door is essential to the appeal of Kylie Minogue.

Figure 12.1 Cover, *Q* magazine, June 2002

---------------- **Persona** ----------------

Kylie is no remote diva, nor icy confection. She is the nation's favourite, a kind of public institution loved from dads down to toddlers. She may be ultra-glam and dead fashionable, but she loves a cuppa and has the same problems wearing short skirts as the next woman. Everyone feels on first-name terms with Kylie.[19]

There is a sense of the ordinary about Kylie that is surely part of her appeal. Academic McKenzie Wark has argued that she and her career represent possibility and the Australian rhetoric of a "fair go."[20] For not only is her story one of an ordinary girl from the suburbs of Melbourne made good, it is also inspirational. While she is ubiquitous through success, Kylie appears to remain relatively grounded. Undoubtedly, her below average height and tiny frame (5ft) allow her to be perceived as inoffensive, banal, or, as one writer argues, the "pop version of a brisk walk by the sea or a nice cup of tea."[21] But this is a carefully constructed campaign, in line with any of the outrageous stunts pulled by (pre-indictment) Michael Jackson. Kylie is everything to everybody, simply because she reveals so little about herself.

William Baker, Kylie's stylist and best friend, agrees that the enigmatic quality of Kylie is part of her appeal: "It goes back to mystery and mystique and that's such a big part of her. She's very cleverly managed to lure people into thinking that they know a lot about her when they actually know very little."[22] Since her chart rebirth in 2000, Kylie has been a regular feature in the UK and, to a lesser extent, Australian newspapers. Stories about her love life are amongst the most prominent, and take their place amongst other features that attempt to pinpoint the personality of Minogue through expert opinions, and the obligatory "close friend who wishes to remain anonymous." In interviews she refuses to give any specific details about her private life, and has never been quoted as decrying the public's attention. When she was reported to have suffered a minor nervous breakdown in 2002, Minogue refused to comment and simply stayed out of the public eye for two weeks while holidaying in Australia. It is in moments such as these that her fans and interested members of the public are able to project their own version of events on to the relatively unknown slate of Minogue's personality. This, in turn, creates a sense of attachment and a sense of allure that allows Kylie to represent various meanings aside from her pop performances.

Some of the meanings that have been ascribed to Kylie were revealed following the events of 9/11. Shortly afterwards, two British journalists wrote opinion pieces about the place of Kylie in the British psyche, with a general agreement being reached that she embodied the opposite of what plagued the public's mind during this explicit display of terrorism. Brian Appleyard in the *Sunday Times* asked "Why Kylie? Why Now?" and concluded: "In a shakier world, we don't want subversion, sneering, alienation or the dark seeds of dance, we want pop, pure and simple. This is what we do: it's the opposite of terrorism."[23] Julie Burchill was a little more direct when she argued:

> I do really believe that Bin Laden and Kylie represent the polar opposites of human nature; the first all about cruelty without beauty, the second all about beauty without cruelty . . . how lucky I am to live in a country where a beautiful, barely-clothed woman inspires affection, adulation and cele-bration, rather than shame, anger and hysteria.[24]

It seems the meanings attributed to Kylie have come full circle – but what was originally used to criticize is now used to celebrate. Pop music sung by a beautiful woman is the antithesis of what many would argue "good music" should be, and this is why in the early stages of her career she was so quickly denigrated. If this is an age of uncertainty, then it is good to know there are still things that can be relied upon. What Kylie thinks of this appropriation is irrelevant – that is not what she does. In the absence of definitive personality traits, she can be all we want her to be, but mostly, she provides a gorgeous form of escapism.

And of course, those who have always known this remain Kylie's most ardent fans – gay males. Kylie is possibly the most prominent gay icon of contemporary times, though no one, including Minogue herself, has pinpointed why. She says, "gay icons usually have some tragedy in their lives, but I've only had tragic haircuts and outfits."[25] Haven't we all! Part of the appeal is obviously Minogue's longevity and music, but her idea of "tragic" seems well placed within contemporary gay culture. As Johann Hari notes, writing about gay icons, artists such as Judy Garland, James Dean, and Marilyn Monroe were tragic, doomed figures that were often iconic as they reflected the fears and loneliness that many gay men felt prior to more liberal times. But, he argues, "as gay people's lives have transformed and improved, so too have their icons changed."[26] Although the author stops short of this suggestion, it is possible to argue that Kylie's iconic status is one that links her own struggle for critical acceptance with that of the gay community's struggle for cultural, political, and social equality. This may be difficult to prove, but it is the little that is known about Kylie that allows her to be a *"bearer* of meanings"[27] to various publics in the public sphere.

Pop

Underpinning the continuing popularity of Kylie is the fact that she is someone who obviously understands the appeal of her music. While Madonna may have alienated some fans with her journey into pseudo-political and religious lyrics and symbolism, Kylie has embraced the form of the innocuous pop song. Sure, she "is no Lou Reed,"[28] but this is obviously part of her appeal, as the failure of her attempt to be treated as a serious artist in the late 1990s adequately displays. It is her return to pure unadulterated pop that has brought her more recent success; a success that found her being the only artist to register in the Top Ten of both singles and albums in the UK in 2001.[29]

As noted earlier, Kylie's musical career has had more twists and turns than a Justin Timberlake dance routine. This is something apparent in the critical appraisal of Kylie's more recent work. For example, the *NME* notes how we "put on a brave face when she makes a wonky record, and put out the bunting when she makes a good one."[30] But the bunting that is put out for Minogue is not typical of that awarded to other musical artists; in Kylie's case, rather than critical acclaim, she is often awarded critical *acceptance*. For example, in a review of her album *Fever*, the *NME* writes that the record "is as effervescent as a foot spa, and with about as much depth. But if you're looking for depth in a Kylie album, you clearly don't know your arse from your [UK Indie band] Elbow."[31]

Similarly, the *Guardian* argues: "No one buys a Kylie Minogue expecting grit and passion. Complaining that *Fever* is soulless and manufactured is like complaining that Radiohead are kind of mopey."[32] If depth is something that is left to more serious, "mopey" bands, then an acceptance of Kylie's music generates a wider examination, something that a review of her 2004 album *Body Language* makes explicit:

> Praising Kylie for a good album is no more logical than praising HM Queen Elizabeth for the success of the England rugby team. Like the

Queen, Kylie is very important but does nothing. Her job is to be the regal, waving figurehead for the cutting-edge and finely-honed creative skills of scores of songwriters.[33]

Although she is often credited with co-writing, it is the choice of collaborators she works with that plays the most important part in her continuing popularity.

The writing credits on Minogue's last three albums demonstrate some of the creative skills that have been employed for this performer. "Light Years," released in 2000, contained a hit single written by Paula Abdul, but it was the work of UK pop phenomenon Robbie Williams and his then song-writing partner, Guy Chambers, that provided the bulk of the album's most flamboyant, and overtly pop, songs. Both of these songwriters continue to have careers in their own right. Rather than replicate a similar set of songs for her following album, Cathy Dennis, a minor pop celebrity in the UK in the 1980s, provided the hit single, "Can't Get You Out of My Head" and several other numbers on the album *Fever*. Dennis has since worked with, amongst others, Britney Spears, Janet Jackson, and Celine Dion. For Kylie's most recent album, *Body Language*, Dennis contributes one song, and is joined by, amongst others, former Scritti Politti front man Green Garside and UK garage sensation Ms Dymanite. At the end of 2004, Kylie released a new single from her *Greatest Hits* album, written and produced by one of the most critically acclaimed acts of the year, the Scissor Sisters.

Music criticism, broadly speaking, relies on a benchmarking system that posits, for example, rock against pop, live music against recorded (DJs) and performing musicians/bands against the solo performer who doesn't write their own material.[34] With Kylie, however, critics themselves are beginning to reassess their own prejudices. Certainly, she has never been credited as anything other than a performer, but her obvious ability to match her persona with her choice of musical material is something that is now granted some credibility. While more traditional rock bands struggle for longevity via their own song-writing ability, the pop star's ability to recognize writing talent and a song's potential should not be underestimated. As the review above suggests, it is true that it is sometimes hard to decide where to grant authority in pop music: to the performer, to the manager, or to the record company A&R department. In this instance though, Kylie's break with her writing/producing team in the mid-1990s (her decision), her own song-writing contributions on her last four albums, her involvement in the planning and design of her performances, and her complete control of her public image suggest there is a talent beyond performance that should be realized. For if success and appeal could simply be equated with the look and the (pop) "hook," then Dannii Minogue (Kylie's very similar looking, pop-singing sister) would be enjoying similar success. (She isn't.)

Treating pop music as an important and relevant cultural force is still difficult. To do so attracts charges of "populism" in academic writing – and even in some music journalism. Pop music can be appreciated in ways similar to other cultural objects, but, in order to understand Kylie's role as the best pop princess, it is necessary to broaden the context. Although Kylie's musical output since the beginning of 2000 is agreed to be her best work, her status in the world of popular music in Australia, Europe, and the UK is a product of more than just her music. It is a combination of Kylie's persona, her performances, and, perhaps most importantly, her perseverance that has allowed her to become a cultural force in her own right. Making judgments about the worth of particular cultural products is difficult, and the criteria offered here cannot be applied indiscriminately to other pop princesses. While pop songs may often evoke a similar feel, each pop performer is unique, and each deserves to be assessed and understood within the limits of their own history, performances, personalities, and musical output.

Coda

I noted at the beginning of this chapter that to many, Kylie Minogue is simply "Our Kylie." This perceived sense of familiarity allows people to make connections between her life and their own. As this chapter was being finalized, we saw an example of just how powerful, and important, this connection can be. In May 2005, Kylie announced to her fans that she would cancel all forthcoming appearances to undergo treatment for breast cancer. News of her condition made front-page headlines in both Australia and the UK; Australian Prime Minister, John Howard, commented that "all Australians [felt] shocked and saddened by the news."[35] And throughout the country, the fact that this ordinary Australian, just like us, was facing this disease, had an unexpected effect. Suddenly, screenings for breast cancer – which public health authorities had been trying to promote for years – jumped by 40 per cent.[36] Kylie embodies ordinary lives, and the perseverance that it takes to live them. As Kylie struggles with this battle, she takes her fans along with her.

Notes

1 Brian Appleyard, "Why Kylie? Why now?" *Sunday Times* (October, 21 2001): page unspecified. September 11, 2005: Factiva.

2 Alan McKee, *Australian Television: A Genealogy of Great Moments* (Sydney: Oxford University Press, 2001), pp. 237–54.

3 Minogue, quoted in Philippa Hawker, "The real thing," *Age* (April, 14 2001): 1.

4 John Hartley, *Popular Reality: Journalism, Modernity, Popular Culture* (London: Arnold, 1996), pp. 171–95.

5 Michael Dwyer, "Kylie: return of the disco queen," *Rolling Stone* (Australia) 579 (October 2000): 69.

6 Adrian Deevoy, "The Tao of Kylie," *Blender* (April 2004): 90.

7 Dorian Lynskey, "Attack of the 5ft women," *Q* (June 2002): 99.

8 Designer Patrick Cox, in ibid., p. 101.

9 Hawker, "The real thing."

10 Caroline Sullivan, "The butt stops here," *Guardian* (November 19, 2003): 25.

11 Dave Simpson, "Camping with Kylie," *Guardian* (March 9, 2001): 21.

12 Siobhan Grogan, "Kylie Minogue: spinning around," *nme.com*, September 25, 2004, <http://www.nme.com/reviews/6730.htm>.

13 Simpson, "Camping with Kylie."

14 Lynskey, "Attack of the 5ft women," p. 97.

15 Alexis Petridis, "Review of the week," *Guardian* (April 30, 2002): 15.

16 Adrian Thrills, "Kylie's highly spectacular," *Daily Mail* (April 27, 2002): page unspecified. September 11, 2005: Factiva.

17 Nicole Lampert, "Kylie fever," *Sun* (April 27, 2002): 37.

18 Lynsey Hanley, "Basques, fishnets and a show to rival Madonna's," *Daily Telegraph* (April 29, 2002): 17.

19 Craig McLean, "Kylie Minogue: pop idol," *Independent* (January 31, 2004): 12.

20 McKenzie Wark, *Celebrities, Culture and Cyberspace: The Light on the Hill in a Postmodern World* (Annadale: Pluto Press, 1999), pp. 86–7.

21 Appleyard, "Why Kylie?"

22 William Baker, quoted in Paul Flynn, "Confide in me," *Attitude* 1/104 (December 2002): 43.

23 Appleyard, "Why Kylie?"

24 Julie Burchill, "Love thy neighbour," *Guardian* (December 29, 2001): 7.

25 Minogue, quoted in Johann Hari, "The gay icon," *New Statesman* 131/4583 (April 15, 2002): 18.

26 Hari, "The gay icon," p. 18.

27 Hartley, *Popular Reality*, p. 178; emphasis in original.

28 Appleyard, "Why Kylie?"

29 Alexis Petridis, "Pop of the tots," *Guardian* (August 30, 2002): 2.

30 Alex Needham, "Kylie Minogue: fever," *nme.com*, September 25, 2004, <http://www.nme.com/reviews/8775.html>.

31 Ibid.

32 Alexis Petridis, "You like it like this," *Guardian* (September 28, 2001): 17.

33 Anna Britten, "Kylie Minogue: body language," *Bang* (December 2003): 80.

34 Roy Shuker, *Understanding Popular Music* (London: Routledge, 1994), p. 36; Sarah Thornton, *Club Cultures: Music Media and Subcultural Capital* (Cambridge: Polity: 1995), p. 1.

35 "Fans rally for Kylie," *Age* online, May 18, 2005, May 19, 2005, <http://www.theage.com.au/news/People/Fans-rally-for-Kylie/2005/05/18/1116361592246.html>.

36 "Cancer screenings rise after Kylie Minogue's cancer announcement," *Medical News Today*, August 7, 2005, August 10, 2005, <http://www.medicalnewstoday.com/medicalnews.php?newsid=28785>.

13

The Best Disco Record: Sharon Redd: "Never Give You Up"

Simon Frith

The Track (1)

"Never Give You Up" opens with six syncopated notes on a cowbell, soon underwritten by a repetitively hard hit side drum.[1] Then we hear a stately five-note keyboard riff, doubled, and syndrums and a brassy fanfare. Even before a voice is heard I've taken up my position on this sound stage, all my attention focused on the relentless *presence* that is disco.

Actually, this is not music that is very easy to describe. This is one reason, I think, that disco is undervalued critically. Critics lack the appropriate descriptive terms. I assume, without knowing, that all these noises are, in fact, electronic, but I don't have the expertise – or the ears – to account for each sound in terms of the equipment or process producing it. And so I hear the track in similes. I describe the music as what it sounds *like*, and however the notes are actually constructed they sound percussive, the noises made by things being struck: bells, bombs, bumps, hand-claps, plucked strings (only the bass playing a continuous line).

There isn't a tune here in the sense of a melodic narrative, parts being fitted together to form a whole which then illuminates the parts so that we listen again to anticipate their completion, the climax, the final chord. Rather, one can only listen to this track *all at once*. It's layered, with all the layers (different settings on computerized gizmos) equally weighted (no foreground, no background). What stands out is determined by an

ever-variable listening focus, a focus determined in turn by bodily concentration. Listening to disco involves not so much thought – let's see
how that works, like opening up an engine – as intellectual distraction
and a constant sense of surprise. One finds oneself following a sound one
had never noticed before (which is one reason why after more than 20
years of listening to "Never Give You Up" I still don't know in advance
what the listening experience will be). The appearance and reappearance
of percussive effects seem random, not choices made according to harmonic rules or the commercial requirements of a three-minute radio
song, but the effects of a continuous exchange of energy between electronic particles in which the listener, as Heisenberg observed, is right in
there triggering the uncertainty.

From the outside, of course, all disco sounds the same and any individual track can be reduced to a single element, the mindless sense of a
beat, repetition as pure boredom. But from the inside repetition isn't
what you hear but the framework of what you hear; it's a way of releasing
dancers from the obligation of listening to time passing so as to be able
to listen as if time stood still. The family resemblance between disco and
minimalism is not just formal – the use of repeated riffs, the refusal of
complex harmonic structures – but philosophical. Both involve the pursuit
of timelessness.

Philip Glass's account of the goal of minimalist music, to enable the
listener to deploy "another mode of listening," could equally describe the
effect of disco, "in which neither memory nor anticipation have a place
in sustaining the texture, quality or reality of the musical experience." In
this listening mode, one enters (in Jonathan Kramer's words) "the vertical time" of a piece. Kramer describes listening to Erik Satie's *Pages mys-
tiques* (four eight-bar phrases played 840 times in succession): "My present
expanded, as I forgot about the music's past and future. I was no longer
bored. And I was no longer frustrated because I had given up expecting.
I had left behind my habits of teleological listening."[2]

Rather than saying that disco is my favorite form of music, then, I
should say that it is my favorite way of listening.

All this high theory and the voices haven't happened yet, which brings
me onto another analogy. Listen to jazz and swing band tracks from the
1920s and 1930s now and one is surprised by how small a musical space
the vocalist occupied. Anyone expecting Billie Holiday, for example, to
stand astride her tracks like a modern star would be thrown by how long
her "accompanists" play before she enters, how short a time she has to

make her point. The voice in jazz and swing was treated as just another instrument, the singer taking a solo like everyone else. But the voice, unlike the other instruments, also provided a kind of semiotic ordering. The emotional meaning of the number was revealed by the singer's way with the lyric; it was the vocal that held up the music *en plein air*. *This*, the singer suggested, is what this song *is*.

With the rise of the crooner and in 1950s pop, the singer began to fill out the song, which was now organized to project their emotions. From this perspective, disco was clearly a return to an earlier method of song construction (one also designed for dancers). In the 1970s disco mixes (contrasted to radio mixes) thus took on the shape of old swing tracks, as producers and engineers expanded on the instrumental bits and made intros and breaks disco's essential architecture. The voice became an occasional feature again, working as a kind of track ident, a reminder of what song we were actually listening to. And this is to draw attention to one of the peculiarities of disco as it developed at the end of the 1970s. This most formulaic of genres, rooted in the calculated manipulation of machines (rather than "spontaneous" interplay of instruments) had at its core a belief in improvisation. "Never Give You Up" was mixed by François Kevorkian, a French musician who had gone to New York in 1975 to immerse himself in the jazz rock scene and cut a deal trading French lessons for drum lessons with the great jazz drummer Tony Williams.[3] What I hear in "Never Give You Up" is not standardization, but someone – Kevorkian – playing *with* the beat.

Still, this is a "Sharon Redd record" and she does at last appear. And if in classic big band jazz the vocal line often seemed lonely, vulnerable amidst the strutting horns, the disco voice (again mostly female) is decid-edly powerful, unconfined by the precision of beats per minute, the fetishized bpm. Disco singing obviously emerged from soul music, still followed soul conventions, emotional expression signed as black (whatever the singer's actual ethnicity). In disco as in soul the feeling of the moment can push the singer across the boundaries of tune or pitch or lyrical sense; in disco, unlike soul, the voice often becomes the only mark of human feeling, rhythmically rough amidst the machinery. At the same time, aesthetically, disco is essentially artificial music and so disco singers have to put quotation marks around their soulful "authenticity." Disco singing, it seemed to me at the time (and I haven't changed my mind) had a kind of theatricality to it, a self-conscious *performance* of human feeling, usually sexual feeling, usually female sexual feeling – as dramatized by men, by male producers and mixers, a touch of camp. Sharon Redd, like many of the disco divas (led by Donna Summer) started her professional singing career in *Hair* (playing the lead role in the Australian production), developed her reputation as the voice of an advertising campaign for Shaffer beer, was a backing singer for Bette Midler.

On "Never Give You Up" the voice (mostly Redd's own, I think) is anyway layered too, divided into three: background vocals, multitracked, part of the rhythmic mosaic; middle-ground matter-of-fact singing, providing the song's narrative drive, telling its emotional story in a straightforward way; and, in the foreground, *over the top*, the sound of a diva diva-ing. Sonically and rhythmically these various vocal elements play off each other in a kind of conversational counterpoint (like an amped-up sixties girl group). Lyrically this is not a song in the conventional pop sense to which one could sing along. There is not even (as in much of the more commercial disco) a chorus for collective bellowing. Rather, the song is made up of lyrical fragments and exploits different kinds of rhetorical device – exhortations, exclamations, commands, boasts. Devices we might expect to hear on a football touchline (from players and spectators alike) or, more to the point, from the congregation of an evangelical church or, more intimately, in bed. "I'll never give you up!" "No, I'll never stop!" "Just keep coming!" "Give it up!" "Keep coming for more!"

What Redd expresses here (and this is what further distinguished disco from the soul music from which it derived) is not need (a kind of feeling) but demand (a kind of performance), a demand for, well, anything really. The pleasure is in the demanding itself, the enjoyment of a performance that is met by its own repetition. ("More, more, more!" is as much the message of this track as of almost all the best disco.) This is music that expresses above all the pleasures of desiring (rather than the different pleasures – and inevitable disappointments – of having those desires met.) And if in this case desire is articulated in terms of its most intimate expressive conventions – love and sex – what the record is actually about in its self-reflexivity (what all good disco records are about) is disco itself. A style of singing that originally, in classic soul, gave form to an intense individuation (of performer and listener) is, in disco, deconstructed or, rather, abstracted, so as to give voice to desire for its own sake, without any object except its expressivity.

There is no gap here between hearing the noise, feeling the noise, and moving to it. To listen to this track *no interpretation is needed*. "Never

Give You Up" is the best disco record because it does best what disco records do: give exhilarating shape to the disco experience.

The Experience

What is the disco experience? Disco was obviously music for dancers and its very usefulness is what, from a rock perspective, makes it lack credibility as music. Music designed to fill dance floors has, by its nature, to follow certain formulae (the right pace, the right sort of easy access, the right gleam). From the start disco was thus denied the possibility of being music-as-art. It couldn't express an artistic sensibility, explore complexities, promise some subtle meaning that would be unfolded only over the course of many listenings. Disco had a job to do immediately; it did this job – getting people moving – more or less effectively. What more can be said?

But this is to undervalue not so much disco as dancing. If, as Roger Scruton has suggested, "dancing to music is an archetype of the aesthetic response," then music designed for dancing contains, at least, the nugget of an aesthetic argument.[4]

For Scruton (writing about high music), even concert-hall listening is a form of dancing – "our whole being is absorbed by the movement to which we attend, inwardly locked in incipient gestures of imitation." For me, disco was the music that paid closest attention to dancing as a way of listening. What, from the outside, seemed like the most physical, *bodily*, of musical genres (and disco was, after all, a repository of bodily exhortations that lent the form well enough to aerobics, Jane Fonda videos, and numerous other forms of physical fitness regime), from the inside felt like the most abstract, *disembodied* musical experience going (there were, among other things, no instrumentalists to play air guitar to). The disco experience involved a loss of will, a ceding of body-consciousness to the beat. In its very functionalism, disco (more than any other popular dance music) substituted text for context. Disco idealized dancing for no purpose.

In analytic retrospect I think what was involved here was a kind of integration of the musical elements of time and space. There certainly was a way in which disco was (as rock ideologues argued) one-dimensional. But this was because the two dimensions of space and time were collapsed into each other. Technology was involved here, elements of science fiction (that would be pushed much further by the later developments of house and techno). The way disco was produced, in layers, the way its rhythm was calibrated, by machines, did give it a kind of other-worldly oddity.

Disco, that is to say, was an *envelope* of sound: one entered *into* disco (it was not music that could be listened to from the outside, as it were; from there it was just a noise). Disco was not, like rock, a spectacle. Disco surround was vertical, a concatenation of sound, and horizontal, everything one would hear, had heard, was present simultaneously. And it was a space that was both material and symbolic. Disco described the place of dance (the floors! the lights! the people!) and its phantasms (disco records always took for granted the ideal disco experience). Such spatial experiences involved a particular account of time. Disco time was circular rather than linear, or, rather, was a continuous present. Disco suspended the experience of time passing, offered an utterly enthralling sense of timelessness. The best disco records, like Sharon Redd's "Never Give You Up," grab one's attention immediately, stop the ticking of the clock and so last for ever.

There's something else involved here too: disco sociability. In *Love Saves the Day*, his inspirational history of "American dance music culture, 1970–79," Tim Lawrence shows that the driving force of the New York underground dance scene in which disco was forged was not simply that city's complex ethnic and sexual culture but also a 1960s notion of community, pleasure, and generosity that can only be described as hippie. What this involved, in turn, was not just utopianism, an individualistic liberation from cultural and sexual mores, but also a kind of selflessness, a dream of bodily dissolution. This may have meant that, institutionally, disco, like rock before it, was doomed to a more mundane kind of dissolution – economic and sexual exploitation, individual hedonistic self-destruction, greed trumping good will. But it also meant that the best disco music contained within it a remarkably powerful sense of collective euphoria.

Disco, in other words, was always a paradoxical pursuit of pleasure. It concerned sexuality but in an undirected kind of way (it wasn't about couples or courting). It involved intensely individual dance floor displays that became part of an experience of collective comfort. Whatever it may have looked like and wherever it may have happened (and I mostly listened to the records at home), disco never meant dancing alone.

————————— The Track (2) —————————

The question remains: why is "Never Give You Up" the *best* disco record?

Well one answer (rooted in the disco experience itself) is, of course, that my choice is random. It could have been many other records but this just happens to be the one I've played more than any other. There are things about it I can only assert: when it comes on I still always stop whatever else I'm doing. I've never ever not listened it. But, hey, this is an academic essay and I'm supposed to be explaining my musical responses, not just recounting them.

It's not accidental, I think (given that I do now have to think) that "Never Give You Up" is late period disco. It works so well because it is standardized. It has nothing of the experimental or tentative or confused nature of the pioneering dance tracks of the 1970s. It is a highly professional number, typical output of the Prelude production line. It was neither a big hit (it never crossed-over to the pop or r&b charts) nor a lasting club cult (though it was widely played for a while). It was, one could say, a routine record of its time, following the standard disco and post-disco dance floor formula of female soul vocals plus drum-machines and synthesizers.

My first argument, then, is that in a genre in which standardization is the name of the game the most standard (or perfect) record is also, by definition, the best.

That said, however perfect formally, no popular music is really satisfying unless it is also engaging, unless it also has a sense of personality. In disco, two kinds of personality matter: the singer in whose names tracks were issued (there partly for this reason, to sell the track) and the producer/mixer, whose musical personality determined how the numbers sound. (The writers of disco tracks, in this case Eric Matthew and Willie Payne, are of no interest at all.)

It is indicative how disco worked in pop terms that while, as a casual fan, I knew about "Never Give You Up"'s mixer François Kevorkian, I knew nothing about the track's singer, Sharon Redd, at all. Kevorkian featured regularly in music press articles on the dance music scene in New York in the late 1970s and 1980s. His name was often used alongside such other studio "legends" as Shep Pettibone to sell the mix compilations that I used to collect. His background and studio career is well documented by such dance music historians as Tim Lawrence. By contrast, I couldn't find any mention of Sharon Redd in any of my reference books and had no idea (having bought her records as 12-inches or on mix LPs) even what she looked like.

Thanks to the vast store of knowledge on record-selling sites on the Internet I know now that Redd was a well-established session singer when she signed to Prelude in 1980, that she was 37 when she cut "Never Give You Up" (a year older than I was when I bought it, which I find remarkable), and that she died of pneumonia on January 5, 1992. She wasn't any kind of star in pop terms, but a highly skilled African American singer from a musical family in Virginia. Her parents and siblings were in the music business. She had classical singing lessons as a child, and a successful career in showbiz, doing all the various kinds of stage and recording jobs available to a singer of her style in the 1960s and 1970s. In the early 1980s this meant performing on disco tracks. There were many women like Redd in the singing business then. A few became stars in their own right; most didn't but were, like Sharon Redd, names attached to more or less successful producers' output.

It's easy enough to read this as a familiarly depressing story of talent wasted and black female skill exploited by white male power. And it's certainly true that disco has its own share of stories of producers using singers like Sharon Redd on dance records who were then dropped for TV and live appearance as too old or unattractive and replaced by someone younger and more telegenic. But this may be to miss the point. Sharon Redd may well have been exploited (I have no idea of the terms of her recording deal) but she was being employed not as an artist but as an artisan. Disco singers like her were the equivalent to an earlier generation of session singers like Marni Dixon, who provided the voice for such stars of Hollywood musicals as Audrey Hepburn and Natalie Wood. The irony here, perhaps, is that Sharon Redd was valuable to Prelude precisely for her ability to *enact* the music she performed.

My point here is that disco music-making was a craft not an art. As a singer, that is to say, Redd's essential quality was self-reflexivity rather than self-expression. "Never Give You Up" is not a record about Redd's feelings but about what it is to express feelings as a kind of music.

Disco is, I believe, a rather cerebral form of music-making, certainly in contrast to rock's romantic sentimentality and neediness. If in "Never Give You Up" Sharon Redd was not really engaged with her own feelings but, rather, with strictly musical matters, then neither were her listeners engaging in their own feelings, in reading Redd's situation onto theirs (or vice versa). My love of this record, to put this another way, is not nostalgic. It doesn't bring back memories of past people or places. To tell the truth, I don't actually remember hearing this in a club or shop or on the radio. I don't even remember buying it. It's just a record I've always had and its pleasure comes not from its past but from its never diminishing ability to take over the present. Until I wrote this essay I didn't think there was anything else I needed to know.

The Judgment

This chapter, like most chapters in this book I would guess, is written with a rather uncomfortable self-consciousness. I don't normally have any anxieties about rating records – I've done it for a living for much of my life. Academically too, I've long understood (at least to my own satisfaction) that the aesthetics of popular music necessarily means considering subjective and objective factors, immediate responses and the detached and socially shaped terms that describe them. This is, after all, what I do: write about the value of popular music, the relationship between high and low cultural concepts. It is, in Bourdieu's word, my claim to academic *distinction.*

Why, then, do I find it difficult to write about the best disco record ever? It wasn't difficult to choose the record, or even to explain that choice; what is difficult is to find a voice in which the argument sounds right. For a while I thought the problem lay in disco itself. Maybe this was a form of music that just didn't lend itself to the kind of serious attention that an academic essay entails. Now though, having done it, I think the problem lies in the nature of judgment *as an act.*

The issue here is not philosophical (what's meant by "value") but sociological: how does one *perform* authority? Scholarly authority is primarily asserted through the display of knowledge. And so here I've deliberately shown off my reading, referred to other writers, deployed footnotes. As a scholarly in-joke I've cited in my support a philosopher, Roger Scruton, who has denounced both popular music and popular music scholars. At the same time I've casually deployed arcane pop knowledge (not that it took much research) about Sharon Redd's life and François Kevorkian's career. This wasn't information that was ever relevant to my appreciation of "Never Give You Up" but it seemed necessary somehow to an academic article about it.

There are formal ways too in which scholarship must be performed in popular cultural studies. Taking seriously something that obviously isn't serious entails various kinds of writing: humor (primarily irony) to let the reader know you're aware of the discrepancy; a defensive pomposity (it's difficult to avoid taking oneself too seriously too); theoretical jargon or, in my case, adjectival abstraction, phrases that float free from any empirical grounding. To perform as a scholar is necessarily to detach oneself from the immediate experience and to connect what one says to broader fields of study and argument.

At the same time, though, to write authoritatively about popular culture is to perform as a witness. For this part of their performance scholars must write from *within* a cultural process and cultural *engagement* (as consumer or connoisseur) involves different kinds of stylistic device (all apparent in this chapter) – reference to one's own memories, the deployment of the right kind of autobiographical fragment. The scholarly authority to write about popular culture in the first place (to display one's knowledge) is rooted, after all, not in that knowledge but in experience, experience indicated either rhetorically ("I was there!") or through the correct use of non-scholarly terms.

This is a long digression but I needed to take this route to get to where I want to end. The problem of writing about "the best disco record" is that not just that I lack both the scholarly and insider authority to make such a judgment stick, but also that disco has so rarely been discussed analytically (by scholars or insiders) that there is no available discourse in which to make such a judgment in the first place. To put this another way, not only would I be surprised if anyone else agreed with my disco pick, I'd also be, I realize, aggrieved! I've always loved "Never Give You Up," but I've always needed to believe too that I was the only person who really, *really* appreciated it.

Notes

1   Written by E. Matthew and D. Payne, produced by Eric Matthew and Darryl Payne, mixed by François Kevorkian, Prelude Records, New York, 1982.
2   Jonathan D. Kramer, *The Time of Music* (New York: Schirmer Books, 1988), pp. 376–81.

3 Tim Lawrence, *Love Saves the Day* (Durham, NC, and London: Duke University Press, 2003), pp. 215–16.
4 Roger Scruton, "Notes on the meaning of music," in Michael Krausz, ed., *The Interpretation of Music* (Oxford: The Clarendon Press, 1993), p. 199.

Conclusion

Alan McKee

Which is the Most Beautiful Beautiful Thing?

Is Kylie Minogue better than a Ducati 916 superbike?

No, seriously, don't laugh – it's not a silly question.

Well, yes it *is* a silly question. But it's also an important question – at least under traditional models of aesthetic value, where every cultural object has an innate worth which can be judged against the innate worth of other cultural objects, in order to say which is "better." Not better *for* anything – just *better*. This is the approach that underlies ongoing public debates about the content of education, for example. Should we be teaching schoolchildren Milton or *Buffy the Vampire Slayer*? Why, Milton, of course – Milton is better than *Buffy*.[1] We don't need to ask whether Milton and *Buffy* serve the same purposes in order to make that judgment – we simply know one must be more valuable than the other.

So, in the same vein of judgment – which is better? Kylie or the 916?

As I suggested in the Introduction to this volume, many journalists and academics worry that if intellectuals aren't telling consumers what is good and what is bad in culture, then we end up with total relativism – a world where anything goes and everything is equally valuable. In this collection we've seen that this isn't true – that within communities of consumption, connoisseurs are able to explain in detail which examples they think are better than others. But perhaps this is just pushing the threat of relativism up a level, still without addressing it? We can say that some disco records are better than others; that some porn websites are better than others – but can we take a step back and say whether disco records are better than porn websites generally? Or more specifically, can we say that, as culture, the work of Brian Michael Bendis is better than the work of Michael Jordan? That the character of Alti is better than the Nike Air Max Classic TW?

This is the level of analysis demanded by traditional approaches to aesthetics. Can I answer these questions? Can I rank the 13 beautiful things described in the chapters of this collection in order of their relative worth? And if not, have I fallen back into the dangerous trap of "anything goes" relativism?

The "Popular Aesthetic"

This raises the question of the level at which we can make meaningful judgments about which is "the best" example of a cultural area. When I invited the authors to contribute to this collection, I told them that part of their job was to decide what was an appropriate level at which to make a judgment:

> It is up to the author of each chapter to decide what is an appropriate level at which to make the decision about a "best object." In the example chapter provided [to the authors], it is sensible to make a decision about "the best *Doctor Who* story"; this is a question which connoisseurs discuss. However, it would not be sensible to attempt to write a chapter about "the best episode of a science fiction television series."

"Who is the best pop princess?" Marc Brennan asks, and makes a case that the answer is Kylie Minogue. He doesn't claim that she is "the best pop singer" – would it even be possible to ask that question? How about: "Who is the best singer?" Or "Which is the best kind of music?" Or at the most extreme, most generalized, abstract level, we could compare all kinds of music with all kinds of literature and all kinds of drama and all kinds of visual arts and all kinds of material culture, and ask "Which is the best form of culture?" and then try to place Kylie Minogue into a continuum of cultural value against not only the Ducati 916, but also Milton and Shakespeare.

We know – and this collection has demonstrated – that there are many different aesthetic systems at work in society, to judge the worth of different "genres" of culture. But can we accept that these systems might have contradictory and "irreconcilable" elements?[2] Or should we rather argue that we need to seek out the underlying structures which bring them all together, insist that there can, at the end of the day, only be one correct way of judging value, and attempt to make all of the various aesthetic systems described in this book fit into it?[3]

This is a familiar philosophical question, most commonly named as the contest between "structuralist" and "poststructuralist" approaches to thinking about representation. A structuralist approach believes that there is a single truth about the world, although it may be hidden beneath the surface of culture; and a poststructuralist one believes that there is no single hidden truth about the world and it is rather the surface of culture which tells the truth – which is that different groups make sense of the world in a variety of ways. The history of philosophical writing on aesthetics has tended to take the first approach, seeking the underlying structures that underlie value judgments at the most general level possible. In the modern history of writing on these questions (from the work of philosopher Immanuel Kant – *Critique of Judgment*, first published in 1790 – onwards[4]), intellectual work on value judgments has tended to reduce all of the competing aesthetic systems in Western culture to a single, overarching binary: some texts are judged to be valuable ("art," or "good taste") and the rest are judged not to be valuable ("not art" – mass, or popular culture, "bad taste" or "vulgarity"[5]). The smaller scale aesthetic systems functioning within these broad, society-wide categories have received little attention. Once you have decided that something is art, or mass culture, traditional philosophy loses interest in the question of how you might decide, within those categories, what is good and bad.

Indeed, in the traditional approach to aesthetics, philosophers have often argued that, by definition, it's not possible to have aesthetic systems within popular culture. From Kant onwards philosophers have argued that art is appreciated intellectually, but that popular culture is designed to create emotional bodily responses, to be consumed without thinking. Kant draws a binary between the ways that art and mass culture are consumed. Art, he says, satisfies the "taste of reflection," which is a thoughtful approach to culture; whereas mass culture satisfies the "taste of sense," producing immediate, physical, bodily pleasures. High culture produces true "pleasure," whereas low culture provides only sensory "enjoyment." High culture is "sublime" and "beautiful," mass culture is only "charming" or "agreeable."[6] Philosophers writing on the evaluation of culture have tended to follow this binary, arguing that the aesthetic of high culture involves suppressing the emotions, and taking a thoughtful approach to texts; while "the 'popular aesthetic'" is about a bodily, immediate, emotional, participatory response to culture – an approach that is not distanced or reflective.[7] Whereas high culture, they claim, is difficult, and needs training to understand and appreciate, popular culture is, purportedly, "easy" or "facile,"[8] designed to be consumed by people with no training, and without thought, responding to it in an emotional and immediate way.

Are these philosophers correct? Is popular culture only about emotions, immediate response, and the body? Is it wrong to try to take a distanced, reflective approach to popular culture – that is, to do exactly what the authors of the chapters in this book have tried to do?

I don't think so – for three reasons.

First, I don't think we can draw a simple line between art and "mass" or "popular" culture. The world is far messier than that. Indeed, I don't like the term "popular culture" at all. You might have noticed that nowhere in this book have I defined the term, even though it supposedly structures the whole project. There's a reason for that. I think that "popular culture" is a useful marketing term for a book addressing the kinds of ideas that this one does – but beyond that, I don't think it has much utility for describing the workings of culture. "Popular culture" is part of a binary with "high culture." And the binary seems to describe "high culture" in quite a specific way – the artistic cultural productions of a certain educated class fraction – and then leave the label "popular culture" for everything else that's left over. Everything that isn't high culture, by definition, becomes popular culture – even minority cultural practices that would be despised by the mainstream (such as the casual gay sex of cruisingforsex.com); and radical cultural practices that would reject and attack the mainstream (such as community media). Such a label seems to me to be too broad to be analytically useful. It is, I feel, much better to think of many different "subcultures" – including "art" as just one more subculture, alongside mainstream entertainment as another particular subculture, alongside sexual subcultures, alternative experimental subcultures, radical subcultures, and so on.

Having said all this, in this Conclusion I've accepted the binary high/popular for argument's sake – simply because that's how writers have traditionally thought about aesthetics.

Secondly, even if we do accept the terms of the binary for argument's sake, I think philosophers are wrong to say that popular culture is designed only to be consumed thoughtlessly; rather, it seems to me that the best mainstream popular culture (as in the examples discussed in this book) is designed to be consumed on a number of different levels. Take Gwenllian Jones' example of *Xena Warrior Princess*. The program is designed to be immediately accessible to audiences who have never watched it before – the narrative, characters, storytelling, and visual presentation work to insure that if a naive viewer, who has never seen the show before, stumbles across "When Fates Collide," they will be able to follow the episode and enjoy it. But a connoisseur of the show can then go further, can learn more about the program, can find out more about the backstory of the characters – she can discover that the character of Xena first appeared in the television program *Hercules* as an evil character and forever lives with the legacy of this past; that Alti is her nemesis, has appeared in the program many times before, and that there is a seductive relationship between them – and then returning to "When Fates Collide" she will find more to enjoy in that episode, will interpret it slightly differently. She can go even further – can investigate the real-world production of the episode, and watch it again in a slightly different way; can research the ways in which the program plays with mythological references, and then explore this in the episodes as they are broadcast, and so on. Popular culture is not *just* easy and accessible. The best popular culture works on a number of levels, is easy and accessible, but also rewards detailed study and appreciation.[9] Not every consumer of *Xena*, or *Red Dragon*, or the work of Brian Michael Bendis thinks about their engagement with the text, or explores it, or communicates their ideas about it in the way that these authors have done. For some consumers, this mass culture is background noise, something to be glanced at, skimmed over, taken in easily.[10] But that is not the *only* way in which it is possible to engage with popular culture. As the authors in the collection demonstrate, there are communities of connoisseurs in each area who do take a thoughtful and reflective approach to what they consume.

Thirdly, I think that philosophers have been wrong in arguing that high culture invites an intellectual response, while mass culture demands an emotional one, because – as Simon Frith has pointed out – this is a false binary. All intellectual responses come from people with bodies; all immediate, sensory responses necessarily involve thinking as well. Even the most embodied, emotional response to culture – such as dancing – involves an intellectual element. Deciding how to dance, how to communicate visually, how to express one's emotions in this physical language, necessarily involves a thoughtful process. Our bodies are not simply connected up to respond mechanically to rhythm – if they were, every time we heard a clock ticking we'd be unable to stop ourselves from jiving.[11] There is some element of reflection, of distance, involved in even the most embodied and emotional responses to culture. And although all of the chapters in this book are extremely intelligent, and carefully reflective, I don't think that this makes them dispassionate – they are not pretending, as does some aesthetic appreciation of high culture, that the writers' emotional responses to the objects under discussion are unimportant. Quite the opposite, in fact. These chapters clearly show that the binary between mind and body, reflection and emotion – between writing and dancing – is a false one. It is possible to do both – although not, perhaps, at the same time.

I Like It. It Is Beautiful

Traditionally, philosophical writing about value judgments has worked at the level of culture as a whole, subsuming all of the varied aesthetic systems by which people decide what is valuable in different parts of culture to a single overarching system, where all examples of culture are compared all other examples of culture, and judged to be "good" or "bad." So, to return to the question I asked above – can we do this with the examples in this book? Can we avoid the messy relativism of "anything goes" by deciding, once and for all, whether cruisingforsex.com is better than *The Silent Village*?

I think the answer to this question depends on first answering another question: "What are value judgments for?"

What a silly question – *Of course* we need to know why some things are better than others . . .

But it's a useful exercise to stop for a moment and ask – why? What purpose do value judgments actually serve? They are not necessarily functional, in the sense of offering practical consumer guidance on what the reader might like. When Harold Bloom makes his judgments about what counts as good culture, he's not providing guidance as to what people will enjoy reading. For most citizens, the works he recommends are remote and uninteresting – they're never going to read Homer or Dante. Rather, Bloom is making moral judgments about what is "good" and "bad," which describe how he sees the world – what he thinks is important, what he thinks is good and true and beautiful and moral.

So what purpose does it serve to know what Harold Bloom thinks is good? Or a film reviewer in a newspaper? Or Will Brooker on Batman stories, or Glen Thomas on romance novelists, John Banks on action console games? What, at the end of the day, is this process *for*?

Since the work of sociologist Pierre Bourdieu in his study *Distinction*, many researchers have suggested the major social function of value judgments is to enable us to form communities. Value judgments help us to find people who are like ourselves – the *right kind of people* – and make connections with them.[12] When Harold Bloom makes a claim about what is good culture, he will attract to him people who agree that this is good culture (and repel people who disagree with him) enabling those people to form communities that have something in common – a strong feeling about what is good and true and right and moral in culture.

This perspective raises an interesting point about the objectivity of value judgments. Again, in traditional philosophical writing about aesthetics, from Kant onwards, there is a firm distinction between subjective judgments about value – "I like it" – and objective judgments about value – "It is beautiful."[13] However, if we accept that value judgments are important because they allow us to find people who think like we do, then this distinction – between what is subjective and what is objective – doesn't work. When Harold Bloom says that Dante is better than Batman comics, he is not simply telling the objective truth, which every informed and reasonable person must agree with. We know this, because there exist informed and reasonable people who disagree with him (hello!). Bloom is presenting *his* version of what is good and bad.

This is not to say that his claims are completely subjective – Bloom is not simply saying that he *likes* Dante. He is making a moral claim that other people should also think that Dante is better than Batman comics. So how does this work? If his claims about the truth of Dante aren't simply "objective" truth, then what is the difference between saying "I like it" and "It is beautiful"?

I agree with the philosopher Barbara Hernstein Smith that the difference between subjective and objective value judgments can be understood in terms of communication. "I like it" is a subjective evaluation because it represents a retreat into your own preferences. If you simply say "I like *Red Dragon*," that demands no response – indeed, there are few possible responses, beyond saying "So do I," "I don't," or "Good for you." There is no next step in the conversation – the listener can't reasonably say, "No, you don't like it. Let me prove it to you."

But to say that "*Red Dragon* is beautiful; it is the best serial killer novel" is to make a *claim* to objectivity, to be saying something more than just describing your own personal response – and this makes your statement available for discussion. What are your criteria for judgment? How does *Red Dragon* – or Kylie, or *The Silent Village*, or the Nike Air Max Classic TW, or *Grand Theft Auto: San Andreas* – fit those criteria? What other examples might meet those criteria? Are the criteria themselves up for discussion?

Of course, you might find that nobody else agrees with you, that you are ultimately in a community of one – in which case, you are back with subjectivity. Smith argues that objectivity is an effect of interaction with other people, so if I am the only person who thinks as I do – that *Forces of Nature* is the best romantic comedy, for example – then that remains a subjective judgment, no matter how much I might claim that "it is beautiful." But the more that we orient ourselves toward others in a community who understand and engage with our processes of evaluation – even if we ultimately do not reach absolute agreement on every point – the more objective our judgments are, for "the more extensive the set of people for whom . . . [the evaluator] believes . . . [her judgment] would be appropriate," the more "objective" it is.[14]

From this perspective, the arguments that we produce in order to prove, objectively, that what we like is in fact the best, are literally rationalizations.[15] Our preferences – shaped by individual experiences of economic and social and cultural and psychological factors – come first. And then we rationalize them – put them into rational discourse – as a way to communicate them to others, to invite responses, to engage with people, to find those people who, although never identical to us, we can believe are similar enough to form a grouping with. And thus communities form.

At the risk of falling back into (what I feel are) the simplistic binaries that the philosophy of aesthetics has traditionally worked with, I think that we can see high cultural aesthetic systems and popular cultural aesthetic systems dealing with this subjective/objective distinction somewhat differently.

The aesthetic systems of high culture tend to be those that are "dominant" in our culture.[16] Obviously popular culture is in one sense "dominant" in Western cultures – it is the culture consumed by, and liked by, the majority of the population; those who produce it can make vast fortunes for themselves, and gain positions of influence in society. But in another sense, traditional hierarchies of value remain firmly in place – as the public debates about Harold Bloom's work remind us. Nobody might want to actually read Shakespeare – but everybody has a nagging feeling that their children should be forced to do so at school, because, somehow, Shakespeare is good. Indeed, more generally, popular culture uses examples of high culture – opera, classical music, literary novels, and, of course, Shakespeare – to validate itself and make itself seem worthy (Jane Austen adaptations; Nessum Dorma as the soccer world cup theme; Baz Luhrmann's *William Shakespeare's Romeo + Juliet*).[17]

The fact that these high-culture aesthetic systems continue to have some purchase across different areas of culture means that those communities that enjoy high culture can feel confident that their value systems are validated. Shakespeare fans just *know* that their aesthetic systems are correct. They don't have to worry that maybe Harlequin-Mills & Boon fans in fact have it right after all and maybe Emma Darcy *is* better than Shakespeare. Educational systems, and general discourses of value – and the history of philosophical writing on aesthetics, of course – reassure consumers of art that their value systems are not only the best ones, but are, in fact, the only *real* systems of judging cultural value. High-cultural aesthetic systems tend, therefore, to be somewhat "ethnocentric" – they assume that their way of seeing the world is the only correct one.[18] An aesthetic system for judging Batman comics? How ridiculous: "I can't understand how anyone can like that!"[19] Indeed, as Simon Frith has noticed, high-cultural aesthetic judgments often do have a moral element – that we must identify good culture, because consuming it makes us better people; whereas consuming bad (popular, mass) culture is actually bad for you – it rots your brain. There is therefore a didactic, or even evangelical purpose to high-cultural aesthetic judgments.[20]

By contrast, the users of popular aesthetic systems are always aware that other aesthetic systems exists – in the educational system, and in wider culture, they are constantly reminded of the high-culture aesthetic system that dismisses their own tastes as worthless. Just as marginalized ethnic groups in society are statistically more likely to be bilingual than members of dominant ethnic groups – because they know a native language and that of the dominant group in society – so users of popular aesthetic systems are likely to be aesthetically bilingual. As a viewer of the soap opera *Dynasty* puts it when interviewed about the value of the program: "I know it's ridiculous, but I enjoy it."[21] This is a similar response to that described by Simon Frith in this collection – the response demanded by: "Taking seriously something that obviously isn't serious" (under a dominant aesthetic system).

For many of the writers in this book we can see that the project they were asked to engage in led them to an investigation of precisely this issue: is it possible to make a claim for objectivity, for being "beautiful," when you're discussing something that "obviously isn't serious"? And in their chapters you can see them negotiating between completely idiosyncratic subjectivity and arrogant claims to be telling "the truth." Frith notes that writers on popular culture often gain their authority from speaking about their own subjective experience of it, presenting "reference to [their] own memories, the deployment of the right kind of autobiographical fragment." Frith does this himself; Clare Gould's account of her own tastes begins with "I blame it on my youth" – as do Turnbull's and Brooker's. And from their own personal, individual, psychological, subjective engagements with the "best" texts, they then begin to move outward to a community of fellow connoisseurs, never losing sight of how that community is constructed – and the fact that it is always in debate, always asking questions, always talking about the issues. They always remember that this is, in fact, the whole point of taste judgments – not to reach a final, definitive answer (for this has never happened, and we have no reason to believe it ever will) – but to keep the conversation going. To keep talking to people – this is, actually, the end in itself.

In his chapter, Thomas McLaughlin notes that the members of the community of baseball connoisseurs

> need only share a loose set of criteria without an established hierarchy, a discourse in which they can agree or disagree meaningfully in arguments about aesthetic judgment. Wherever two basketball players or fans gather, they will argue about the game, proving by their very disagreements the fact that they share an unspoken aesthetic, and proving by their emotion that their disagreements have a moral dimension.

The old binary of subjective/objective breaks down. The point of community, of conversations about value judgments, is to strive to reach beyond the solipsism of pure subjectivity, of "I like it," by making claims that "It is beautiful": and it is through the connection with others – the conversations held with them, the agreements and the disagreements we have with them – that objectivity (our ideas interacting with those of other people) is formed. In order to make the claim that "It is beautiful," you do not have to believe that you are simply speaking the truth – you merely have to want to communicate with other people about your tastes. As Lawrence Levine describes his own attitude toward his aesthetic values, they are: "attitudes I hold, values by which I make judgments, but not necessarily universal truths."[22] Popular cultural aesthetic judgments don't have the same didactic impulse as those of high culture. There is little sense in the writing that those people who disagree about what is the best Batman comic or sneaker are in any way failing as human beings; while in Harold Bloom's work on the Western canon this is obviously the case.

Secret Masters of Fandom

All of this might make popular aesthetic systems sound like utopian sites of tolerance and supportiveness, where everyone's view is taken to be just as important as everybody else's.

This is not the case.

It is true that those consumers who use popular aesthetic systems know that there are other aesthetic systems in place, and that those aesthetic systems devalue what they love – that is, they are always aware that their own value judgments are not the only truth about culture. But this does not mean that they fail to stand up for their judgments and argue passionately for them. All communities are riven and unstable phenomena, involved in a continual play between similarity and difference, ritual celebrations of what we have in common, bitter arguments about what makes us different, with allegiance forever shifting as new threats come along or new forms of commonality are identified. In this collection, Henry Jenkins points out that:

> Comic fans are sharply divided into two camps: on the one side, there are fans of comics as popular culture (with a focus on the creative reworking of genre elements and plays with continuity) . . . on the other side, there are fans of comics as art (with a focus on aesthetic experimentation and unconventional content).

Gould notes that: "it is important to emphasize that there are two types of trainer buyer. In the broadest sense, there are those who use them to play sports, and those who use them to play." And Turnbull claims:

> I do take very seriously the recommendations of fellow crime readers and knowledgeable reviewers who can place a crime novel within its specific sub-generic context, or make an association with another author's work, giving me enough information to ascertain whether or not it is worth tracking down. After a while, you get to know whose recommendations to trust even among your otherwise valued friends: who shares the same aesthetic criteria and sensibilities, who knows a "good" crime novel when they read one.

Consumers of all kinds of culture are involved in ongoing discussions about value. And in this process, some people's opinions matter more than others. Partly this is due to personal attributes – some people are more rhetorically skilled, better at getting their point across in ways that are convincing, amusing, interesting, or just better suited to the audience they are addressing. But there are also structural issues in place. In questions of cultural evaluation, some people have control over what is published and distributed. In high-cultural aesthetic systems, these people include publishers, booksellers, librarians, museum and art gallery owners, the people who award grants to artists, booking agents, state censors, and those who set school curricula. Others have an authorized position in society which grants them the right to say what is good and bad – and expect to be listened to. This category includes university lecturers, critics in the media, judges who hand out awards, members of learned societies. These two groups of people have cultural power to back up their beliefs about what constitutes good culture – for they can control what people have access to, or can expect readers to give respect to their opinions. In the case of high culture, it is formal education which has been the most powerful institution in teaching its aesthetic systems as an objective truth about cultural value.[23]

We can see similar processes operating in popular aesthetic systems. Some people have institutional authority (although, unlike high cultural examples, they tend not to get that prestige from universities). This allows some of them to express their beliefs about what is good by deciding what gets produced and distributed – A&R departments, television's commissioning editors, and the publishers in mainstream publishing houses, for example. And other people get to present their beliefs about what is good in a format where they can expect to be listened to and taken seriously.

This latter group includes professionals – such as film, TV, and music reviewers in the media. But, importantly, it also includes non-professionals. The consumers of popular culture have much more access to institutional power to validate their opinions than do the consumers of high culture – simply because the official (educational) systems have shown little interest in colonizing this ground, and thus it has been free for "fans" – connoisseurs of popular culture – to create those validating institutions for themselves.

In his discussion of the two "camps" of comics fans, Jenkins points out that each has its own journal representing it (*Wizard* for fans of comics as popular culture; *Comics Journal* for those who see comics as art); while Turnbull pays attention to at least some published "reviewers." Some consumers have access to publication in these sites of institutional power – and thus their contributions to the discussion about what is good and bad reach more people, with a greater expectation of being listened to. The anthropologist Camille Bacon-Smith, for example, in her study of the culture of science-fiction fandom, points out that there exists a group of fans who run the convention circuit. This provides them with a cultural power to decide whose work is given space at the circuits, and with a privileged position from which to disseminate their own ideas about what is good science fiction. Within the community, she notes, these fans are given the label ("ironic, if sometimes bitterly applied") "secret Masters of Fandom."[24]

Some connoisseurs have more power than others to disseminate their ideas about what makes the best culture. But it remains true that in popular aesthetic systems, institutions of authority are more porous and less intractable than in traditional aesthetic systems. It is very difficult (though not impossible) to start a new university. It is much easier to start a magazine; even easier to start a fanzine; and easier still to start a webzine. Even if you do manage to start a new university, it is extremely hard to get it recognized as a respectable and reputable institution, with the right to speak on issues of cultural evaluation (ideally, you would still like to be at Harvard, Yale, Oxford, or Cambridge to claim the ultimate authority in such matters). But as several of the authors in this collection demonstrate, the primary institutions for managing debates about cultural value in many areas of popular culture are either fanzines, magazines, or Internet sites. The authors find conversations about the best things in popular culture on websites such as chud.com, SF-Z.com, dorothyl.com, amazon.com, thescene.com.au – and not in university publications.

All of this means, of course, that you shouldn't just – as one had to do with Shakespeare in the bad old days of schooling – learn the canon of popular things presented in this book off by heart and reel it off at parties – "But, darling, *of course* Alti is the best *Xena* villain!" That would be to miss the point of the collection entirely. Each of the claims for what is "best" is, in a sense, a provocation. There are informed and intelligent connoisseurs of Batman who, as Brooker points out, would say that *The Killing Joke* is the best story – and they're not wrong. There is never absolute agreement, no possibility of pure "objectivity," in claims about cultural value – whether we are discussing the best Shakespearean tragedy or the best pair of sneakers. It is the discussion that is important – the fact that people are moving beyond the selfish claim about their "favorite" to find out what other people's favorites are, and to engage them in discussions about what's good.

"The Fact that It Lacks Mass Appeal Makes It all the More Alluring"

Forming communities involves two simultaneous processes. On the one hand there is the inclusion of those who are like us; on the other, the necessary exclusion of those who are not like us.[25] Pierre Bourdieu pointed out that one of the important social functions of taste judgments was to allow communities to exclude those who were not like them – the process of "distinction" or "discrimination." His particular focus was on the way that the dominant groups in society used knowledge of high culture and good taste as a way to keep the riff-raff out; but we can see a similar process working in all aesthetic systems. As well as keeping the conversation going with others with whom we share some level of judgment about taste, there is also a strong element in the popular aesthetic systems – as we see in several of the chapters collected here – of keeping others out; and in particular, keeping out "the masses." Claire Gould discusses the question of distinction:

> This is a very real issue for the hard-core trainer lover. While the fact that we have something so aesthetically pleasing on our feet is important, the

real challenge and appeal is to find a shoe that is reasonably unique and not particularly commercial. This may sound a little odd, since shoe manufacturers produce trainers as a business, in the hopes of making a huge mark-up – but you only have to visit the millions of discount outlets around the globe to know that what tickles the fancy of the shoe-buying public can be worlds apart from what the shoe company expects. Thus, when trainer freaks find that "special" shoe, the fact that it lacks mass appeal makes it all the more alluring.

In their chapters, Sue Turnbull and Thomas McLaughlin also draw on the image of the mass public, against whom the connoisseur can judge themselves and feel more informed; while Simon Frith goes further still, arguing that because he hasn't found a community of disco connoisseurs with whom he can develop the sense of objectivity that comes from discussing these issues, "not only would I be surprised if anyone else agreed with my disco pick, I'd also be, I realize, aggrieved! I've always loved 'Never Give You Up' but I've always needed to believe too that I was the only person who really, *really* appreciated it." It is possible, then, to use popular cultural capital for purposes of distinction, to mark oneself out from the outsiders who do not know as well as you.[26]

Bourdieu goes further. He points out that knowledge of high-culture aesthetic systems can also be converted into social and economic capital. If you know a lot about why Shakespeare is good, you can convert that into a job at a university for example. He also suggests that knowing about good taste may be useful for winning entry to the more powerful echelons in society (although recent writers have questioned how true this remains[27]). But it's not so clear whether knowing a lot about gay porn web sites can so easily be translated into social or economic power. Perhaps this is best left as a question: what is the relationship between popular cultural capital and social and economic systems? The academic writers in this book are not going to make money out of their chapters; but the reference will go on their CVs and publishing resumés, and might get them jobs or promotions. As for the reader of the collection, who can now expound with confidence her reasons for believing why Emma Darcy's romance novels are just so good – what economic or social benefit might that bring her? Perhaps she might aspire to become a "secret Master of Fandom" in her area of interest, winning bitter recognition of her power from other romance connoisseurs? More research is needed – if you get a promotion because of something you learned from this book, write and tell me.

"There's No Basis for Making a   _____
          Meaningful Comparison"

And so I return to the questions that opened this Conclusion. First: Is Kylie Minogue better than a Ducati 916 superbike? And secondly: do we need to ask this question?

As I have explained above, I believe that the purpose of making value judgments in culture is not to speak a truth that must be heard, but to engage communities in conversation. From this perspective, it is certainly *possible* to make a decision about which is better (for argument's sake, let's use the criteria "Who's got the better pipes?" and give the laurels to the 916[28]). But answering that question doesn't actually serve much purpose. There isn't a community of people who care about the answer, who feel that it matters, who could agree on criteria – in short, who could make it an objective choice. As Henry Jenkins argues in his chapter: "There's no point comparing Bendis with Stan Lee, the writer who created so many of the Marvel characters that Bendis is now retooling. Lee and Bendis wrote in such radically different contexts, for such different audiences, and under such different constraints that there is no basis for making a meaningful comparison."

This is the problem with the work of writers like Harold Bloom – their work is so subjective. They speak only to a community of literature readers, but claim to be addressing all readers everywhere. In fact, as Bloom dismisses Batman comics, he isn't speaking to the people who read Batman comics – he doesn't know enough about Batman comics to engage them. If he limited himself to addressing literature scholars with his arguments about which are the best books *within* the realm of literature, then his pronouncements would be more meaningful.

I would argue, then, that there is no need to judge whether Kylie or the 916 is better. Our culture is not harmed by the fact that we don't make that decision – no one needs to. Think about it – in which situations would anybody have to make such a choice? One possible answer would involve governments – arts councils, for example, might have limited funds to support cultural development, and might have to decide whether that money should go to subsidize the cultural production of romance novels by Emma Darcy, or the comic book adventures of Batman. But of course, this is silly, because governments don't support the production of popular culture. They support the production of high culture. So even they will not need to make these comparative decisions. A second, more realistic situation might come – as suggested above – when somebody has to make the decision about what to teach at a university or in a school syllabus: should we teach Milton or *Buffy*? Shakespeare or soap operas?[29] For me, though, this isn't a problem – it's not a question that I need to ask, never mind answer. For me, teaching about culture is not about teaching students to appreciate a small number of great texts – it's about showing them how we, as a society, decide what's good and bad – and why those decisions matter. You can use Shakespeare to teach that, or you can use *Xena: Warrior Princess*, or you can use both. Those academics, like Harold Bloom, who want to teach appreciation of great texts, will indeed have to make the call, and decide whether Kylie is better than a Ducati. I'm afraid that I'll have to leave it to them to explain how they do it.

And does this mean that I am embracing relativism, and saying that anything goes? That gay sex websites cannot be compared to comic books, that Shakespeare cannot be compared to pop music? I don't think so. All I'm saying is that not everything has to be compared to everything else, all the time. Sometimes we do indeed need to make these judgments – and when we do, *then* the discussion begins about how to do that.

John Frow has pointed out that you can bring together different aesthetic systems, not by deciding that one is superior to the other, but by letting them engage with each other in dialogue, as equals.[30] One example of this might be the discussions between radical feminists and conservative Christians. Although there is no agreement between these groups about how their value systems work, through their discussions they have found a point of commonality – their hatred of pornography – that is important enough to allow them to work together as allies, even though both would argue that aspects of the others' value system are wrong.

Or we can take a more positive example – the collection that you hold in your hands. Marc Brennan has explained why he believes that Kylie Minogue is the best pop princess, giving readers some insight into the criteria that might be employed and the ways in which Kylie Minogue gives pleasure to the pop connoisseurs who love her. Margaret Henderson has told us about the importance of the Ducati 916 Superbike, of why you would call it "the best" in the area and what it is that motorbike experts celebrate about it. And now, after taking part in this collection, each of them also knows how the other – and the rest of the contributors to this collection – makes their judgments. And – importantly – they also know that *doesn't take anything away from their system!* In order to explain how she judges Ducatis, Margaret doesn't have to attack or denigrate the ways in which Marc judges Kylie. Marc can understand how Margaret thinks about motorbikes without feeling threatened in his love for the best pop princess. Understanding each other's systems adds to the sum of their knowledge. We don't need to believe that there's a limited amount of judgment to go around. In order for Marc to be right, he doesn't have to prove that Margaret is wrong. They can both be right. Everybody wins!

And, importantly, the systems are not cut off from each other in a relativist nightmare where there is no communication between the areas. They can begin a dialogue, *ask* whether they have anything in common, whether there are areas of overlap in judging what is good and what is bad, check whether they can, in fact, survive in the same world together.

Translators become particularly important in this process – those who can understand more than one system, and communicate to people outside of their own community, to people who do not immediately share their own tastes.[31] There is a history of intellectual writing which has attempted to take popular aesthetic systems on their own merits, and describe them for readers outside the immediate communities of connoisseurs.[32] This book may help contribute to this ongoing process, making these forms of knowledge available to readers who previously would not have realized that they even existed, never mind being experts in them.

I Love This Book

I love this book. I think I'm allowed to say that as I didn't write any of the chapters. I think that the essays that are collected here are intelligent, funny, insightful, generous, original, informed, and informative. I learned something from reading them – information and ideas that I didn't know before. But more than this, from each chapter I got a glimpse of something else that I didn't know before: the sense of joy and excitement that connoisseurs of motorbikes, romance novels, Batman comics, basketball, or action console games experience from engaging with the objects of their affection. Reading the first drafts of the chapters as they came in, I experienced something I hadn't expected – a physical reaction, shivers of delight down my spine. As I argued above, I don't think that intellectual and emotional responses are separate. The writers collected in this book have written creatively and beautifully in ways that not only provide the bare bones of information about the popular aesthetic systems in their areas of expertise – but also make you understand why they matter.

After reading them, you – or at least, I know for myself that I – have a sense of what it's like to love and argue about and become a bit obsessed with serial killer novels, disco records, and propaganda movies. I will never myself feel a sense of passion about a motorbike, but thanks to Marg Henderson's evocative writing I have some sense of what such a passion feels like. Comic books don't engage me, but Brooker and Jenkins help me to understand why they do engage some people, and how colorful and powerful a medium they are for that audience. I'm even looking at my feet in a new way since I read Gould's chapter.

Kylie Minogue, I have to admit, I already knew about . . .

These writers are translators who explain to outsiders like myself why they love the kinds of culture that they do – things which I have never personally been drawn by, but which I have now experienced vicariously at their hands. And knowing that there are people who do love and think about and discuss things that don't engage me isn't a threat to my way of thinking. It's a source of delight. The more joy that's in the world, the better for all of us, I say. I hope that you've had the same experience reading this collection. Hopefully you've enjoyed it, learned something from it, and it's made you think. As I said in the Introduction, many of our attitudes toward popular culture are rooted in profound ignorance. We assume that nobody could make an intelligent decision to consume action console games or romance novels or gay online pornography, because we don't know many intelligent people who make those choices and are willing to take the time to explain them to us. "I can't understand how anyone can like that!" – well now I do understand how someone can like *Grand Theft Auto: San Andreas*, Emma Darcy's novels, and cruisingforsex.com.

I hope that you can understand it too.

Notes

1 Emma Tom, "Buffy slays the stuffy in classroom standoff," The *Australian* (August 10, 2005): 11.

2 Simon Frith, *Performing Rites: Evaluating Popular Music* (Oxford and New York: Oxford University Press, 1998), p. 75.

3 John Frow, *Cultural Studies and Cultural Value* (Oxford: Clarendon Press, 1995), p. 131.

4 Immanuel Kant, *The Critique of Judgment*, trans. James Creed (Oxford: Clarendon Press, 1952).

5 Tony Bennett, Michael Emmison, and John Frow, *Accounting for Tastes: Australian Everyday Culture* (Cambridge: Cambridge University Press, 1999), p. 38.

6 Pierre Bourdieu, *Distinction: A Social Critique of the Judgment of Taste* (Cambridge, MA: Harvard University Press, 1986), p. 489.

7 Ibid., pp. 4, 5, 32.

8 Ibid., pp. 486.

9 Frow, *Cultural Studies and Cultural Value*, p. 68.

10 Joke Hermes, *Reading Women's Magazines: An Analysis of Everyday Media Use* (Cambridge: Polity Press, 1995).

11 Frith, *Performing Rites*, p. 131.

12 Bourdieu, *Distinction*, p. 241; Frith, *Performing Rites*, p. 4, 18; Barbara Hernstein Smith, *Contingencies of Value: Alternative Perspectives For Critical Theory* (Cambridge, MA and London: Harvard University Press, 1988), p. 13.

13 Smith, *Contingencies of Value*, p. 86.

14 Ibid., p. 92.

15 Bourdieu, *Distinction*, p. 67.

16 Bourdieu, in Frow, *Cultural Studies and Cultural Value*, p. 32.

17 Jim Collins, ed. *High-Pop: Making Culture Into Popular Entertainment* (Malden, MA: Blackwell Publishers, 2002).

18 Bourdieu, *Distinction*, p. 493.

19 Ibid., p. 61.

20 Simon Frith, personal communication, August 23, 2005.

21 David Morrison, *Invisible Citizens: British Public Opinion and the Future of Broadcasting* (London: John Libbey/The Broadcasting Research Unit, 1986), p. 17; see also Ien Ang, *Watching* Dallas: *Soap Opera and the Melodramatic Imagination* (London and New York: Methuen, 1985), p. 104.

22 Lawrence W. Levine, *Highbrow/Lowbrow: The Emergence of Cultural Hierarchy in America* (Cambridge, MA: Harvard University Press, 1988), p. 3.

23 Frow, *Cultural Studies and Cultural Value*, p. 40.

24 Camille Bacon-Smith, *Science Fiction Culture* (Philadelphia: University of Pennsylvania Press, 2000), p. 23.

25 John Hartley, *The Politics of Pictures: The Creation of the Public in the Age of Popular Media* (London and New York: Routledge, 1992), pp. 206–10.

26 See also Sarah Thornton, *Club Cultures: Music, Media and Subcultural Capital* (Cambridge: Polity, 1995); and Mark Jancovich, "'A real shocker': authenticity, genre and the struggle for distinction," *Continuum: Journal of Media and Cultural Studies* 14/1 (2000): 23–36.

27 Frow, *Cultural Studies and Cultural Value*, p. 14.

28 Joke copyright Margaret Henderson, 2005.

29 Ibid., p. 15.

30 Ibid., p. 142.

31 Ibid., p. 154.

32 See Frith, *Performing Rites*, pp. 19, 26, 49–50, 73, 94. Also Gilbert Seldes, *The Seven Lively Arts* (New York: A. S. Barnes, 1962[1924]); Stuart Hall and Paddy Whannel, *The Popular Arts* (Boston: Beacon Press, 1967[1964]); Horace Newcomb, *TV: The Most Popular Art* (Garden City, NY: Anchor Press/Doubleday, 1974).

Index